~~Borough of~~ [Sunder]land | Town of Sunderland | ~~Village of~~

Age of Males	Age of Females	Rank, Profession, or Occupation	
	31		Newcastle upon Tyne
[illegible]			Durham Sunderland
	7		Do
	4		Do
[illegible]			Do
	5		Do
[illegible]		Stone Mason	Durham Brancepeth
	23		Northumberland N. Shields
	1		Durham Sunderland
[illegible]			Do
5[illegible]		Coal Trimmer	Durham East Rainton
	36		Northumberland Blyth
	6		Durham Ryhope
	30		Northumberland Blyth
	37	House Keeper	Durham Sunderland
[illegible]		Joiner	Do Houghton le Spring
[illegible]		Stone Mason	Scotland
	37	Rail. Lab. Wife	Yorkshire Stansfield Todmorden
5		Scholar	Buckinghamshire Castlethorpe
	13	Do	Do
	12		

WHO DO YOU THINK YOU ARE?

Discovering the heroes and villains in your family

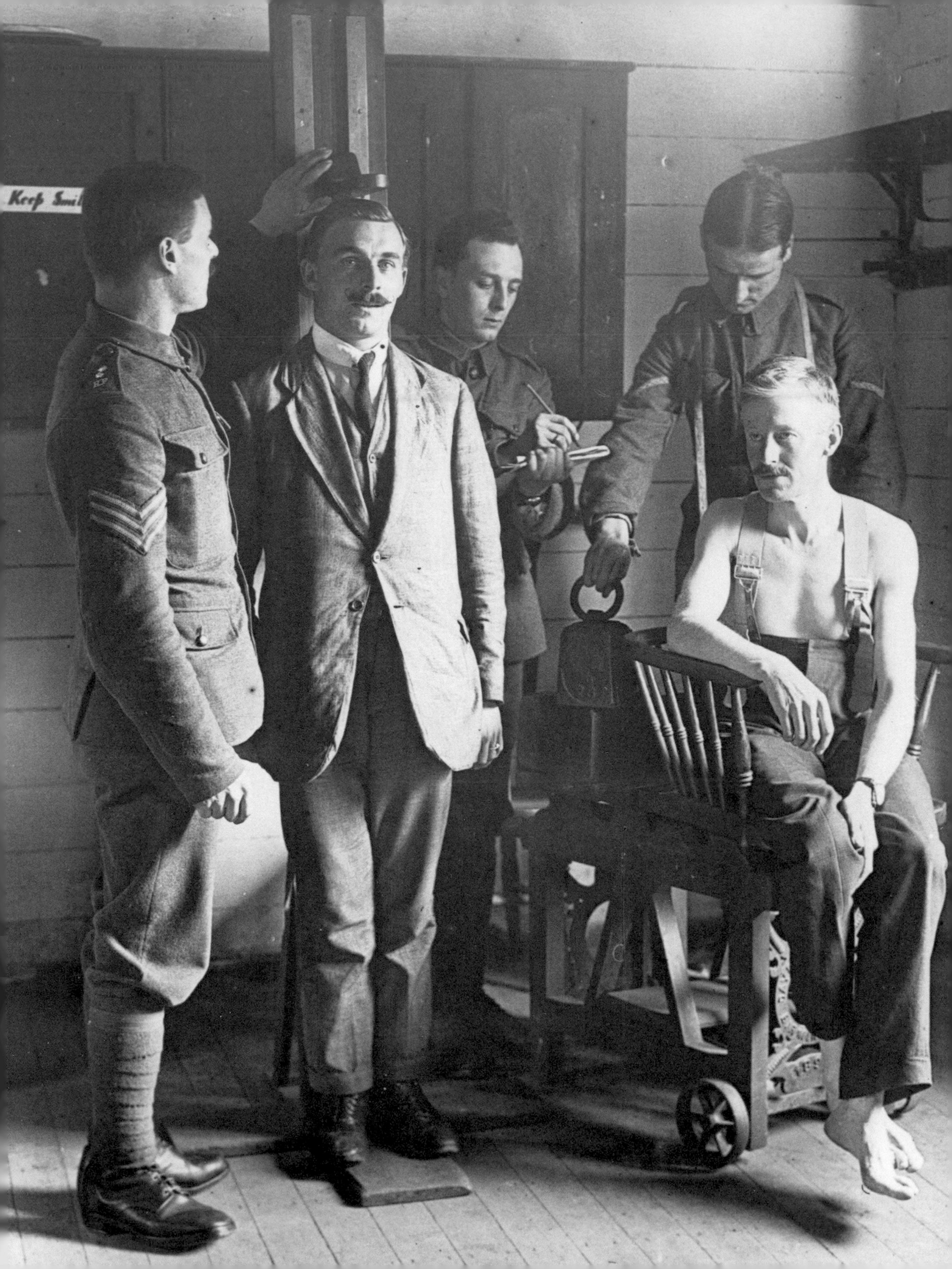

WHO DO YOU THINK YOU ARE?

Discovering the heroes and villains in your family

DAN WADDELL *and* NICK BARRATT

HarperCollins*Entertainment*
An Imprint of HarperCollins*Publishers*

HarperCollins *Entertainment*
An Imprint of HarperCollins*Publishers*
77–85 Fulham Palace Road,
Hammersmith, London W6 8JB

www.harpercollins.co.uk

Published by HarperCollins *Entertainment* 2006
1

A CIP catalogue record for this book is available from the British Library

ISBN-13 978-0-00-722089-2
ISBN-10 0-00-722089-8

Printed and bound in Great Britain by Butler and Tanner, Frome

PICTURE CREDITS

Crown © material is reproduced with the permission of the Controller of HMSO.
AKG Images: p182 (Archie Miles); The Art Archive: p31 (Pasteur birthplace Dole / Dagli Orti); The Bridgeman Art Library: p39 (© Guildhall Art Gallery, Corporation of London, UK), p41 (Bibliotheque des Arts Decoratifs, Paris, France), p145, p149; Corbis: p113 (© David Cumming; Eye Ubiquitous); Mary Evans Picture Library: p10, p16 (Joanna Sanderson / Crown ©), p17 (Joanna Sanderson / Crown ©), p18 (Joanna Sanderson / Crown ©), p21, p32, p37, p44, p45, p50, p53, p54, p56l, p56r, p58, p60, p72, p80, p89, p90, p91, p103, p104, p106, p116 (Maurice Ambler), p132, p133, p134, p136, p138, p140-1, p143, p146, p148, p160, p161, p162, p166, p170, p173, p181, p184bl, p184tr, p185 (Margaret Monck Photographs), p186, p190, p191, p199, p201, p202; Getty Images: p9, p20 (Terence Spencer / Time Life Pictures / Crown ©) , p42-3 (Keystone Features), p51 (Three Lions), p76 (Roger Fenton / Hulton Archive), p102 (Topical Press), p107 (Hulton Archive), p110 (Topical Press Agency), p117 (Mansell/Time Life), p121, p122, p150, p180 (Fox Photos), p187 (Henry Guttmann), p192 (Otto Herschan), p203 (Hulton Archive); Imperial War Museum: p2 (Q.30064); National Archives: p22 / Crown ©, p24 / Crown ©, p25 / Crown ©, p26 / Crown ©, p27 / Crown ©, p28 / Crown ©, p29 / Crown ©; Peter Newark's Historic Pictures: p61, p73, p74, p81, p88, p93, p94, p95, p165; Topfoto: p30, p35, p48 (© The British Museum), p57, p78, p79, p82-83, p87, p108-9, p112, p118, p139, p167, p188, p193, p194, p196, p197, p198; Wall to Wall Media Limited: pp64, 96, 126, 154, 174, 200.

All celebrity family photographs are the copyright of the respective families.

Contents

Introduction

L.P. Hartley, at the start of his novel *The Go-Between*, proclaimed famously: "The past is a foreign country: they do things differently there."

In the same way that most of us would not dream of visiting a foreign country without consulting a guide to its customs, habits and traditions, or doing some sort of research beforehand to get the most out of our trip, so this book will give you a background to the times in which your ancestors lived to help you make the most out of the journey along your ancestral trail.

The book is split into three distinct sections: the first is a thorough, yet succinct, guide to tracing your family tree. If you are new to the subject, it is here that you will find the information you need to learn who your ancestors were, what they did for a living and when they were born, married and died. However, this is only the first step. The fun in family history comes when you attempt to discover how they used to live: how did they end up in a lunatic asylum? What were the reasons behind the war in which they fought and what were the conditions that killed them? Why do they appear in one census married to one person, then turn up on another married to someone else without any sign of a divorce? Picking your way through such conundrums and picturing your ancestors back in the time in which they lived is the true essence of family history – not simply sketching an ornate family tree.

To that end, the second section of this book provides you with the information you need to help explain the lives of your forebears. We have limited ourselves, on the whole, to discussing the early part of the nineteenth century onwards, mainly because the existence of records and other sources make it the most fertile ground for family historians.

As such, this second section is split into six themes, all of them common to many family histories:

Skeletons – every family has its hidden secrets that fall from the family tree once it is given a good shake, such as: illegitimacy and lunacy – particularly the differing attitudes about both.

Military – most of us have ancestors who fought in the world wars of the last century; one in seven of our forefathers fought in World War II.

Immigration and Emigration – millions of us are here today because of ancestors who came to this country from elsewhere, while many of us will find that our families have at some time left this Sceptred Isle in search of better things.

Occupations – finding out how our ancestors earned their daily bread is a fascinating glimpse into the way they lived and the struggles they faced.

Social Migration – how and why our ancestors moved around the country.

Everyday Life – discovering how our ancestors spent their leisure time and family life.

The final section can be used as a guide to finding the relevant records and documents, with useful places to visit and helpful websites to browse. Armed with this information, we hope to help you to do more than simply discover who your great-great-grandfather was, we hope that you will be able to plot the fascinating story of his life.

Along the way, you will also encounter the family histories of the six celebrities featured in the second series of *Who Do You Think You Are?*, including a piece written by Nick Barratt telling how he and his team pieced together Jeremy Paxman's story. Celebrities, however, are not the only people to have colourful family histories, which is why we have included several extraordinary stories from ordinary members of the public. When we came to put this book together, we made an appeal to you, through the National Archives, to send us your stories; the response was overwhelming, and our favourites are reproduced here. We have also included a case study or two, including the life and times of William Towers; a fascinating example of how exciting a seemingly humdrum life can be once you get beyond the basic details of birth, marriage and death.

There is so much more to family history than dry facts; there is always a story: a narrative and a plot in which your ancestors and your family are the main characters.

Section 1

Starting Out

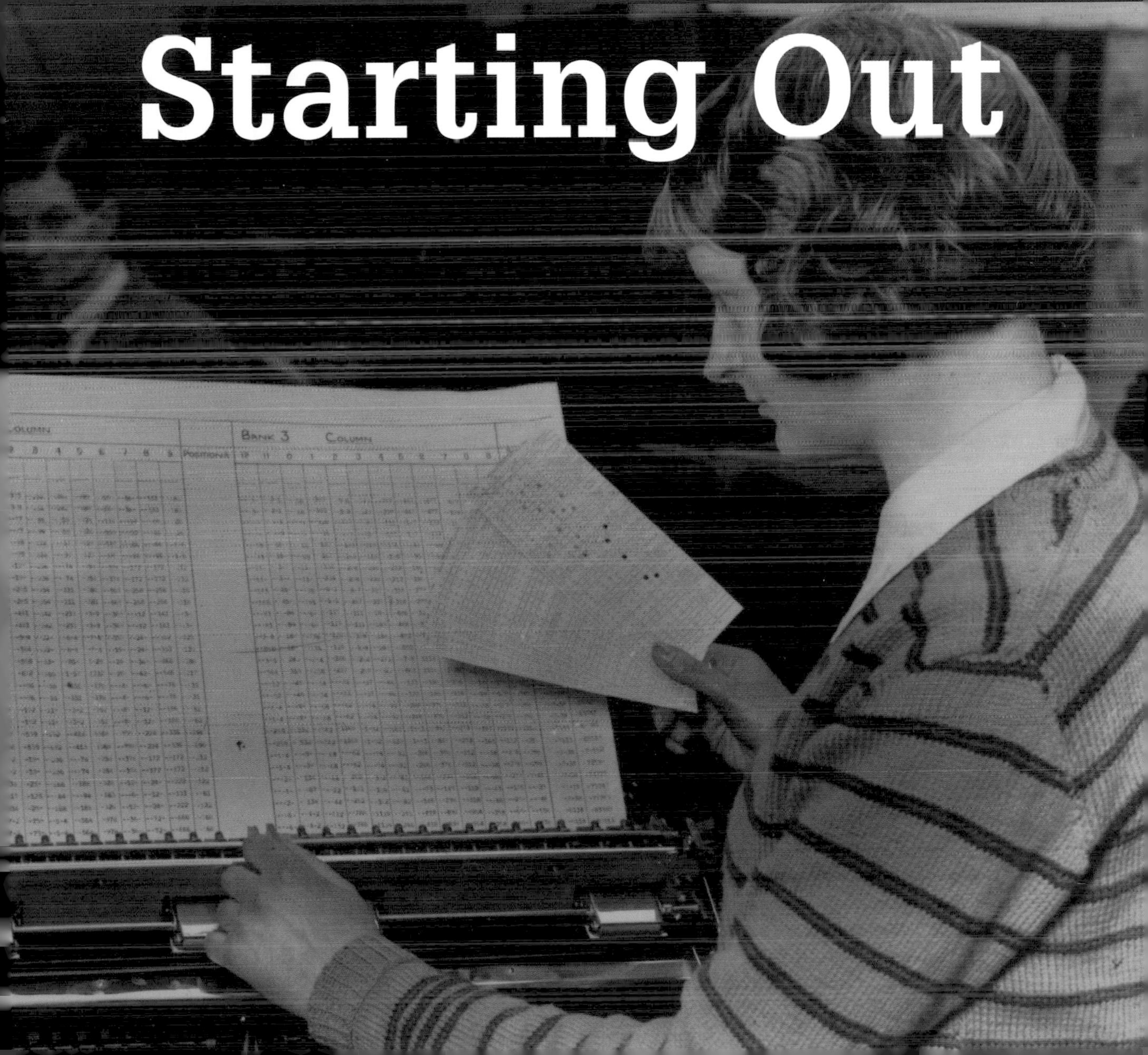

Simply by buying this book you have taken an important step towards gaining a better understanding of your family history. One striking aspect of genealogy is the number of times people say, 'I'd like to know more about my ancestors but I don't know where to start.' Or, 'I would trace my family tree but I don't have the time.' This first section of the book seeks to conquer both these excuses. We will equip you with the basic skills to start your search, before giving you the information, know-how and confidence to be able to sketch your family tree as quickly as possible.

Alternatively, you may have started tracing your family tree and hit a dead end (or should that be a withered branch?). In that case we hope this section outlining the four building blocks of family history – birth, marriage and death certificates; census returns; probate records; and parish records – will give you some fresh ideas or new paths to follow in order to complete the picture of your family's past.

Secrets and Lies

The aim of this first section is to provide beginners and novices with the tools they need to sketch the bare bones of their family history; subsequent sections will supply the meat. For the authors of this book, it is not your genes that count, but the stories that you can tell about your ancestors. The bald facts that so and so was born in 1845, lived in the village of Byheckerslike and is genetically related to you leave us a bit cold. However, it is necessary to find this out before investigating their lives in more detail. Consequently, learning that they had an illegitimate child, or lost their first wife through tuberculosis, then moved the family to the city in search of work and so radically altered the path of their family, facing all manner of setbacks with quiet determination and courage because 'it was the way of the world' at the time, is a gripping concept. The idea you share the same genes as this person is an immensely powerful thought: history is made personal.

Be warned: genealogy is a compulsive hobby. Dan speaks here from personal experience. Until his first child was born, like Jeremy Clarkson, one of the celebrities featured in the first series of *Who Do You Think You Are?*, he was a bit of an agnostic on the subject. Clarkson, famously, when asked to take part in the show, responded by saying: 'Why? My ancestors are too boring.' Turned out they were anything but.

Like most people, Dan was aware of a few family stories and legends but it didn't seem relevant somehow, certainly not that racy or exciting. Then his son was born and he remembered, oddly, feeling proud that the Waddell name would live on. Why? Dan realized it was because he was vaguely aware that the name stretched back hundreds of years and wanted it to carry on for a few more generations. He wanted to know more ...

First thing he did, like all the books tell you to do, was to contact his family and ask a few questions. His father had made a few tentative steps in tracing the Waddell family tree. Not one to let the truth get in the way of a good story, he told Dan that he'd heard of some Waddells who fought in the American Civil War. Dan knew it might be better to start a bit closer to home. First things first: he asked his father when his grandparents, now both dead, got married.

'Well,' he said, 'I was born in 1940, and they met about four years before I was born, so 1936 or so.'

Dan went to the Family Records Centre and started searching. At first he couldn't believe how many people were there. He thought some sort of event was going on, some sort of open day. He walked up to a member of staff behind the customer services desk and asked who all these people were. The response was quizzical. 'Ordinary people,' the staff member said.

Dan managed to fight his way through the scrum to the marriage certificates indexes for 1936 and started looking. Nothing there. He found the 1937 indexes. Same again. Nothing. OK, he thought, my dad is a couple of years out: it must be 1938. Still nothing. 1939 drew a blank also. It was at that point he thought he had gone too far forward in time. So he checked 1935. Zero. As were 1934, 1933, 1932 and 1931. Dan was puzzled. Perhaps their marriage had not been registered. If so, why? For the sake of completeness, he checked 1940,

Clarkson, famously, when asked to take part in the show, responded by saying: 'Why? My ancestors are too boring.' Turned out they were anything but.

though he knew that if they had got married then his grandmother would have been pregnant on her wedding day, and, as she was a good Catholic woman, that was most unlikely. Well, of course, there it was: in May 1940, four months before his father was born, his grandparents got married.

Family history often throws up dilemmas such as this; Dan was faced with a common one. Here he was faced with a piece of information, a secret that had lain undiscovered for more than half a century. What should he do? Keep it to himself? Or share it with his family and accept some might not know what to make of the news? He decided on the latter and rang his father. He told him the news and he was, as you might expect, shocked: Dan wondered whether he had done the right thing. But an hour or so later his father called back and said how it explained so many things. It had actually added to his understanding of his parents. Think about it: it was 1940; most of the eligible men were at war, which at that point was going against the Allies. The atmosphere must have been one of fear, of not knowing what was looming in the future. Dan's grandfather was a coalminer and so didn't go off to fight, which made him one of the few eligible bachelors around. Obviously they met and the rest is family history.

Dan was knocked off his feet. Here he was, two hours into researching his family history, and already he was unearthing family scandals. In a past life he had been a tabloid journalist, so scandal and gossip were his staple diet; this was manna from heaven.

> **Here he was faced with a piece of information, a secret that had lain undiscovered for more than half a century. What should he do? Keep it to himself?**

He couldn't believe how many myths he exploded. One family legend that everyone took for granted was that of his great-grandfather's death: the story was that he fell into a water-wheel at a malting. Dan remembered as a child being fascinated by this grisly story, always getting his granny to tell it again and again. (He was a pretty morbid kid, obviously.) Shortly after discovering the news of his grandparents' shotgun wedding, he pulled out his great-grandfather's death certificate and was crestfallen to learn that he had, in fact, died of kidney cancer. God knows where the water-wheel came into it. Other legends turned out to be true. Immediately Dan learned how compulsive a hobby it is: before he knew it, he was packing sandwiches and a Thermos flask with weak milky tea in preparation for an all-day stint at the Family Records Centre. Each time he rang his parents, one of them would answer and groan when they realized it was him. 'God, what have you found out now?' they'd ask.

Dan learned many things from this cursory expedition into his past: he learned never to believe a word anyone told him about his ancestors until he had checked it out for himself; he learned that time takes on a different aspect when you're flicking the Births/Marriages/Deaths indexes – hours race by; he learned that he hated microfilm more than any other substance on the planet; but most of all he learned that family history is without doubt one of the most fascinating subjects that exists.

By contrast, Nick has a more mercenary interest

in the subject; coming from an archival and historical background, he has undertaken only the most rudimentary research into his family's past, mainly because kindly great-uncles had done most of the work for him. These days, most of the genealogy he undertakes is done for others – hired historical help, if you like. However, the thrill of the chase and the 'eureka' moment when an elusive quarry finally gives up its secrets is not diminished by the fact that the research is not relevant to his family. Each case becomes a unique detective trail, with clues to be uncovered and problems to be solved. This is the excitement of family history – you never know what you are going to uncover next. Anyway, there are plenty of mysteries still to be uncovered in Nick's family tree – a mysterious grandmother with connections to Arthur Chase of the Chase Manhattan Bank, spirited away from Amsterdam before the outbreak of the First World War – but in the meantime, *Who Do You Think You Are?* and other projects keep him fully entertained.

In order to uncover the skeletons rattling around in your family's closet, you need to know a few basics. Armed with those, you will be able to try and see how your ancestors lived. People moan about history today and how it's taught; 'people don't learn enough about the Victorian era', they say, 'or the age of Empire'. But family history is a gateway to these bigger topics, a journey undertaken through the eyes of our ancestors, and a real opportunity to immerse yourself in the events that shaped this country. But it's an alternative version of history; not one where great dead white males are the heroes, but one where your own ancestors lived through the grime and smoke of the factories, the poverty and hardship of the urban slums, and the killing fields of the Somme. It's the history of Britain told through the life of its people. That is the pleasure of the television series: it's not about seeing Stephen Fry's ancestors and thinking how much they look like him; it's about seeing how the events of the last 150–200 years affected ordinary people, and discovering who were the linchpins in each of the celebrity's families, the person who changed the ultimate destiny of their descendants. We all have them, waiting to be discovered.

Starting Out

It is a good idea when you decide to take the plunge into your ancestral past to speak to members of your family first. This not only gives them a chance to divulge those dark, undisturbed secrets before your sleuthing does, it also will give you the vital crumbs of information you need to focus your search. No scrap of information should go unrecorded. Ask your relatives, if they are minded to help, to have a look in their bottom drawers or attic to see if there are any relics or heirlooms that have been handed down through the generations. The more information you can extract, the more straightforward your search will be. In particular, any of the following will be a massive help:

- ***Birth, marriage and death certificates.*** The information these hold is invaluable. See below.
- ***Photographs.*** When it comes to evoking the past, nothing beats old pictures of

ancestors. Find out from which long-dead relative you inherited your Roman nose, high forehead or wing-nut ears. Check on the back to find out details of names and when the picture was taken because that was often where people put such information.

- ***Letters.*** We are lucky: the most popular way our ancestors used to communicate was mail. However, our descendants will be less fortunate. Emails, phone calls and text messages are not recorded and kept – well, not unless you believe the conspiracy theorists – so our thoughts, hopes and dreams will not outlive us. Treasure any letters you can get hold of: they can offer a fascinating, detailed glimpse into the lives of our predecessors. Don't throw away the personal 'stuff of history'.
- ***Family Bible.*** Not every family has one, but if one does exist it is likely that the person who owned it has inscribed their name inside the front cover together with the day they inherited it. You may also find an inscription to the first recipient, along with the date of baptism.

It is also well worth contacting any surviving grandparents, aunts and uncles to see what clues they can give you. Of course, nothing beats oral evidence, so if the fount of all your family's knowledge is alive and willing to speak, pull up a chair, switch on a tape recorder and preserve those memories while you can. Just be wary of family myths and the fact that a few uncomfortable family secrets might have been airbrushed out of history. Try to get as many versions of a family legend as possible; where accounts tally, it is more likely that there's a grain of truth hidden amongst the embellishments added over time, and so these small nuggets of information should be followed up first in the search for further information.

First Steps

For some people it is the most difficult challenge of all. How do you go about organizing the information you already have, in order to carry out your search as quickly and efficiently as possible? And once a search has started and information comes pouring in, how do you manage and order it in a legible way?

Basically all you need is a pen and some paper. Start by sketching out a rough plan of what you know about your family. Write down all the names, dates and basic relationships that you know about, or have heard during your initial 'ask the family' stage of work. Place yourself at the centre of your family tree; after all, you will be doing all the hard work! Everyone else is then described in relation to you. Add your children below you, and then any grandchildren below them. Next, add your siblings and their children. Finally place your parents – an older generation – above you, and continue working back in time up to grandparents, great-grandparents and so on. By repeating this process you can quickly see at a glance what you know about your family, and – more importantly – where the gaps in your knowledge are.

It's best to work with several copies of your family tree as you go along. As you progress you will create various working copies that you can amend, scribble over, delete and doodle on when you reach a dead end; you may want to make abbreviated versions of your tree so that you can take them into archives with you to help you focus on one particular branch of the family. However, you should always maintain a master copy, on which you can record known or verified facts. On your working copy, make a note in pencil of evidence gathered from talking to other family members, such as presumed birth, death and marriage dates of possible relations. These can then be researched and added to the master copy when you get confirmation. Where possible, try to keep separate research notes for each family member, on an index card or a page in a notepad or exercise book. If you can develop some form of reference system that links your notes to the people on the family tree – perhaps using a card index system if you are not working on a computer – it will help you keep a clear idea of where you are going. Make sure that you keep abbreviations in notes and on the family tree as consistent as possible. There's no point coming back to your research after a couple of weeks and not being able to understand what it is you've written down on your working copy. Try to compile your own glossary of abbreviations as you go, adding new ones to the list as your family tree becomes more complex. There are standard terms of reference – b for birth, d for death, ch for christening, m or = for marriage – but you may want to formulate your own system. With all the information that you will be processing, it's pretty likely that your working copy will get quite confusing. When this happens, start again with a fresh version and date it. Keep the old one for reference; there's nothing worse than doing hours of research, managing to trace your family back to the Domesday Book, only for you to lose your notes and have to start again.

Births, Marriages and Deaths

The extension of the State into people's lives has been a controversial topic, like many other subjects, throughout modern British history, and not just a present-day obsession. But while many people have grumbled and mumbled about creeping bureaucracy, there is one large and expanding group of people who are profoundly thankful for the State's love of red tape, registration and regulations; family historians. Without records, returns and registrations, tracing one's ancestry would be impossible. Civil registration and census returns in particular,the introduction of which engendered frenzied debate and protest in the 19th century, have become essential to anyone seriously interested in tracing their family tree.

Since 1 July 1837, every birth, marriage and death in England and Wales has been required by law to be officially registered at a local Registrar's Office, and a certificate was then created to record details of the event. Before the introduction of civil registration, the Church had the responsibility for recording details of our ancestors' christenings, weddings and burials in local parish registers. Whilst these ecclesiastical records continued, and indeed

BIRTHS AND DEATHS REGISTRATION ACT, 1874.

CERTIFICATE of REGISTRY of BIRTH.

I, the undersigned, Do hereby Certify that the Birth of Margaret Allan born on the 18th day of July, 1884 has been duly Registered by me.

Witness my hand, this 9th day of September 1884.

Geo Watson, Registrar of Births and Deaths.

South Bishopwearmouth Sub-District.

[OVER.

Please Return.

London:—Printed by Authority of the Registrar General, by W. J. Johnson.

Above: This is an example of a short birth certificate, which carries basic genealogical information. Order a full certificate for more details.

are still created, the population at large adopted the new system remarkably quickly, though many people still did not bother until regulations were tightened in 1875, forcing greater compliance with the law. The resultant certificates provide crucial evidence for the family historian, not just about the person concerned but also about their relatives. It is possible to purchase duplicates of these certificates: these should be the first documents that a new family historian should tackle. Why? Certificates record a person's journey through life, or the major staging posts at least: when they were born, when and whom they married, and when and how they died. By careful manipulation of the data they contain, not only should you be able to add additional lines and branches to your family tree, but also begin to understand more about the lives of your ancestors.

For example, from looking at BMDs for one of your ancestors you can usually tell what socio-economic group they might have been born into by the occupation of the father on a birth certificate; the social mores of the day by their age upon marrying; and the social conditions they lived under by their cause of death. On each type of certificate, you will also find addresses, which will be useful when it comes to using census returns.

The rapid population growth of the early 19th century, together with concerns over the implications of rapid urban expansion on public health and poverty, led to the creation of the Office of the Registrar General. Its job was to collect statistical data on demographic trends, which would be used to govern the country more effectively. One of the most important strands in this policy was the introduction of civil registration for births, marriages and deaths. Local Registration Districts and Sub-Districts were created, initially based on Poor Law Union boundaries, each district covering a defined

(Page 128) **Certified Copy of an Entry of Marriage.**

Pursuant to the Acts Anno Sexto et Septimo Gulielmi IV, Regis, ... Cap. lxxxvi, et Anno Primo Victoriæ Reginæ cap. xxii. 61 and 62 Vic. Reg, ch. 58.

1908 Marriage Solemnized at the Parish Church in the Parish of Bishopwearmouth in the Counties of Sunderland & Durham

No.	When Married.	Name and Surname.	Age.	Condition.	Rank or Profession.	Residence at the time of Marriage.	Father's Name and Surname.	Rank or Profession of Father.
255	Twenty-Ninth September 1908	John Robert Sanderson	28 years	Bachelor	Railway Clerk	29 Low Row	Robert John Sanderson	Commercial Traveller
		Margaret Allan	24 years	Spinster	–	44 Harrogate Street	Robert Todd Allan	Master Mariner

Married in the Parish Church according to the Rites and Ceremonies of the Established Church, by Superintendent Registrar's Certificate by me J. J. McKitterick Curate

This Marriage was Solemnized between us, John Robert Sanderson, Margaret Allan; in the Presence of us, Robert Cairns, Elizabeth Allan

I hereby Certify the above to be a True Copy of the Entry No. 255 in the Marriage Register, for the said Parish of Bishopwearmouth the said Register being legally in my custody. Witness my Hand this 29 day of September

J J McKitterick Curate 29.9.08

Above: A full marriage certificate. From this we learn not only Margaret Allan's age at marriage, her occupation and who she married, but also the name and occupation of her father.

geographical area. From 1841, these districts were the same as the census districts, allowing you to move effectively from one source to the next when hunting down your ancestors. After three months, each local registry would produce an index of all births, marriages and deaths, and forward this information to the Registrar General's office. Central indexes incorporating all registration districts were compiled, referenced by the code allocated to every local district.

If you know where an event took place, you can search the local indexes – held at your nearest major library – and apply for a duplicate certificate. However, don't forget that the local and central indexes are not the same, so never order a certified copy from the central register using an index reference obtained from the local registry – you'll receive the documentation of a complete stranger! The national indexes are stored at the Family Records Centre, London (they can also now be viewed in their entirety on the website www.1837online.com, though you will have to pay to see the results of your search). The FRC is the first place aspiring family historians should visit, a veritable treasure trove of information. By preparing well, asking for advice from any members of staff and with a fair wind in your sails, it is possible to trace your family back a few generations in one visit. To order from the central index, either place a request online at www.gro.gov.uk, make a postal application to the Registrar General's Office (part of the Office of National Statistics) at Southport or fill out an application form at the Family Records Centre.

In theory, it should be possible to identify the date of any birth in England and Wales between 1837 and the present day; however, in practice this can be harder to achieve. There are several reasons why an event might not be recorded. For

IH 125680

(Printed by authority of the Registrar-General.)

The Statutory Fee for this Certificate is 2s. 7d. If required subsequently to registration, a Search Fee is payable in addition.

CERTIFIED COPY of an ENTRY OF DEATH.
Pursuant to the Births and Deaths Registration Acts, 1836 to 1929.

D. Cert.
R.B.D.

Registration District SUNDERLAND

1943. Death in the Sub-district of SUNDERLAND NORTH in the COUNTY BOROUGH OF SUNDERLAND.

No.	When and where Died.	Name and Surname.	Sex.	Age.	Rank or Profession.	Cause of Death.	Signature, Description, and Residence of Informant.	When Registered.	Signature of Registrar.
114	First September 1943 12 East View U.D.	John Robert Sanderson	Male	63 years	Railway Clerk (Retired)	1a Pulmonary Tuberculosis Certified by H.H. Dale Anderson M.B.	W. Chambers Brother-in-law In attendance 18 Sandringham Terrace Sunderland	Second September 1943	R.A. Wilkinson Registrar.

Insert in this Margin any Notes which appear in the original entry

I, RICHARD ALBERT WILKINSON, Registrar of Births and Deaths for the Sub-District of SUNDERLAND NORTH, in the COUNTY BOROUGH OF SUNDERLAND, do hereby certify that this is a true copy of the Entry No. 114 in the Register Book of Deaths for the said Sub-District, and that such Register Book is now legally in my custody.

WITNESS MY HAND this 9th day of September, 1943. R.A. Wilkinson Registrar of Births and Deaths.

CAUTION.—Any person who (1) falsifies any of the particulars on this Certificate, or (2) uses it as true, knowing it to be falsified, is liable to Prosecution.

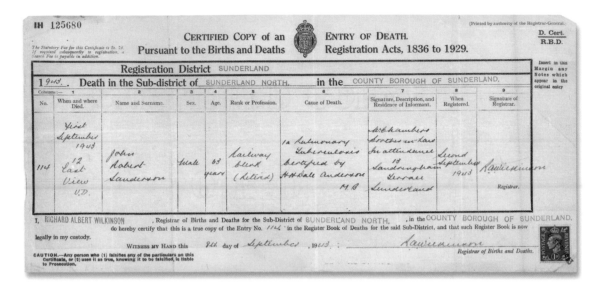

Above: *The death certificate of John Sanderson, Margaret Allan's husband. He died of tuberculosis during World War II.*

a start, errors are known to have occurred during the transfer of data from the district registries to the Registrar General's Office, and so the central lists may be incomplete or incorrectly indexed. Perhaps more significantly, there was no penalty for non-registration before 1875, and therefore no compulsion to come forward with information. If you can't find your relatives listed prior to 1875, try looking in local records such as parish or nonconformist baptism records. You should also consider the possibility that they were entered in the indexes under a different first name; we often refer to relatives by their nicknames, pet names or by an abbreviated version. Similarly, the registrars often wrote down what they heard, and so spelling errors might produce variant surnames.

Despite these pitfalls, birth, marriage and death certificates remain the building blocks of family history and can be used to construct a basic family tree. Start from a known date and work backwards. This may mean looking first of all for the death certificate of a relative to obtain their age, and then using this information to trace their birth certificate. Similarly, if you know when someone got married, order the marriage certificate to find the age of the bride and groom, and then look for birth certificates. Usually, the birth certificate will provide the names of both parents and allow you to repeat the process, so adding a new generation to your family tree.

From a birth certificate you can obtain your relative's date and place of birth, the name and residence of their mother (and sometimes her maiden name – for you to follow up later). The name and occupation of the father is also added to the certificate. A marriage certificate provides you with the full names of each spouse and the date of the marriage – more useful clues for further researches. You will also discover the names of the fathers of both bride and groom. From a death certificate you'll discover the date of death and final residence of your deceased ancestor. Perhaps of even more interest, though, is the name of the person who informs the authorities that a death has occurred. This is often a relative who can also be traced, thereby setting up another set of searches.

It is likely that not all of your ancestors were born, married or died in England and Wales. Many people gravitated to those countries from Ireland and Scotland. Researching their stories might involve a trip to those countries. Here is a brief guide to researching your Scottish and Irish roots.

Scotland

Having Scottish ancestors can be more fun than having English or Welsh ones for the simple reason that Scottish bureaucrats gave away more information. Civil registration did not begin until 1855, but when it did commence it was far more revealing. Birth certificates contain all the information of their English counterparts, but also the date and place of the parents' marriage. This saves masses of time, allowing the researcher to head straight for the marriage index and find the corresponding certificate without any need to rifle through the files. But that's not all: Scottish marriage certificates also feature the father *and* mother's names of both bride and groom. Death certificates also feature the name of the deceased's mother and father.

The General Register Office in Edinburgh holds all records. All the indexes are on computer, and you can view actual images of the records themselves without having to wait for duplicate certificates. Indeed, for a fee you can even search and view records online at www.scotlandspeople.gov.uk. To find out more about Scottish registration, visit www.gro-scotland.gov.uk.

Ireland

Civil Registration in Ireland began in 1864. At the General Register Office in Dublin (www.groireland.ie) you can search the records for all Ireland up to 1922, and the Republic of Ireland thereafter. There are no consolidated indexes; the records for each county are filed separately. The certificates offer virtually the same information as their English and Welsh counterparts, apart from death certificates, which don't offer information about cause of death.

Northern Ireland

Following the partition of Ireland in 1922, all records pertaining to Northern Ireland are held at the General Register Office in Belfast (www.groni.gov.uk/index.htm).

> **Having Scottish ancestors can be more fun than having English or Welsh ones for the simple reason that Scottish bureaucrats gave away more information.**

Death and Disease – You Can't Beat 'em

It may seem morbid to say, but death certificates make for fascinating reading. Far more than either a marriage or birth certificate, they can tell you a great deal about the life the deceased led.

Take their age at death. By 1901, for example, the upper classes' average life expectancy was 60, so if your ancestor made it to that great age then there was a good chance they lived the well-fed, healthy existence that usually stemmed from having money. If they were unfortunate enough to be poor then they would be lucky to get past 30. Disease and epidemics stalked the poorest areas of Britain, the cities in particular. This is where the cause of death can tell you a great deal; perhaps your ancestor was one of many who contracted and died of tuberculosis, or any number of other ailments. Sometimes, particularly for the working classes, their deaths may have been linked to the conditions in which they worked. Don't be put off by an unfamiliar or archaic name in the cause of death column. Either seek out a medical dictionary, or, even quicker, type the cause of death into an Internet search engine and see the results.

IC 648206

CERTIFIED COPY of an ENTRY OF DEATH
Pursuant to the Births and Deaths Registration Act, 1953

Registration District KENSINGTON

1965. Death in the Sub-district of ... in the ROYAL BOROUGH OF KENSINGTON

No.	When and where died	Name and surname	Sex	Age	Occupation	Cause of death	Signature, description, and residence of informant	When registered	Signature of registrar
10	Twenty fourth January 1965. 28 Hyde Park Gate, Kensington	Winston Leonard Spencer Churchill	Male	90 years	The Right Honourable, K.G, O.M, C.H, Statesman	I(a) Cerebral thrombosis (b) Cerebral arteriosclerosis II Congestion of lungs Certified by Moran, M.R.C.S.	S. A. P. Montague Browne Present at the death 44 Eaton Place, S.W.1	Twenty sixth January 1965.	J. Hebborn Registrar.

I, JOHN HEBBORN, Registrar of Births and Deaths for the Sub-district of ..., in the ... do hereby certify that this is a true copy of Entry No. 10 in the Register Book of Deaths for the said Sub-district, and that such Register Book is now legally in my custody.

WITNESS MY HAND this 26th day of January, 1965. J. Hebborn
Registrar of Births and Deaths.

CAUTION.—Any person who (1) falsifies any of the particulars on this certificate, or (2) uses a falsified certificate as true, knowing it to be false, is liable to prosecution.

Above: *The death certificate of Sir Winston Churchill.*

Census Working Overtime

On Sunday 29 May 1831, Mr Richard Stopher made his way around the village of Saxmundham, Suffolk, calling at the houses of his friends and neighbours. His task was to collect important statistics as part of the nationwide census. By the end of the day, Stopher's notebook had been filled with the number of occupied and unoccupied houses, families, men and women, occupations, and statistics for baptisms, marriages and burials.

Although only numerical totals were officially required, Stopher jotted down the names of the head of each household as well. He had a deep interest in the history of his community, and, when he returned home, he added the names of former occupants of each property, as far back as the 1790s.

We should be thankful for these census pioneers. The population of 19th-century Britain, not unlike their 21st-century counterparts, were deeply suspicious of any encroachment by the state into how they lived their lives. The introduction of the census was greeted with immense scepticism, even downright hostility, which is why the early censuses were simply exercises in statistical data, a mere head count of the population and no more. By 1831, however, enlightened souls such as Mr Stopher were going further, and scenes like the one outlined above were repeated across the country; this thirst for knowledge was reflected in the new census forms issued in 1841. For the first time, enumerators were asked to collect the name, rough age and place of birth for each household member. This was, once again, not without controversy, but the argument was won: it was not only important for a nation to know how many people lived within its borders, but also how they lived and where. The modern census started here.

Above: *An 1870s illustration showing census-taking, from the wealthy to the destitute.*

So, when it comes to using the census, bear in mind that only those from 1841 will be of use. Also note that census records are closed for 100 years, and at present you can only view the returns for 1841–1901.

The 1841 census is less informative than those for 1851–1901, as it only records the full name, age, gender and occupation for each individual in

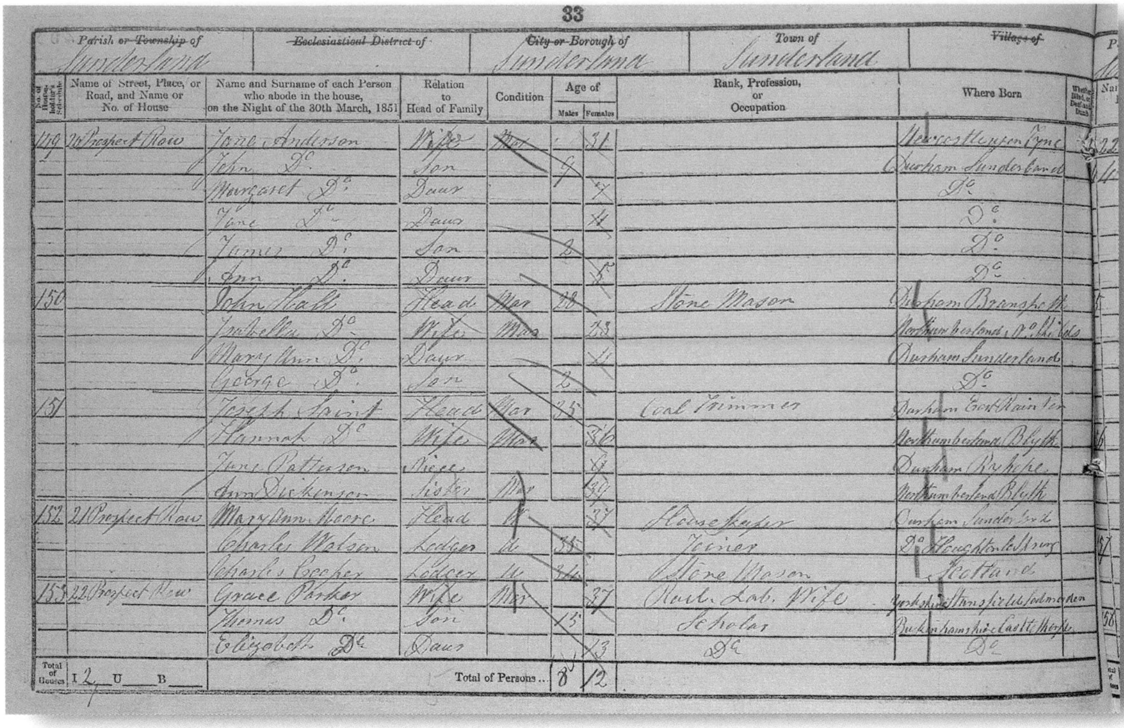

33

Parish ~~or Township~~ of Sunderland	~~Ecclesiastical District of~~	~~City or~~ Borough of Sunderland	Town of Sunderland	~~Village of~~

No. of Householder's Schedule	Name of Street, Place, or Road, and Name or No. of House	Name and Surname of each Person who abode in the house, on the Night of the 30th March, 1851	Relation to Head of Family	Condition	Age of Males	Age of Females	Rank, Profession, or Occupation	Where Born
149	20 Prospect Row	Jane Anderson	Wife	Mar		31		Newcastle upon Tyne
		John Do.	Son		9			Durham Sunderland
		Margaret Do.	Daur			7		Do.
		Jane Do.	Daur			4		Do.
		James Do.	Son		2			Do.
		Ann Do.	Daur			5		Do.
150		John Hall	Head	Mar	28		Stone Mason	Durham Brancepeth
		Isabella Do.	Wife	Mar		23		Northumberland, No. Shields
		Mary Ann Do.	Daur			4		Durham Sunderland
		George Do.	Son		2			Do.
151		Joseph Saint	Head	Mar	35		Coal Trimmer	Durham East Rainton
		Hannah Do.	Wife	Mar		36		Northumberland Blyth
		Jane Patterson	Niece			8		Durham Ryhope
		Ann Dickinson	Sister	Mar		39		Northumberland Blyth
152	21 Prospect Row	Mary Ann Moore	Head	W		37	Housekeeper	Durham Sunderland
		Charles Watson	Lodger	U	35		Joiner	Do. Houghton le Spring
		Charles Cooper	Lodger	U	24		Stone Mason	Scotland
153	22 Prospect Row	Grace Parker	Wife	Mar		37	Rail. Lab. Wife	Yorkshire Stansfield Todmorden
		Thomas Do.	Son		15		Scholar	Buckinghamshire Castlethorpe
		Elizabeth Do.	Daur			13	Do.	Do.
Total of Houses	I 2 U B		Total of Persons..		8	12		

Above: *A census return from 1851. Note that 14 people were living at 20 Prospect Row.*

every property on the day of the census. Everyone over the age of 15 had their age rounded down to the nearest five years, so care should be taken when attempting to use this data to confirm birth dates. People are grouped into households within a particular property. From 1851, however, it gets more fun: you will find the full name, precise age and marital status of every person within each household. You will also find their relationship to the head of the household, their gender and their occupation, as well as the parish and county of birth for every person within each household.

So, how do you use the census returns to further your search? The fact is they provide far more information about our ancestors than birth, marriage or death certificates do. When you find your ancestors on the census, look at the entries for surrounding houses on their street. How many people lived in one house? What were the occupations of their neighbours? It was common for people engaged in similar jobs to live near each other. This information will give you an insight into the social conditions in which your ancestors lived.

One idea is to attempt to track your ancestors from the 1841 census to 1901, to see how their occupations, conditions, indeed their whole lives changed. And for those who are seeking to trace their family trees beyond 1837 and the beginning of the era of civil registration, the ages given on the census will give you clues about birth dates, allowing you to narrow your search when the time comes to scour parish registers.

Censuses are invaluable for troubleshooting or locating that elusive ancestor who may have slipped through the net. Most family historians encounter one ancestor who seems to have evaded civil registration, or whose trail goes suddenly cold. Then it pays to turn to census returns to see if you can locate them there. If you are successful, then an age will allow you to find a birth certificate, or even a marriage certificate if they have tied the knot.

Census records for England and Wales are stored on microfilm at the Family Records Centre, London; Scottish records are at New Register House, Edinburgh. You can also access relevant copies at county record offices, or at family-history centres maintained by the Church of Jesus Christ of Latter-day Saints. Sadly, Irish records for the 19th century have not survived, but you can view records for 1901 and 1911 (which are largely complete) at the National Archives, Dublin, with copies available at the Public Record Office of Northern Ireland, Belfast.

For the purpose of the census, the country was divided into registration and sub-registration districts, and the process generated enumeration books that covered districts of several hundred houses. It is vital for those researching their family history to know in advance roughly where their relatives lived, and preferably their street address if they lived in a city or large town. Fortunately, there are place and street indexes available, to help narrow down the relevant documents.

> **One idea is to attempt to track your ancestors from the 1841 census to 1901, to see how their occupations, conditions, indeed their whole lives changed.**

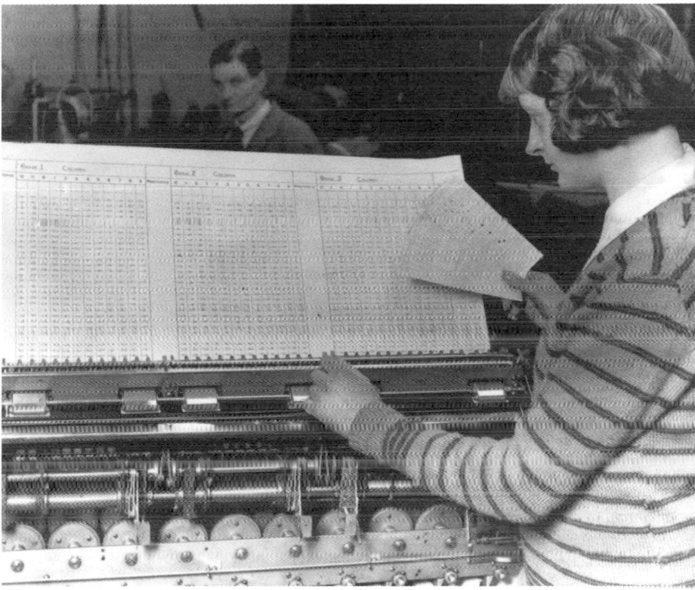

Above: *Machines producing census results in 1931.*

Census Records Online

In January 2002, the 1901 census was launched with a great fanfare to the waiting world as the first major family-history dataset to be viewed online. Unfortunately it promptly crashed, the server being knocked over by the sheer weight of numbers trying to access the material. Since then, things have calmed down a little but the 1901 census can now

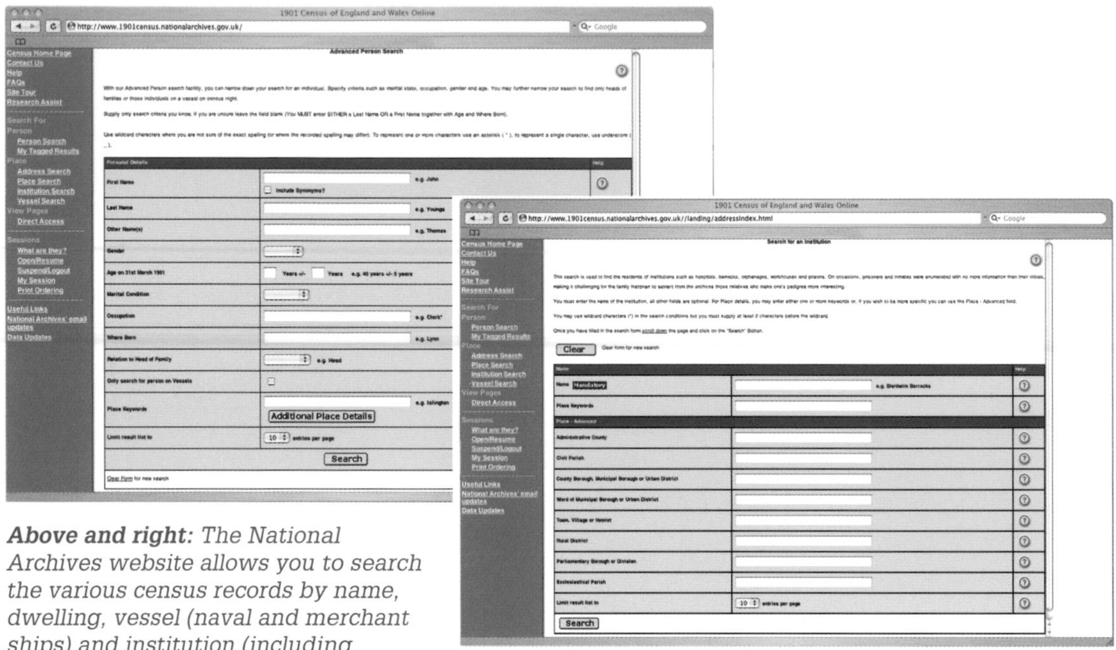

***Above and right:** The National Archives website allows you to search the various census records by name, dwelling, vessel (naval and merchant ships) and institution (including hospitals, orphanages, prisons, barracks and workhouses).*

Ancestry.co.uk – 1901 England Census

http://content.ancestry.co.uk/iexec/?htx=List&dbid=7814&ti=5538&r=5538&o_xid=18685&o_lid=1

Ancestry.co.uk
Discover Your Family Story

Home | Search | Family Trees | Ancestry Community

You are here: Search > Census > UK Census Collection > 1901 England Census

1901 England Census

Ranked Search | Exact Search

Enter as much info as you can – even a **guess** can help. See search tips

First name | Last name

Residence
County or island: All available counties | Civil parish | Town

Personal
Gender: Any | Relationship to head of household | Birth Year +/- 0

Birthplace
Country | County or island | Parish or place

Census
RG13/ Piece | Folio | Page # | Keyword(s)

Search

To browse census images, click on a county link below. Subsequent screens will allow you to choose a civil parish and an enumeration district.

***Above:** Ancestry.co.uk holds a range of records from the UK, including census, ecclesiastical, parish and immigration records.*

be seen as a trail-blazing success. The National Archives have formed a partnership with Ancestry, and to date the 1851–1891 records are also available online, with free access to those who view the records at the National Archives or Family Records Centre, or via subscription at www.ancestry.co.uk.

To cater for those without access to the Internet, the 1901 returns are also available on microfiche at the National Archives and the Family Records Centre, London. Copies are also available, as for other censuses, at relevant county record offices and local libraries.

In the years leading up to the release of the census returns in 2002, over 1.5 million pages contained in the enumerators' returns were transcribed, with the resultant data entered into a series of linked databases that include every person named in the census, along with their place of abode, family or household members, age, place of birth and occupation. These transcriptions have been checked for accuracy, although it is likely that some errors may still have occurred. A similar process has generated searchable databases for the other census records as well.

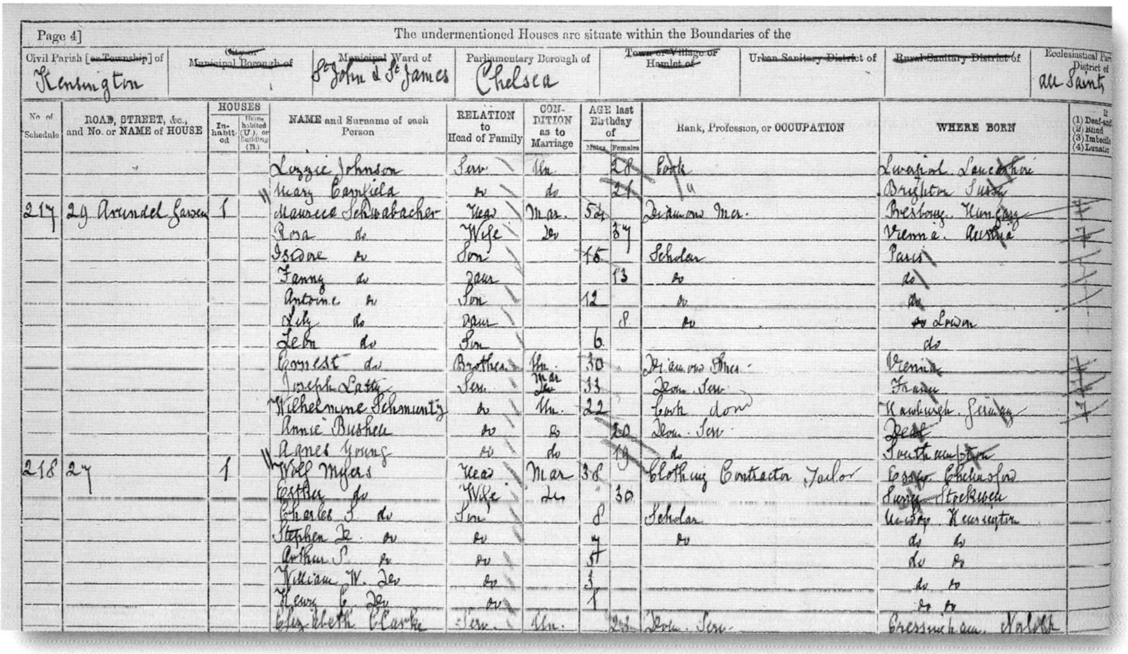

Way Back ...

A less straightforward but often invaluable source of information can be found in many parishes, in their registers of baptisms, marriages and burials. From 1538 in England and Wales, and 1555 in Scotland, each parish in the kingdom was required to keep these, and they are very useful to genealogists. However, it is important to stress that most of the records prior to 1837 do not provide

Above: *Census returns are a mine of information, allowing you to pinpoint your ancestors at a moment in time*

an actual date of birth or death, but only the date of the event that followed it (baptism or burial).

Parish registers are not a comprehensive record, as they were maintained at the discretion of the local vicar. If he was a diligent chap, who at the end of each week or month noted down all the baptisms, burials and weddings he had administered, then the records will be of great use. However, if he was a dilettante, an irregular keeper of records, then the register may be of little help to family historians. It's all down to luck. Again, how much detail the vicar recorded was his decision. Some entries are sparse to say the least: a record of baptism, for example, may only give the date, the name of the child and the name of the father. Just pray you don't have to go searching through the

The Life of William Towers

As an example of what you can learn from certificates and census returns, we took the life of one man and used birth, marriage and death certificates, coupled with census returns, to determine what screenwriters would call the 'narrative arc' of William Towers, but what we call the simple facts of his life.

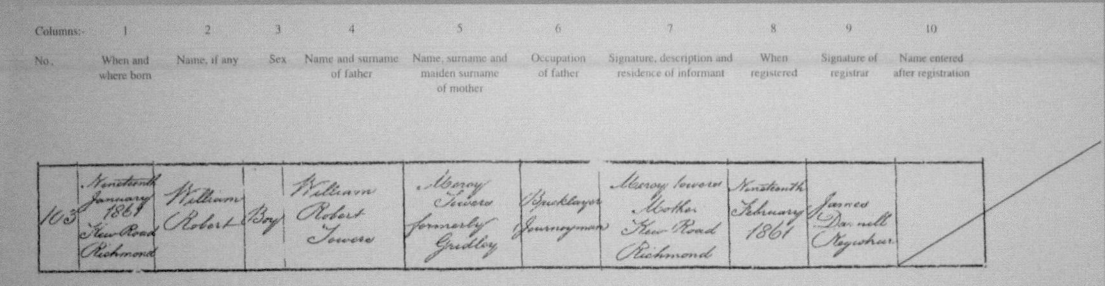

Columns:-	1	2	3	4	5	6	7	8	9	10
No.	When and where born	Name, if any	Sex	Name and surname of father	Name, surname and maiden surname of mother	Occupation of father	Signature, description and residence of informant	When registered	Signature of registrar	Name entered after registration
103	Nineteenth January 1861 Kew Road Richmond	William Robert	Boy	William Robert Towers	Mercy Towers formerly Gridley	Bricklayer Journeyman	Mercy Towers Mother Kew Road Richmond	Nineteenth February 1861	James Darnell Registrar	

Above: *The birth certificate of William Towers.*

William was born in 1861 in Surrey on 19 January at Kew Road, Richmond; this was also the family's home as the address of his mother on the birth certificate, the wonderfully named Mercy Towers, née Gridley, attests. His full name was William Robert Towers; his father's full name was the same. It was common for sons to be named after their fathers in such a way, where now it is less so. William senior was a journeyman bricklayer, which means he worked wherever the work was.

The next time William junior (let's call him Will to differentiate him from his dad) encounters civil registration is the census of 1871. Here he is 10 years old, and the family is still living in Richmond, though at a new address, 9 Bottoms Place. This census tells us that Will is William and Mercy's second child; their eldest is 11-year-old Elizabeth. But since Will's birth the couple have been busy: there are five other children listed at the address, all of them boys – Henry (7), George (6), Edwin (5), James (2) and 9-month-old Thomas. It appears that none of the Towers children are being educated because the word 'scholar' does not appear next to any of their names, nor does any occu-

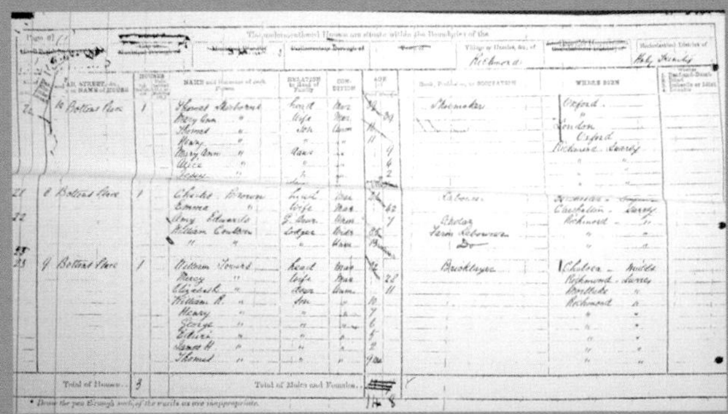

Above:: *William appears on the census return of 1861.*

Above: The marriage certificate of William Towers.

pation. The family are living on the wages brought in by William's bricklaying job. Either side of the Towers live Charles Sherborne, a shoemaker, his wife and six children; and Charles Brown, a labourer, his wife, granddaughter and two lodgers. From this we can confirm that this was a working-class area.

Scroll forward to 1881. The family have moved to George Street in Battersea, closer to the heart of London. Elizabeth has left home, presumably to get married (or to escape all those brothers: since the last census the Towers have added two more children, Jim and Arthur, both boys, taking the tally to seven boys, one girl. The census also tells us that Will and Henry have both followed in their father's footsteps and become bricklayers, while George has become a grocer and Edwin is idle, it seems. Thomas, Jim and Arthur are all at school, but then an education act in 1880 made school compulsory.

Later that year, on Christmas Day to be exact, Will, aged 21, married Louisa Johnson, 21, at Christ Church in Battersea. Louisa's

Above: William appears again in 1881.

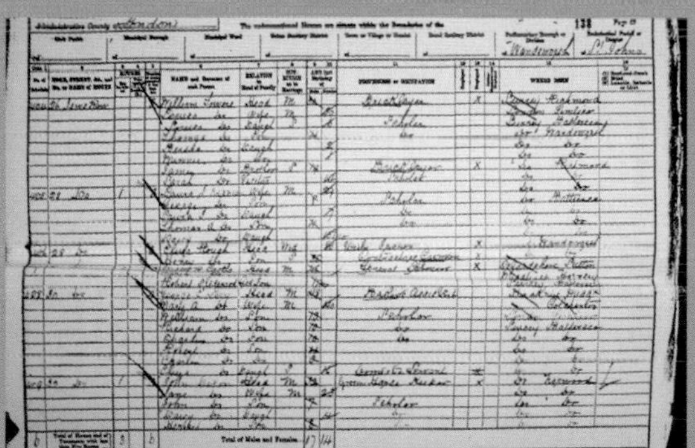

Above:: And once again in 1891.

The Life of William Towers

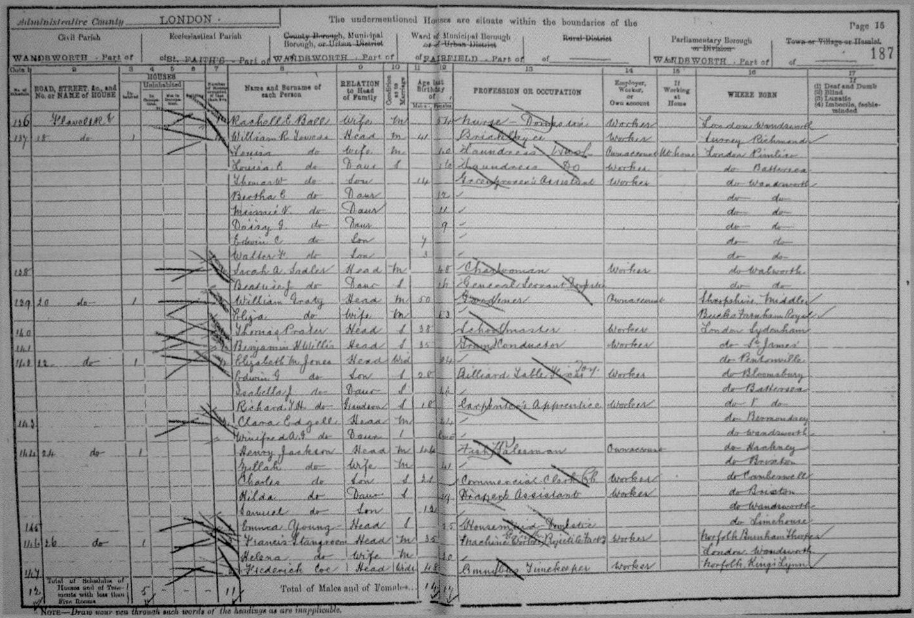

Administrative County LONDON. The undermentioned Houses are situate within the boundaries of the — Page 15

Civil Parish WANDSWORTH Part of — Ecclesiastical Parish of St. FAITH'S Part of — ~~County Borough~~, Municipal Borough, ~~or Urban District~~ WANDSWORTH Part of — Ward of Municipal Borough ~~or of Urban District~~ of FAIRFIELD Part of — ~~Rural District~~ of — Parliamentary Borough ~~or Division~~ WANDSWORTH Part of — ~~Town or Village or Hamlet~~ of — 187

No. of Schedule	Road, Street, &c., and No. or Name of House	Houses Inhabited	Name and Surname of each Person	Relation to Head of Family	Condition as to Marriage	Age (Males)	Age (Females)	Profession or Occupation	Employer, Worker, or Own account	If Working at Home	Where Born
136	Flavell Rd		Rachell E. Ball	Wife	M		57	Nurse – Domestic	Worker		London Wandsworth
137	18 do	1	William R. Towers	Head	M	41		Bricklayer	Worker		Surrey Richmond
			Louisa do	Wife	M		40	Laundress Wash.	Own account	At home	London Pimlico
			Louisa E. do	Daur	S		16	Laundress Do	Worker		do Battersea
			Thomas W. do	Son		14		Greengrocer's Assistant	Worker		do Wandsworth
			Bertha E. do	Daur			12				do do
			Minnie V. do	Daur			11				do do
			Daisy J. do	Daur			9				do do
			Edwin C. do	Son		7					do do
			Walter F. do	Son		3					do do
138			Sarah A. Sadler	Head	M		45	Charwoman	Worker		do Walworth
			Beatrice J. do	Daur	S		16	General Servant Domestic			do do
139	20 do	1	William Goaty	Head	M	50		Gardener	Own account		Shropshire, Middle
			Eliza do	Wife	M		53				Bucks Farnham Royal
140			Thomas Prater	Head	S	38		Schoolmaster	Worker		London Sydenham
141			Benjamin H. Willis	Head	S	35		Tram Conductor	Worker		do St James
142	12 do	1	Elizabeth M. Jones	Head	Wid		64				do Pentonville
			Edwin J. do	Son	S	28		Billiard Table [illegible]	Worker		do Bloomsbury
			Isabella J. do	Daur	S		16				do Battersea
			Richard J. H. do	Grandson	S	18		Carpenter's Apprentice	Worker		do " do
143			Clara Edgell	Head	M		24				do Bermondsey
			Winifred A. J. do	Daur			2 mo				do Wandsworth
144	24 do	1	Henry Jackson	Head	M	44		Fish Salesman	Own account		do Hackney
			Zillah do	Wife	M		41				do Brixton
			Charles do	Son	S	21		Commercial Clerk	Worker		do Camberwell
			Hilda do	Daur	S		19	Drapers Assistant	Worker		do Brixton
			Samuel do	Son		12					do Wandsworth
145			Emma Young	Head	S		35	Housemaid Domestic			do Limehouse
146	26 do	1	Francis Stangroom	Head	M	35		Machine Worker Projectile Factory	Worker		Norfolk Burnham Thorpe
			Helena do	Wife	M		30				London Wandsworth
147			Frederick Coe	Head	Wid	48		Omnibus Timekeeper	Worker		Norfolk, Kings Lynn
12	Total of Schedules of Houses and of Tenements with less than Five Rooms	5	Total of Males and of Females			14	17				

Note—Draw your pen through such words of the headings as are inapplicable.

Above: *William appears for the last time in 1901; he was to die 5 years later of 'Locomotor Ataxy'.*

father George was a plasterer, which allows us to speculate whether their fathers worked together, or whether Will worked with George, and that's how the couple came to meet. It seems more than likely.

Ten years later, in the 1891 census, Will and Louisa have settled down in Wandsworth, on the rather politically incorrectly named Jews Row. They have three daughters: Louisa junior (6), Bertha (2) and Minnie (1), and one son, 4-year-old Thomas. Will's younger brother James is also living with the family, and they have a 'visitor', Sarah Towers. Perhaps, given her surname, she was a cousin but not named as such.

The 1901 census reveals the family to have moved once more: to Flavell Road in Wandsworth. They now have seven children: Daisy (9), Edwin (7) and Walter (3) completing the brood. Will is still bricklaying at 41, but Louisa is now working as a laundress, as is Louisa junior. We could infer that they have hit hard times, or the building trade did, so forcing the two eldest women to supplement the family's income. Their eldest son Thomas is a greengrocer's assistant, and it is possible that he is working for his Uncle George.

Will's end came in January 1906 at the home in Flavell Road. He was 45 when he succumbed to 'Locomotor Ataxy'; '8 years' is scribbled next to it, which indicates how long he might have suffered from the disease. Asthenia is also mentioned. So how did he die? Locomotor Ataxy, or Locomotor Ataxia, is, basically, syphilis of the spinal cord. It was progressive – as the '8 years' suggests – and means that Will's movements would have become increasingly uncoordinated and clumsy, perhaps even to the point of paralysis (though his death certificate indicates he was still working as a journeyman bricklayer). It could have been endemic syphilis, which occurred only in areas of very poor hygiene (it has long since been wiped out everywhere apart from the tropics), a factor which might have applied to a poor part of a deprived area of London, like the one in which Will and his family lived. But it is unlikely. More likely is that it was venereal syphilis: 'the pox' to give it its colloquial name of the time.

The pox might have been transmitted from his mother and lain dormant, or he could have contracted it through sex – though had it been the former he would have been lucky to make it past late childhood. The syphilis would have gone through several stages, locomotor ataxia being the final, fatal stage. It is fair to say the previous eight years would not have been much fun for Will, and he might have shown outward signs of the disease other than his gait or clumsiness. Asthenia is a medical term for 'weakness'; it seems he became so weak he died, although it can be used as a euphemism for tuberculosis, but it is unlikely that a physician would employ such weasel words about that disease when he did not pull punches when it came to syphilis. Syphilis was not curable until well after the discovery of penicillin in 1928.

CERTIFIED COPY OF AN ENTRY OF DEATH

GIVEN AT THE GENERAL REGISTER OFFICE

Application Number Y570883

REGISTRATION DISTRICT Wandsworth

1906 DEATH in the Sub-district of Southfields in the County of London

Columns:– 1 No.	2 When and where died	3 Name and surname	4 Sex	5 Age	6 Occupation	7 Cause of death	8 Signature, description and residence of informant	9 When registered	Signature of registrar
159	Twenty fourth January 1906 18 Havell Road	William Robert Towers	Male	45 years	A Bricklayer Journeyman	Locomotor Ataxy 8 years Asthenia certified by Henry Carmichael M.B.	[illegible] Towers Widow of deceased present at the death 18 Havell Road Wandsworth	Twenty fourth January 1906	W. V. [illegible] Registrar

Above: The death certificate of William Towers.

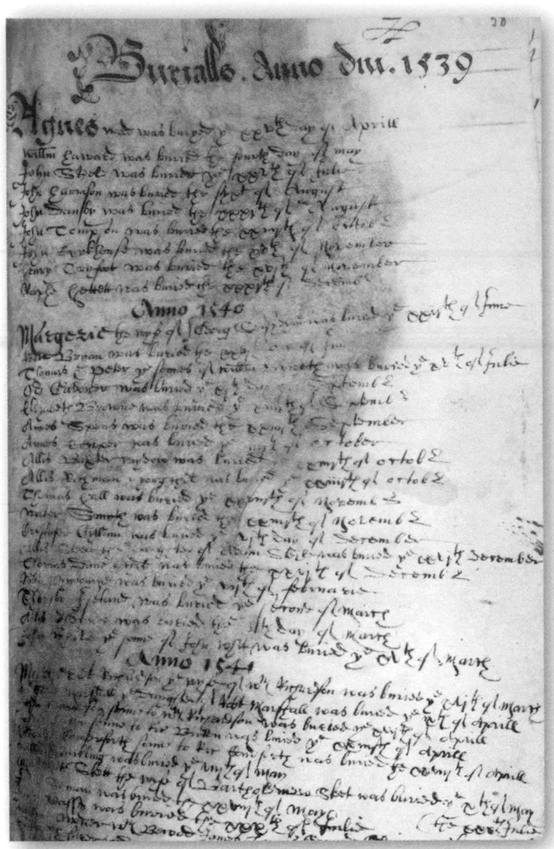
Burialls. Anno Dni. 1539

Anno 1540

Anno 1541

Above: *Burial entries from the parish register of St Peter's Church in Dunwich, the Suffolk town which was swallowed by the sea in 1697.*

parish register files for St Peter's, Dorchester, for a burial in 1645. 'In twelve months there died 52 persons whose names are not inserted, the old clerk being dead who had the notes,' it reads.

Likewise, luck can play a part in deciphering the texts. Some are easy to read, others extremely difficult, according to the handwriting of the person charged with making the entries. If you are having problems making sense of the handwriting you encounter in some parish registers, then ask a member of staff in the record office you are using. Most have experience of old handwriting and should be able to provide you with help.

Most of the records can be viewed on microfiche. Theoretically, you should be able to obtain the name of the individual you are interested in, the date of specific events and, in the case of baptisms, the parents' identity.

Try scanning several years to pick up all family members. You may also need to look through records of neighbouring parishes to pick up everyone of potential interest. In many areas, printed transcripts have been prepared that will save you squinting at the fiche.

It is important to note that, until 1752, the start of the year in England was 25 March, not 1 January – so you may come across entries such as '24 February 1678/9', indicating both possible dates.

For those to whom the idea of developing a bout of myopia or a migraine while squinting at a barely legible scrawl made by a vicar more than 250 years ago is anathema, there is a possible alternative: the International Genealogical Index, prepared by the Church of Jesus Christ of Latter-day Saints (better known as the Mormons). They provide this sterling service because it is their belief that those who convert to the Mormon faith should baptize their ancestors, so being able to trace one's genealogy is hugely important. The IGI covers every part of the British Isles, usually subdivided into county or region, and is arranged alphabetically, by surname. However, it doesn't include most burials, and doesn't cover all parishes. You will need to have an idea of the geographical location of your family's origins, and you may need to travel to distant archives. Or you can log on to www.familysearch.org, the IGI's website. It is by no means complete or entirely accurate, but it is easy to navigate and often a good place to start.

There are also some registers for foreign churches and non-Anglican religions, such as Quakers, Roman Catholics, Muslims and Jews. Many of these were deposited with the Registrar General when official registration was introduced in 1837, and will be with the National Archives. Modern records are likely to be with the relevant organization or place of worship, for example a mosque or synagogue.

> **Until 1752, the start of the year in England was 25 March, not 1 January – so you may come across entries such as '24 February 1678/9', indicating both possible dates.**

Where There's a Will ...

One of the best ways of gleaning information about family relationships is via an individual's will, which usually contains specific bequests to family members. From this you can make a host of deductions, most significantly about who was and who wasn't in favour. Often who isn't included is more revealing than who is. If someone is bequeathed a sixpence, you can take it they were not in that ancestor's good books, but had to be given something to prevent them from objecting. The details of a will, listing a person's possessions for example, can offer you a glimpse into their personality, which is not something that leaps from a marriage certificate or a census return.

Before 1858, the executor or executrix would register the will in the relevant ecclesiastical court to obtain a grant of probate, thereby allowing the bequests to be fulfilled. After 1858 a Central Court of Probate was established, where all wills for England and Wales were registered. Nowadays wills are registered at the Principal Probate Registry.

If an individual died without a will, then letters of administration would be granted permitting the heir

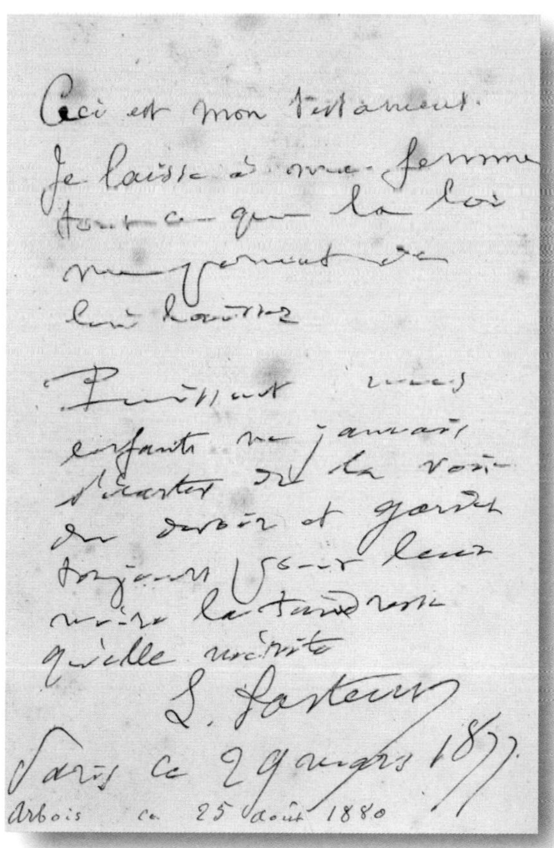

Ceci est mon testament.
Je laisse à ma femme tout ce que la loi me permet de lui laisser.
Puissent mes enfants ne jamais s'écarter de la voie du devoir et garder toujours pour leur mère la tendresse qu'elle mérite.
L. Pasteur
Paris ce 29 mars 1877.
Arbois ce 25 août 1880

Above: *The will of Louis Pasteur, from 1887.*

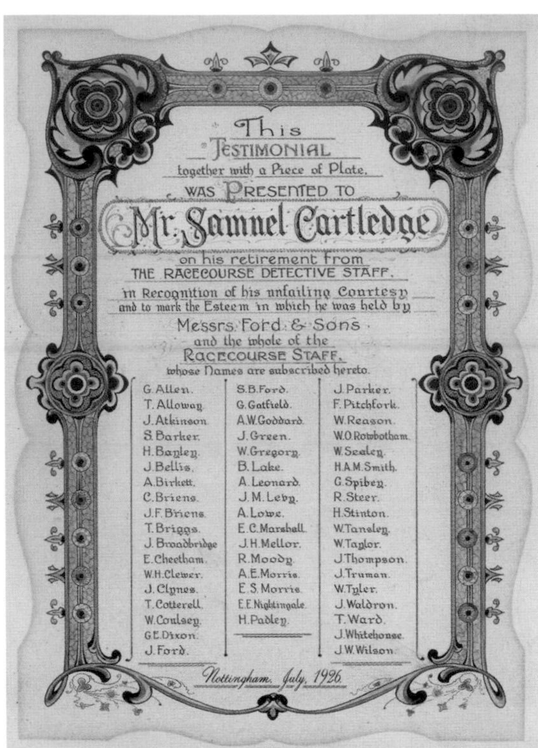

This Testimonial
together with a Piece of Plate,
was Presented to
Mr. Samuel Cartledge
on his retirement from
THE RACECOURSE DETECTIVE STAFF,
in Recognition of his unfailing Courtesy
and to mark the Esteem in which he was held by
Messrs. Ford & Sons
and the whole of the
Racecourse Staff,
whose Names are subscribed hereto.

G. Allen.
T. Alloway.
J. Atkinson.
S. Barker.
H. Bayley.
J. Bellis.
A. Birkett.
C. Briens.
J.F. Briens.
T. Briggs.
J. Broadbridge.
E. Cheetham.
W.H. Clewer.
J. Clynes.
T. Cotterell.
W. Coulsey.
G.E. Dixon.
J. Ford.

S.B. Ford.
G. Gatfield.
A.W. Goddard.
J. Green.
W. Gregory.
B. Lake.
A. Leonard.
J.M. Levy.
A. Lowe.
E.C. Marshall.
J.H. Mellor.
R. Moody.
A.E. Morris.
E.S. Morris.
E.E. Nightingale.
H. Padley.

J. Parker.
F. Pitchfork.
W. Reason.
W.O. Rowbotham.
W. Sealey.
H.A.M. Smith.
G. Spibey.
R. Steer.
H. Stinton.
W. Tansley.
W. Taylor.
J. Thompson.
J. Truman.
W. Tyler.
J. Waldron.
T. Ward.
J. Whitehouse.
J.W. Wilson.

Nottingham, July, 1926.

Above: *This retirement certificate from 1926 is just one example of many other documents that can help you to fill gaps in your family tree.*

at law or next of kin to dispose of the estate. Furthermore, from 1796, death duty was payable on the estate, and the registers often detail next of kin, as well as later annotations.

In terms of locating family members, wills are the most important of the sources you are likely to find. In England and Wales you will find separate will registers for the Prerogatives Courts of Canterbury (at the National Archives) and York (at the Borthwick Institute, York) that go up to 1858. Thereafter all English wills have been registered centrally (and copies of wills can be obtained from the Principal Probate Registry, London).

Remember to use probate copies. Handwriting on original wills may be awkward to decipher, so it may be easier to check the registered copies.

Wills registered in local diocesan courts can be found at the relevant county or diocesan record office. A separate system exists in Scotland, and its records can be found in Edinburgh. Irish wills are mainly kept in Dublin, with copies available in Belfast (although most wills prior to 1914 have been destroyed).

Bear in mind the following hints when working with wills:

- ***Remember to use probate copies.*** Handwriting on original wills may be awkward to decipher, so it may be easier to check the registered documents in the probate courts, where more legible copies will have been created and kept. In any case, most original wills no longer survive as they were essentially private documents.
- ***Be flexible about date of death.*** Wills are not always listed in the same year that a person died, as the actual grant of probate can take some time. It is always worth checking lists from a year or two after a known date of death, especially for disputed wills, which can take even longer.
- ***Remember exceptions.*** You should be able to obtain the names of family members who received bequests in any will, along with their relationship to the person who wrote it.

The Internet

Throughout this first section we have given the email addresses of certain sites we feel might be useful in aiding your search. Recent years have witnessed an explosion in the number of sites geared towards genealogy. Researching a family history is the third most popular pursuit on the Internet, behind porn and personal finance. Once your search is established this mass of information can be enormously useful. However, in answer to the question, 'Can I do it all on the web?' our answer is a categoric 'no'.

The Internet is a very useful research tool, nothing more. When it comes to starting your search, there is no substitute for looking through the BMD indexes and ordering the certificates in person. As for the census, the 1901 online is a marvellous resource, but it remains the only census available to all for free (and even then you have to pay to see the results of your search), whereas at the Family Records Centre, for example, you can search every census return since 1841 without spending a penny. (Many more records are coming online every day, however.)

Another caveat about the Net: do not take everything at face value. Remember that people have often transcribed documents while putting them on their sites, and mistakes do happen. This can even be seen on the 1901 census online: there are numerous examples of the transcriber misreading the name on an original census return and typing in a different name. Place names are commonly misspelt. Bearing things like this in mind will help you avoid frustration when the person you are looking for can't be found.

If you discover something through researching on the Net, always try to corroborate with another source. This can stop you being led on a wild goose chase, and finding out the information that sent you on it in the first place turned out to be erroneous. Here are two more sites that are worth a visit once you are up and running:

- www.1837online.com is a site, as the title suggests, that possesses searchable indexes of all births, deaths and marriages since 1837. Searching is simple: select the event; select a date range; then type in the first three letters of the surname for which you are searching. There is a charge for viewing the pages you might require. The 1861 census is also available here.
- http://freebmd.rootsweb.com is a very popular site, with good reason. Transcribed by volunteers, it features free, searchable indexes to BMDs between 1837 and 1983. The number of records transcribed is constantly growing, though coverage for some years is better than others, so it can be a bit hit and miss. But as a cross-referencing tool and a way to further your search from home it is very useful.

However, important members are sometimes excluded – as may be the case with an heir at law, who would naturally receive the estate without the need for a bequest. Hence the first born or eldest surviving male may actually be omitted from the will.

- ***Avoid assumptions.*** This tip is worth heeding at all stages of your research, not just when dealing with wills and probate records: never assume you are receiving all the facts – corroborate your findings against other sources.

Many people head straight to wills and probate records when they become involved in family history out of curiosity to see whether there is an unclaimed fortune lurking in the family's past.

Forgotten Fortunes ...

Many people head straight to wills and probate records when they become involved in family history out of curiosity to see whether there is an unclaimed fortune lurking in the family's past. It has to be said that such occurrences are extremely rare, so if you have been peddled a family myth about Uncle Arnold marrying again but no one knew what happened to the money, or so-and-so couldn't claim the money because of a lack of evidence and we never heard what came of it, then take it with a hefty dose of salt. That isn't to say such stories do not occasionally turn out to be true, however. There exists a department at the Chancery Court that since 1876 has taken care of money deposited by solicitors who have been unable to track the next of kin or beneficiaries cited in a will. If you can prove you have a beneficial interest, they will allow you to take a look. Good luck ...

Section 2

The Themes

chapter 1
Skeletons

Few of our ancestors left much of a paper trail unless they stepped outside society's norms and were recognized by the authorities and institutions such as the criminal justice system, asylums, prisons, orphanages and the workhouse.

It is the one subject that most excites – or agitates – people when they research the lives of their ancestors: unearthing family secrets. Some people set out on the journey along their family's path to the present specifically to solve a puzzle in the past. Perhaps it may have been whispered *sotto voce* by elderly relatives; or maybe one person has been airbrushed from a family's official history – an outcast, a black sheep; then again, conceivably there is an issue or an event your relatives steadfastly refuse to discuss. All of these reasons and many more lead us to delve into our family history, to play detective and solve that elusive mystery. Just don't expect some members to dance with delight when you inform them of your genealogical quest. Some people prefer secrets to remain exactly that.

Then again, we may start researching our family history unaware of any shame or scandal. But as we peel back the layers of history, as we sketch out our family tree and start revealing the stories of our ancestors – living, breathing human beings, who loved and lived as we did, who were as flawed and fallible as we are – we may disinter a host of unknown incidents and episodes that were swept under the ancestral carpet long ago. Sometimes those skeletons can be centuries old; or they can be from the recent past. Be aware that occasionally you will discover something that affects people still alive today, and that those individuals may not greet the news you have rooted out with much joy. Discovering family secrets is one of the most fascinating aspects of genealogy, but with it comes a great deal of responsibility.

Be thankful for the black sheep you do uncover. Few of our ancestors left much of a paper trail unless they stepped outside society's norms and were recognized by the authorities and institutions such as the criminal justice system, asylums, prisons, orphanages and the workhouse. It is impossible to predict what secrets, if any, you will discover (which is part of the fun) but there are several recurring themes that crop up in many family histories. The aim of this chapter is to set some of those themes in context. Bigamy, for example, seems shocking to us today, each rare occurrence guaranteeing acres of tabloid newspaper coverage. But more than a few of us are likely to weed out an ancestor who was guilty of the crime. The fact is that until 70 or 80 years ago it was not uncommon, and there were explicable social reasons why it was more prevalent than we would imagine: namely, the impossibility for all but the rich of obtaining a divorce. By setting it in context here we hope you will understand why your bigamous ancestor performed an act that has become taboo.

Bigamy, for example, seems shocking to us today, each rare occurrence guaranteeing acres of tabloid newspaper coverage.

Illegitimacy

We have become squeamish about the word 'bastard', unsurprisingly given its pejorative use. But going back to medieval times, men often celebrated the fact that they were descended illegitimately, though only if the father was a person of importance or status. Hence why the surname Bastard came into use – and why it has disappeared over the last century. Go back to the 1901 census online, type in the surname Bastard, hit 'Search' and you will be told, rather prissily, that your enquiry returned too many results and to narrow your search. Actually, on the 1901 census there are 443 people with the surname Bastard. In 1801 there would have been more. But the name has died out, which is ironic given that illegitimacy, the birth of a child to a father out of wedlock, is an everyday occurrence, and no longer such a source of great shame and ignominy.

Of course, there was a pecking order among bastards in the past. Those who were sired by a rich man who had taken a mistress, for example, or the child of a couple who had been together for some time or were planning to marry, met with less opprobrium than a young woman who became pregnant after a fleeting encounter with a man she barely knew, or the result of an affair conducted by a married woman. (Actually, it is funny how those latter events still excite public disapproval – look at how the reproductive antics of young working-class

Going back to medieval times, men often celebrated the fact that they were descended illegitimately, though only if the father was a person of importance or status.

single mothers still attract the odium of some newspapers.) Among the upper classes, the prefix 'Fitz' was often added to a surname to declare someone was a bastard rather than a 'natural son'. Fitzgerald, for example, might mean the bearer of the name was the bastard son of Gerald.

Going back to the era before civil registration – before the point where many of us will encounter illegitimacy in our family history, represented on a birth certificate by a horizontal line or the word 'unknown' where the name of the father might have been – among ordinary working folk the incidence

Below: *'Forgiven' by Thomas Faed, showing a woman 'ruined' by the birth of her illegitimate child.*

of illegitimacy was high but it was not often a cause of teeth-gnashing. If the family was tight-knit and able to support another child then often little fuss was made. Ideally, the couple involved were encouraged to get up the church steps to the altar before the baby was born. But if the family was too poor to support the mother and prospective child, or unwilling, the parish became involved, because it was its job to oversee the poor. So, a bastard was placed under the care of the parish in which it was born. There were incidences of the parish throwing the offending woman out of the area to save itself the trouble, though they were rare. Instead the more usual course involved the woman being forced to name the father, who was then summoned. He would then be offered several options:

- Marry the woman. In this case the parish might assist in helping them set up home.
- Agree to support the child and its mother through what was called a Bastardy Bond. Alternatively he could come to a private arrangement with the mother and her family.

Of course, these choices did not suit every man. Often, the named father would flee the parish. The parish might make efforts to track him down, and if they did so would bring him back and pressure him into facing up to his responsibilities or risk punishment and possibly jail. However, by joining the army or navy the man could protect himself from a civil prosecution, a protection which helped swell the numbers of those who enlisted.

> **Among the upper classes, the prefix 'Fitz' was often added to a surname to declare someone was a bastard rather than a 'natural son'. Fitzgerald, for example, might mean the bearer of the name was the bastard son of Gerald.**

It was a different matter entirely if the woman in question was from a higher social stratum (not so if the man was: in that case he would pay, and often make certain his name was kept off any parish registers). And if a woman became pregnant with the child of a man from a lower class then the 'crime' was aggravated. Then what happened next was entirely down to the woman's parents. Sometimes the woman would be cast out, or married quickly before word crept out. Perhaps the woman might even be sent on a nine-month holiday to an accommodating great-aunt in another town or village some distance away, and the child put up for adoption, officially or unofficially.

The Victorian Era

Official civil records began in 1837 and the standard way of recording an illegitimate birth was to name the mother but not the father. Some fathers did agree to be named. And sometimes the couple would pretend to be married when it came to registering a birth and risk the rare chance of their deception being uncovered. If the parents actually went on to marry, the child remained illegitimate in the eyes of the law. Bastards were not legitimized by their parents' marriage until 1926 in England

Sex outside of marriage, or inside it for that matter, was not something discussed or even acknowledged in civil society; there were tens of thousands of prostitutes in London and Paris to cater for that sort of thing.

and Wales, and 1931 in the Republic of Ireland.

The introduction of civil registration was followed swiftly by the start of the Victorian era, where it became increasingly common for families of most classes to try and cover up such a shameful episode. Sex outside marriage, or inside it for that matter, was not something discussed or even acknowledged in civil society; there were tens of thousands of prostitutes in London and Paris to cater for that sort of thing. However, simply because people did not speak of sex and illegitimacy was so frowned upon – perhaps even because of those attitudes – it did not die out. The rise in the number of households employing domestic staff, usually young working-class women, led to the birth of numerous bastards, as either the father or the son of the house found himself incapable of conforming to the strict mores of the time. More often than not the young servant would end up out on her ear, jobless and pregnant with no prospects, often left with no choice but to head for the poorhouse, all to preserve the reputation of the father of the unborn child.

***Above:** A French cartoon depicts a gentleman being shown his illegitimate child.*

For middle- and upper-class women the dishonour was difficult to bear. Hasty wedding arrangements were often made, and the birth stage-managed so that the child was born 'prematurely' six or seven months after the wedding. Among the lower classes less severe, though more deceptive,

Above: Disabled boys in a Barnardo's home in the 1860s; Doctor Thomas Barnardo opened his first home for destitute children in 1870 in Stepney Causeway, London.

remedies were sought. It became increasingly common if the mother was young for her parents to 'adopt' the child and bring it up as their child, the secret known only by a select few and hidden from the child. Family historians report many incidences of a 'mother' on a birth certificate becoming a 'sister' on a census return.

By the close of the 19th century these social pressures had played a part in reducing illegitimacy rates, though the increase in the use of contraception might have had some effect on that, as had the spread of some herbal and other remedies, such as guzzling copious quantities of gin, to bring about a miscarriage. In the mid-19th century, as a percentage of live births, illegitimacy was at 6 per cent; by 1900 it was 4 per cent. Of course, in terms of numbers there were many more illegitimate births, simply because of the rapid rise in population during the latter stages of the 19th century. In the early 19th century 40 per cent of brides were pregnant when they got married; by the early 20th century it was closer to half that number. Illegitimacy was also

deemed to be more prevalent in the countryside where attitudes were less disapproving.

Adoption

Many illegitimate children were put up for adoption, some through more circumlocutory routes than others. Before 1927 adoption was rather haphazard and disorganized. Most unwanted or orphaned children were taken in by voluntary, charitable or religious organizations, such as Dr Barnardo's. From there, the fortunate might find themselves adopted by a family; the less lucky might have been corralled into one of the several child-emigration schemes: it is estimated that between 1618 and 1967 some 150,000 children were dispatched to the British colonies, mainly America, Australia and Canada. The height of this practice, now viewed as rather dubious, was between 1870 and the outbreak of the First World War, in which it is estimated that around 80,000 children were sent to Canada.

Others were more fortunate; perhaps there was an aunt, or grandparent or other family member willing to take responsibility for the child. For centuries this was done without formality, and

***Above:** Barnardo's girls learned domestic skills at the Girls' Village Homes in Barkingside.*

awkward questions about the child's provenance were deflected. Often, the child would grow up unaware that it was informally adopted and there was no compunction to set it straight. When the child was older, a boy might be 'adopted' by a childless wealthy man seeking an apprentice, or a girl might be brought into domestic service. For the most part, such arrangements were to the benefit of the child.

In 1927 the National Adoption Register was introduced, bringing some formality and legislation to bear on the practice. The person adopting had to be more than 21 years older than the adoptee (30 for a child of the opposite sex). Each adoption was registered, with certificates bearing the child's date of birth and the name of the adoptive parents; no mention is made of the natural parents.

Of course, such a system made it immensely difficult for adopted children to locate their birth parents, because their past was officially erased. An act of 1974 altered this, allowing adoptees over the age of 18 to apply and gain access information about their birth, albeit strictly controlled. But it does allow them to answer the obvious questions they have about why they were adopted, and give them the option of tracing their natural parents should they still be alive.

Foundlings

Some children were unwanted from the moment they were conceived. Perhaps the mother did not want the shame of an illegitimate child, or felt she was unable to feed and clothe her offspring. Therefore, one course of action was merely to abandon a baby – if they were lucky, in a place where they would be found, hence the term 'foundling'. In the eighteenth century they were a feature of life: the sight of dead or dying babies lying in the filth-clogged gutters of Georgian streets was not uncommon. In response to this problem, social reformers such as Thomas Coram clamoured for something to be done, and eventually foundling hospitals were opened. Not everyone was in favour of such institutions: the jaundiced view was that they encouraged wantonness and prostitution. Despite these protestations, Coram got his way and foundling hospitals were opened up in several areas, giving homes and care to thousands of unwanted and abandoned children who otherwise might have died.

***Opposite:** Foundling hospitals were a product of the wave of philanthropic activity in the 18th century for the 'maintenance of exposed and deserted young children'.*

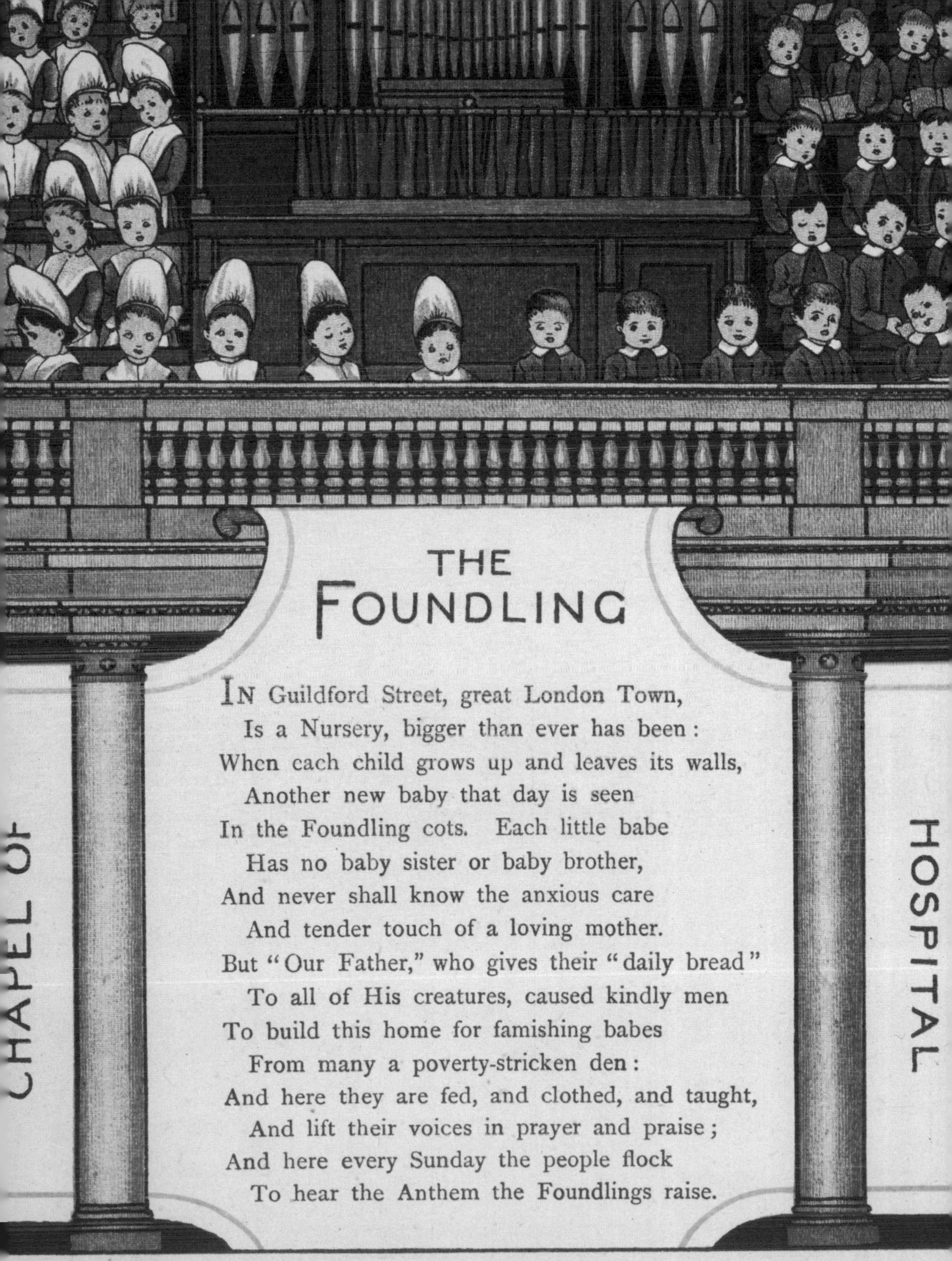

THE FOUNDLING

IN Guildford Street, great London Town,
  Is a Nursery, bigger than ever has been:
When each child grows up and leaves its walls,
  Another new baby that day is seen
In the Foundling cots. Each little babe
  Has no baby sister or baby brother,
And never shall know the anxious care
  And tender touch of a loving mother.
But "Our Father," who gives their "daily bread"
  To all of His creatures, caused kindly men
To build this home for famishing babes
  From many a poverty-stricken den:
And here they are fed, and clothed, and taught,
  And lift their voices in prayer and praise;
And here every Sunday the people flock
  To hear the Anthem the Foundlings raise.

Rosie Ansell: **'Benjamin the Bigamist'**

Phoebe Pratt, my great-great-great-grandmother, married Benjamin Headley in 1852; their daughter Ann was born in 1853. Yet by the time of the 1861 census, Benjamin had vanished. Instead, Phoebe was living with Benjamin's brother, Peter. The couple went on to have 11 children.

But where was Benjamin? I discovered that he died in Portsmouth in 1880. His death certificate recorded him as being a sergeant in the Royal Marine Artillery. He had joined in 1856, after serving in the West Kent Militia. He was aged 21, six feet and one inches, brown hair, grey eyes, complexion fair, and his occupation was labourer. His discharge papers revealed that he sailed on HMS *Caesar* in 1858, visiting Plymouth, Ireland, Jamaica and Cuba; in 1859, he went to Gibraltar and spent two years cruising around the Mediterranean. His next posting was on the HMS *Salamander*, which took him to Sydney. Three years later they sailed back, and Benjamin spent the rest of his career in Portsmouth, becoming sergeant in 1870.

Benjamin 'married' Martha Mickelwight in 1872, claiming to be a bachelor; his new wife was the widow of a colleague in the Royal Artillery. Martha had four children already, and in 1881, the year after Benjamin's death, the census revealed she had six children. Her name was given as 'Hendley'.

Interestingly, a year after Benjamin died, Phoebe and Peter finally got married.

The problem of 'foundlings' has never really gone away – 27,000 children passed through the doors of London's Foundling Hospital between 1739 and 1954, and even now we read reports of some desperate mothers abandoning their babies on doorsteps – but foundling hospitals changed the way in which they were treated by society.

Divorce and Bigamy

By the 19th and early 20th centuries many married couples came to live apart, by mutual consent because of irreconcilable differences, or because one of the parties deserted the other. These separations could be of long standing; however, sometimes one or both of the partners wished to marry again. The problem was that for most people divorce was out of reach. But if people were to remarry, such unions were bigamous: a felony in English law. Some were naturally unwilling to risk such charges and so cohabited (in sin) or parted. Many others decided to risk a second ceremony and possible prosecution, while others were deceived into marrying into bigamous partnerships.

Matrimonial law underwent great changes during the 19th century as Parliament created provision for civil marriage and divorce. Married women achieved greater legal status. At the same time, people's understanding of what marriage meant began to change. In early modern times, divorce lay within the jurisdiction of the ecclesiastical courts and it was virtually impossible to obtain the equivalent today of a divorce *a vinculo matrimonii* (from the chains of

The problem was that for most people divorce was out of reach. But if people were to remarry, such unions were bigamous: a felony in English law.

marriage). More readily it was possible to obtain the equivalent of a judicial separation.

In the 1660s, civil divorce was introduced, which permitted remarriage but required a private Act of Parliament which cost (in the nineteenth century) £1000. It was only the rich who could afford such princely sums: the lower classes had to be more creative when it came to separation. By the 1840s there was much agitation for reform of the divorce laws. In English law, only four women had ever successfully divorced their husbands. Judges started to recognize that this was an intolerable situation and a cause of bigamy as people sought a way round a restrictive law. Increasingly, the law expressed sympathy for those convicted of bigamy, as the following example displays, though it was qualified:

> ***In 1845 Lord Justice Maul told a man he convicted of bigamy that he ought to have tried to obtain a divorce. He instructed him as to the steps he should have taken: he should have brought an action against his wife's seducer (cost £100); sued in the Church courts for a divorce a mensa et toro (cost £200); and appealed to the House of Lords (cost £1000).***
>
> ***'Altogether you would have to spend***

about a thousand or twelve hundred pounds,' he told him. 'You will probably tell me that you've never had a thousand farthings of your own in the world.'

Lord Justice Maul's compassion only went so far.

'But prisoner, that makes no difference,' he concluded. 'This is not a country in which there is one law for the rich and another for the poor.'

Though, of course, it was. The man was set free having already served the day in prison he was to be punished by.

Below: 'Retribution' *by John Everett Millais, 1854. A man is caught out in his attempt at bigamy, with an astonished fiancée horrified at the other woman's wedding ring.*

A fairer balance was struck by the 1857 Matrimonial Causes Act, which took jurisdiction over marriages out of ecclesiastical courts and made it a civil procedure. This undercut the ecclesiastical ideal of the indissolubility of marriage by making statutory provision for divorce on the grounds of adultery. It planted the idea that marriage was a matter of *contract* rather than *status*, and adultery became the gateway for divorce. A court could order a husband to pay

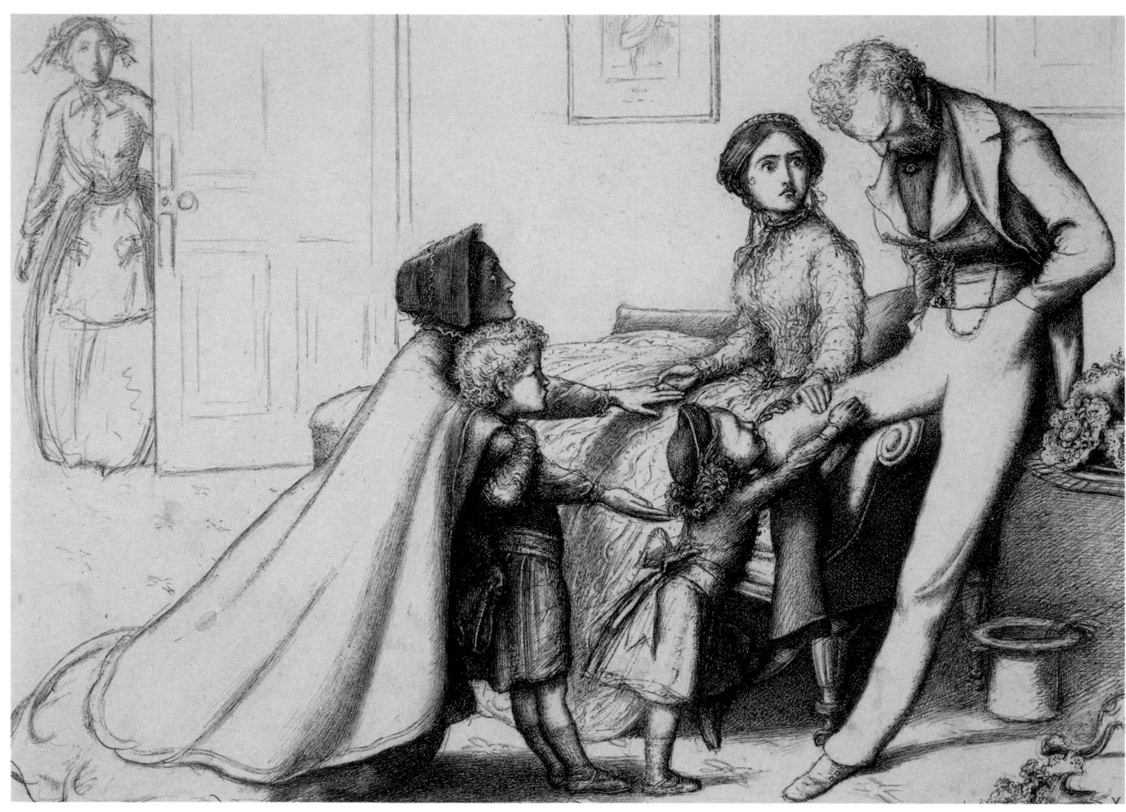

maintenance to a divorced or estranged wife. A divorced wife could inherit or bequeath property in her own right and protect her earnings from a husband who had deserted her. This did not open the floodgates, however. Divorce remained a wealthy privilege. And equality was some way off: a husband only had to claim that his wife had committed adultery, and if it was proved she lost all legal right to her children; meanwhile, a wife had to prove adultery *plus* one of incest, bigamy, cruelty or desertion, which was not often easy.

It was not until 1937 that major changes were made and divorce became an option for all classes, namely by the introduction of legal aid for divorce cases. Subsequent acts have made getting a divorce progressively less restrictive.

The Extent of Bigamy

To the modern eye, the number of bigamy cases tried at local assizes and reported in the county press is surprising:

- According to *Judicial Statistics for England and Wales*, there were 5,327 bigamy trials between 1857 and 1904, and an average of 98 cases a year in the county assize courts.
- Even as late as 1910, judge Justice Ridley was complaining about the increase in bigamy cases in his court.
- Numbers of cases of bigamy rose with the increasing population: an average of 85 cases a year in the 1850s rose to 112 in the early 20th century. But it did not rise as quickly as the population. Either the courts were ignoring more cases or bigamy was becoming harder to detect.
- It is important to realize, though, that these cases represent only the very tip of the iceberg. Most often the two people involved would simply move away from each other and nobody would be any the wiser. Bigamy was usually either accepted by the parties involved, and so never reported and tried in court, or else concealed from one or other of the parties, so that it was never detected.

Acceptable Bigamy

Bigamy was acceptable amongst local communities who developed and enforced (in a world where divorce was unattainable) their own practicable understandings about what was right and proper in relationships between men and women:

- Among the poor, folk customs were followed which enabled them to 'unmarry' and remarry. These included wife sales in local markets in which the consent of the wife was sought and proceedings were carried out in a jocular manner. In more anonymous settings, such as large towns, people separated and remarried without recourse to ritual.
- Judges too accepted bigamy, even though it was a crime. They were suspicious of partners from a first marriage who prosecuted their absent spouse upon a

second marriage. Such prosecutions were often born of malice rather than a sense of injustice. One judge, refusing costs, said that he 'could not allow public money to be spent on gratifying the anger of a woman who had left her husband'. Prosecutions launched by first husbands were even more suspicious: men could support themselves and so were not deemed victims when their wives found other mates. First husbands were scolded from the bench for bringing bigamy charges far more often than first wives.

Above: *A depiction of a trial in the Divorce Court in London in 1900.*

Unacceptable Bigamy

Bigamy was only 'acceptable' if both parties were aware of the situation and acquiesced to it. Bigamy by deception was not acceptable to society, and was often the cause of scandal. The lack of economic options available to women meant that they were viewed with great sympathy when duped by a bigamous male. A judge in 1885 told one bigamist that he had given his victim an 'injury which will never end until she dies'.

Proving a charge of bigamy required proof of both marriages, preferably including the marriage registers. A wife could not testify against her spouse in a criminal trial – but others could testify on her behalf. The conviction rate for cases that came to trial was 80 per cent. Men made up nearly 80 per cent of those charged, and were convicted at a rate of 85 per cent. Women lost their chastity in fraudulent marriages, and as a consequence their children were rendered illegitimate. However, a bigamy charge could not be brought against anyone who had not heard from their spouse for seven years.

Over the centuries, punishment for bigamy became increasingly lenient. In the 1600s bigamists were occasionally executed; by 1840 men were transported, while women were sent to jail for a few months. By the 1860s men were receiving three to seven years' penal servitude, down to a few months of the same sentence. By 1900 only 19 per cent of bigamists were receiving a year or more in prison.

However, sentences were longer for those who tricked their spouses into marriage. In a case from 1880, Judith Killen insisted she did not know her husband Robert Steventon was already married, and she also accused him of selling all of her property and living off her parents. The judge complained that 'the prisoner has basely and wickedly deceived the second wife ... this was not an ordinary case of bigamy but one of cruel deception.' He sentenced Steventon to five years' hard labour.

Bigamy cases in Victorian England in particular were big news, guaranteeing rises in newspaper sales and reported with lip-smacking relish. In the second half of the 19th century, a whole genre of sensational literature emerged, teeming with secrets and lies from the past coming back to haunt the present; bigamy was a recurring theme. These potboilers proved to be enormously successful.

Bigamy continued well into the 20th century, but the increasing accessibility of divorce put an end to it as a common practice, with the odd high-profile exception.

Lunatics, Imbeciles and Idiots

Discovering the presence of an ancestor with mental-health problems, or at least what our forebears considered as mental-health problems, is more common than perhaps some people think. That's because census returns from 1871 onwards, in the final column, record if a person was deemed to be a lunatic, an imbecile or an idiot. The first was someone who was prone to losing his or her reason though experienced moments of clarity; the second was someone who was judged to have fallen into a state of insanity in later life; while the third suffered from congenital mental problems. If you discover any of these terms used in relation to an ancestor, bear in mind that they were not applied scientifically or even with that much rigour, and that some methods of diagnosis seem antediluvian: women who had suffered post-natal depression, for example, were seen as suffering from a form of mania, which is why it is not exceptional for a woman with a new-born to be recorded as a lunatic.

Having a lunatic ancestor is nothing to be ashamed of. It is reasonably likely that that person was not mad: slightly eccentric was enough to alert the authorities in the past, and there is every chance they might have been suffering from some form of physical or mental handicap. A lack of knowledge and medical study led to many disparate mental-health problems being lumped together under one label, with the tragic consequence that many people with different needs and types of problems were gathered together in the same asylum and offered similar treatments.

Before 1800 it is likely that their own family looked after any mad ancestors, though if the family could not afford it the poor unfortunate might have been sent to the local workhouse. Prior to the Victorian era there were few asylums, the most notorious exception being Bethlem Hospital in London, better known to us as 'Bedlam'. But on the

Above: *The original caption to this drawing read: 'The sins of the drunken father are visited in the heads of the children – a thief and a woman of shame visit their lunatic father in a criminal lunatic asylum.*

Roger Guttridge:
'Roger the Dodger: My Ancestor and Other Rogues'

When I was a boy, my maternal grandfather Jim Ridout delighted in passing on legends about our smuggling ancestors. The stories focused on the leader of the gang, Roger Ridout, whose armed men ferried cargoes of spirits, wine, tea and tobacco from the coast in a convoy of horses and wagons. My grandfather told a story of how Roger once beat up an Excise man who dared to challenge him; he bribed magistrates with tubs of brandy; and how he was eventually jailed and visited by his wife with a bladder of ale hidden in her clothing.

I began my research and soon found that Roger Ridout, my great-great-great-great-great grandfather was one of Dorset's best-known smugglers. He was mentioned in books and articles, including one written in 1895 by the grandson of the magistrate who allegedly took the bribe of brandy. The book even gave the name of Roger's horse: Stumpted Tail.

The most exciting documents I found were legal ones. Roger was listed in the prison registers for 1787 after being fined £40 for smuggling – and was released two weeks later when he paid the fine in full! The Poole Customs Collector reported in 1770 that Isaac Gulliver, William Beale and Roger Ridout ran 'great quantities of goods' on what is now Bournemouth beach. The Dorset Assize records mentioned a murder trial of 1781, when Roger, his wife and eldest son were all among the defendants, though all were acquitted.

My first book, *Dorset Smugglers*, was published fifteen years ago – and in a way I owe it all to the skeletons in my ancestral cupboard.

whole there was less motivation in wanting to rid the streets of the mad and the mentally ill; it was a fact of life, and the village idiot, while a figure of fun, was never a source of shame. Like so many other social stigmas, this arrived with the Victorians.

The Lunatics Act of 1845 ushered in the biggest change. By law, every county was required to build and run an asylum for poor lunatics (or 'Madhouses' as they became colloquially known). The compulsion to keep records was also tightened. By the mid-19th century madness was a growing industry, and the new asylums were often packed with patients. There are many reasons for this: Victorian attitudes that frowned upon madness and eccentricity and wanted 'persons of unsound mind' locked away from sight. There was no 'cure' and therefore few asylum inmates were released, so numbers piled up. It was not uncommon for someone to spend their whole life in an institution.

The tragedy is that many people spent years in an asylum when in fact all they suffered from was an inability to fit in with the times, or experienced a brief bout of mania. Women suffered the most, being seen as weak, vulnerable and prone to madness. Those who gave birth to an illegitimate child, for example, were often deemed to be morally insane, and dispatched to asylums. Treatment could vary – the commonly held view was that madness was a physical problem, not a mental one – but popular courses of action were baths: warm ones to help the melancholic; cold ones to aid the manic. Gradually those responsible for treatment began to see the value in treating each patient differently, but it was not until the early part of the 20th century that drugs or tranquillizers were introduced, around the same time that the likes of Sigmund Freud were becoming prominent and treatments such as psychiatry started to develop. However, some of the old Victorian asylums remained open until the second half of the last century.

Above: *Patients in the gallery at St Luke's Hospital, London c.1810, which housed pauper lunatics in the more tolerant pre-Victorian era.*

For wealthy people who were deemed to be insane, and therefore unable to manage their affairs, there were other problems: namely the eagerness of the state to get their hands on that person's money. In the late 18th century, it was the case that the state took over the property of the rich if that person was rendered insane. By 1833 an act decreed that the mental state of an alleged lunatic would be investigated at an inquiry and a decision reached as to whether they were in sound mind.

By the mid-19th century madness was a growing industry, and the new asylums were often packed with patients.

The Chancery would then decide whether to intervene and administer the estate. These people were known as 'Chancery Lunatics'.

__Above:__ Patients eating in the communal dining hall of the Larbert Asylum, Scotland in 1899.

Crime and Punishment

Nothing adds a bit of colour or intrigue to the pursuit of family history like the discovery of an ancestor who found himself in trouble with the law. For a start, criminal and prison records are a wonderful source of genealogical information; you can glean priceless details, such as a physical description of your ancestor, that you would not stand a chance of finding anywhere else. Even better, should your forebear have been nicked in the Victorian era, there may even be a sepia-tinted police mugshot of him or her, staring glumly into the camera.

To condense the history of the criminal justice system of these isles into a few thousand words is an impossible task, and there are many hundreds of crimes your ancestor may have committed. But should they have been found guilty, your ancestor would have been punished, usually harshly, given that previous generations, the Victorians in particular, were keen to cut the crime rate. An examination of how criminals were dealt with gives an insight into our predecessors' attitude to law and order.

Hanging

Hanging was the ultimate punishment. Records show that between 1800 and 1900, 3,524 people were hanged in England and Wales. Some 1,353 of those were executed for murder, and many others for serious offences such as rape. But on several occasions it was used as a punishment for lesser offences. A glance through a list of executions in Durham between 1732 and 1909 confirms this: among the murderers and rapists are the likes of John Moses, who was hanged for stealing drapery goods from a shop in 1803. Other offences that were rewarded with the death penalty were forgery, though by the mid-18th century hanging was reserved almost exclusively for murder. In 1868 it was also decreed that hanging should take place within a prison's walls, where previously it had been a public spectacle, a wildly popular one, too, despite or because of the gruesome scene on display. Pity poor Mary Nicholson, who was hanged for poisoning her mistress, Elizabeth Atkinson, at Little Stainton, in 1798. This is an account of her demise:

> ***The rope broke after she was thrown off, and another rope had to be procured. An hour elapsed before this could be done, and in the interval she recovered her faculties and conversed with her relatives until the resumption of the execution, when she was launched into eternity amidst a scene of painful excitement amongst the spectators.***

The reason the Victorians became squeamish about public executions – before then it was the commonly held view that public punishment acted as an effective deterrent to criminals – was their popularity. As is well known, hangings attracted an almost festive atmosphere, fun for all the family. It also became clear that rather than discouraging crime, these events contributed to an increase in crime rates. While people enjoyed themselves at the hanging, petty criminals took the opportunity to steal from their houses, while the more dexterous mingled among the large crowds and helped themselves to the contents of their pockets. The Victorian authorities also took less relish in sending criminals to the gallows: a high of 209 people were hanged in 1801; between 1840 and 1899 the highest annual number of executions was 22. They also reduced the number of capital crimes from 17 at the beginning of the 19th century – in practice, that is, though there were more than 200 crimes that could attract the death penalty – to just four by 1861, those being high treason, piracy, murder and arson in the Royal Dockyards. In effect, the act meant that from that point onwards only murderers would be hanged.

Though hanging took place in private from 1868, newspaper reporters were often allowed to attend the condemned's final minutes. They would file reams and reams of breathless prose, describing in minute detail the prisoner's every last cough and spit, which would then be splashed all over the next day's newspapers. The following extract, an account of the execution of the notorious thief and murderer Charles Peace, who was hanged at Leeds' Armley Jail on two counts of murder, is taken from the *Scotsman* in February 1879:

Above: *A prisoner recognises that Sabbath-breaking is the second step that has led him to the gallows.*

Above: *A depiction of the execution of William Burke in 1828 – Burke was one of the Westport Murderers, famous for selling bodies to the Edinburgh Medical College.*

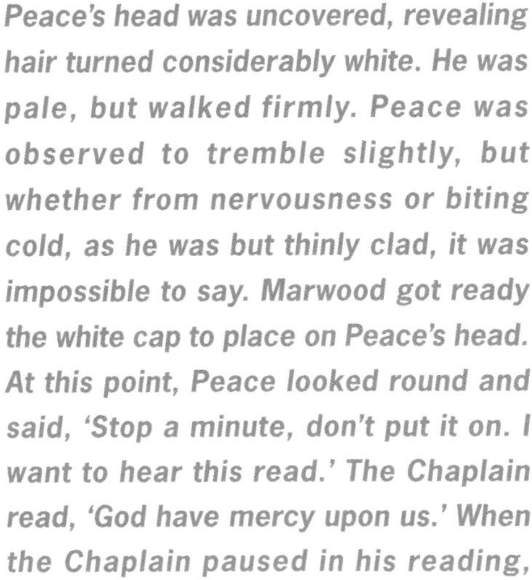

Peace's head was uncovered, revealing hair turned considerably white. He was pale, but walked firmly. Peace was observed to tremble slightly, but whether from nervousness or biting cold, as he was but thinly clad, it was impossible to say. Marwood got ready the white cap to place on Peace's head. At this point, Peace looked round and said, 'Stop a minute, don't put it on. I want to hear this read.' The Chaplain read, 'God have mercy upon us.' When the Chaplain paused in his reading, Peace, bracing himself, said, 'I am prepared for the great judgement day ... I am ready if you are.'

Marwood adjusted the white cap. When it had been pulled down over the face, Peace again spoke, 'Take care, I have got but little wind. It is too tight.' 'No, no,' said Marwood, 'be quiet, it is all right. I won't hurt you.' One of the warders said, 'Are you ready?' Peace replied, 'Yes, God bless you all.' The bolt was withdrawn, the drop fell, and Peace died without a struggle.

After the First World War, however, reporters too were barred from witnessing a hanging, and most took place in secret, with few people aware they were even happening until the death was announced. From 1920 the number of prisons able to carry out executions was reduced, and it became an increasingly less common event. The last hangings were in 1964, and in 1969 Parliament confirmed the abolition of capital punishment for murder.

Transportation

Unsurprisingly, for our ancestors this was a popular way of dealing with criminals. For a start, beyond the initial outlay of paying to get the prisoner dispatched overseas, it was cheap. And there was no need to worry about them reoffending, as there might have been if they had been sent to prison and they were released or escaped. It became an alternative to hanging, and should any prisoners transported to the colonies reappear on British soil before the term of their sentence had been served, the response was simple: you hanged them. The belief was that if criminals were out of sight, out of mind, would-be felons would be less likely to emulate them.

Around 50,000 men and women, and some children, were transported to the Caribbean and America between 1615 and 1776. The American Revolution soon put a stop to that and a new dumping ground was required. For more than a decade the prison population exploded, and prisoners had to be kept in floating jails on the Thames, called 'hulks'. In 1787 a new penal colony was established, founded by a first fleet of 11 ships that set sail for Botany Bay, Australia. Between 1787 and 1867 it is estimated that approximately 165,000 men, women and children were transported to New South Wales and Van Diemen's Land (now known as Tasmania), while around 9,000 were dispatched to Western Australia between 1850 and 1868.

Terms of transportation were often for seven or fourteen years, though in reality being sent to Australia was for life because there would be no easy way back once your sentence was served. Some prisoners facing death sentences had it commuted to transportation, it being seen as the more humane alternative to hanging. In reality, the conditions of many of the ships they were sent on were so poor, and the journey to Australia so long and arduous, that many died en route.

Above: *A prisoner's hand being branded on a convict ship.*

While, post-1788 in particular, it was seen as an alternative to hanging, it was not just serious crimes that were dealt with by transportation. Crimes we may now see as petty, sheep-stealing for example, would often result in the convict being sent to the other side of the world. Often on board a convict ship, a pickpocket might find himself manacled to a murderer, or a sheep-stealer to a rapist.

The Victorian era saw a rapid and almost immediate scaling back of transportation, recognition that it had little effect on overall crime rates. Rising prosperity in Australia and the discovery of gold also made the sentence seem less of a punishment, more of an opportunity. The emerging population of the colonies were not too pleased by the continual dumping of England's least wanted on their doorsteps. From 1840 onwards the process was wound down and abolished in 1868.

Left: *Women prisoners, many with children, in the Pass Room at Bridewell Prison, London.*

Prison

The most likely punishment for any of your errant ancestors was imprisonment. Prior to the 19th century, prisons were appalling, overcrowded places, with men, women and children locked together under the same roof, criminals of all hues, lunatics too, and disease and death rates were rampant. They were privately run, which meant if you had some money you could pay the gaoler to obtain better treatment, while if you had none you had no choice but to suffer. You had to pay to leave when your sentence was served, which meant those unfortunates who had no money often ended up languishing in prison despite having served their term.

Prison reformers in the late 18th century and early 19th century went some way towards improving conditions; sanitary conditions were less dire, and prisoners were increasingly segregated according to the crimes they had committed, for example. But it was not until the advent of the Victorian era that real progress was made. Law and order was a major issue in the 1840s; between 1800 and 1840 the crime rate had quadrupled. Something needed to be done. The prevalent, emphatic belief of the time was that prison worked. Between 1842 and 1877, 90 new prisons were built as the view became widespread that the best way to deal with serious criminals was to lock them up. And even though conditions were less brutal than they had been – fewer people died of disease, for example – the idea was that the prisoner still be made as uncomfortable as possible to deter others from committing crimes. Pointless hard work was introduced, such as the 'treadmill', whereby a

William Towers and the Case of the Stolen Rabbits

Children and crime were an obsession during the 19th century. Dickens's *Oliver Twist* highlighted the plight of children, orphaned and poor, being recruited by adult criminals and organized into gangs of pickpockets. Which is why in the early part of the 19th century in particular, there were no qualms about trying children as adults. They were tried in the same courts as adults, transported to penal colonies like adults, and some were even executed – in 1814 five children under the age of 14 were hanged at the Old Bailey, the youngest being just 8 years old.

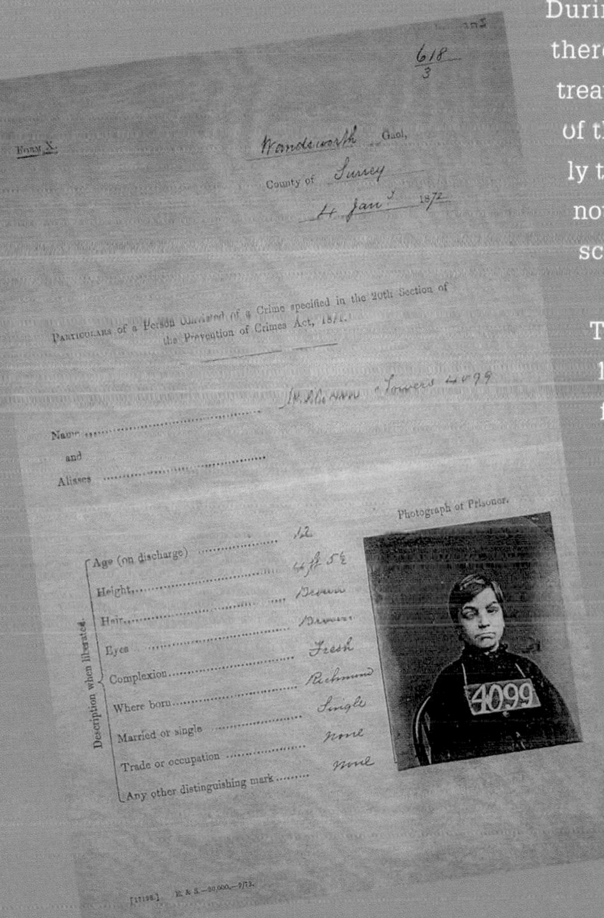
618
3

Form X.

Wandsworth Gaol,

County of Surrey

4 Jany 1872

Particulars of a Person Convicted of a Crime specified in the 20th Section of the Prevention of Crimes Act, 1871.

Name and Aliases: William Towers 4099

Photograph of Prisoner.

Description when liberated.

Age (on discharge): 12
Height: 4 ft 5½
Hair: Brown
Eyes: Brown
Complexion: Fresh
Where born: Richmond
Married or single: Single
Trade or occupation: None
Any other distinguishing mark: None

During the course of the 19th century, there was a change in the way the law treated child offenders. By the beginning of the 20th century they were less likely to be sent to prison; more often than not they might be sent to a reformatory school.

But that did not help young Will Towers. He was only 12 years old in 1872 when he was convicted with a friend of stealing two 'live, tame rabbits'. His police mugshot shows a young boy – he was only four feet, five inches in height – glumly staring out, his number around his neck. Today, he might have been given a fine, or perhaps a caution. In 1872 he was sentenced to one month's hard labour at Wandsworth Gaol.

Above: *Inmates writing letters at Wandsworth Prison in 1900.*

prisoner walked the wheel, occasionally to power a mill, but more often than not as a back-breaking punishment. Another mind-numbing task was 'Picking Oakum', in which the prisoner was tasked with unpicking the strands of a rope. This became known as the 'Silent System', its motto 'Hard Labour, Hard Fare, and a Hard Board'. In other words, mind-numbing, lengthy periods of monotonous work, dull tasteless food and a wooden bed with no mattress. Hard labour was eventually abolished in 1898.

Suicide

Until the 1960s, suicide was against the law. While the Victorians, for example, taking their lead from their Queen who mourned her husband's death publicly for several decades, were fascinated by death, and sensationalized murder in the press, they made less of a fuss over suicide. The commonly held view was that suicide was unchristian – suicides were not to be buried in consecrated ground – and the poor souls who took their own life had in some way taken leave of their senses. Hence, in many inquests into suicides, such as the one reported

Above: Walking the treadmill was a popular Victorian 'pastime' for prisoners: isolated and repetitive, it was thought to break their will and self-respect.

below, the view was that the deceased was insane, temporarily so, when they killed themselves.

If you discover an ancestor who took their own life – the death certificate may refer to the mode of death 'while insane' or 'during a fit of insanity' – it may be difficult to understand the reasons for their actions, simply because their suicide was probably a cry for help and went ignored by doctors and other specialists. Press reports provide the best clues, given that the mental state of the deceased was the subject of investigation. While not exciting the feverish amount of lip-smacking detail that a murder case did, the suicides that went unreported generally had an air of resigned sympathy. For example, this report of one desperately unlucky man's death from *Bell's Weekly Messenger* on Sunday 11 September 1931.

> ***We have to record a suicide of the most melancholy nature, committed by Mr. W. Lewellyn, of Bloomfield Place, Kennington Oval, whose particularly distressing circumstances have excited the universal commiseration of his neighbours. Misfortune had caused his failure in business a few years ago, and had since pursued him with relentless persecution. He retired from a respectable and comfortable station in society, to one of comparative humiliation, and with a constitution worn by anxiety, and broken by ill health, was reduced to subsist on a small life annuity payable to his wife, who died in March last. His son, a fine young man of 20, now devoted himself to the support of his father and sister, till about a month since he fell into a copper of the brewery at Knightsbridge, and was scalded to death. Such a shock almost overpowered the old man; but a few Sundays since his troubles were increased by his daughter communicating, during a visit from her***

situation, that she was enceinte [pregnant] in consequence of her seduction by one of his neighbours; this proved too deeply mortifying to his pride – he became melancholy – when, as if circumstances could never tire in persecuting the ill-fated man, his landlord sent down a distraint upon his goods for rent. He refused an entrance to the brokers, to whom he spoke from the window, telling them that he would not open the door, and desiring they would desist from knocking. They continued their efforts to obtain an entrance the whole of the next day, and on the third day bribed a lad in the neighbourhood to enter by the window; he ascended for that purpose, when he discovered the unfortunate man suspended from the bed-rail, entirely dead. An inquest was held on the body, when the Jury returned a verdict of Hanged himself in a fit of Insanity.

> **In a century plagued by two devastating, bloody world wars, it became difficult to argue that depression was a form of insanity and not an illness.**

The increasingly secular nature of life during the 20th century gradually removed some of the stigma from suicide. In a century plagued by two devastating, bloody world wars, it became difficult to argue that depression was a form of insanity and not an illness. But it was still swept away from view, not talked about or debated in any detail, and it remained illegal until the 1960s. While in many respects suicide is still a taboo subject, there is a greater understanding today about its reasons and causes.

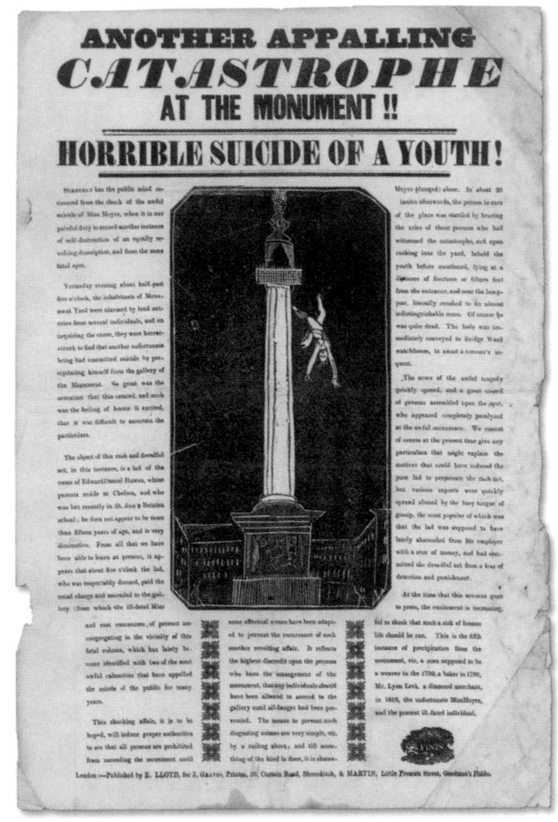

ANOTHER APPALLING
CATASTROPHE
AT THE MONUMENT !!
HORRIBLE SUICIDE OF A YOUTH!

Scarcely has the public mind recovered from the shock of the awful suicide of Miss Moyes, when it is our painful duty to record another instance of self-destruction of an equally revolting description, and from the same fatal spot.

Yesterday evening about half-past five o'clock, the inhabitants of Monument Yard were alarmed by loud outcries from several individuals, and on inquiring the cause, they were horror-struck to find that another unfortunate being had committed suicide by precipitating himself from the gallery of the Monument. So great was the sensation that this created, and such was the feeling of horror it excited, that it was difficult to ascertain the particulars.

The object of this rash and dreadful act, in this instance, is a lad of the name of Edward Daniel Hawes, whose parents reside at Chelsea, and who was but recently in St. Ann's Britain school; he does not appear to be more than fifteen years of age, and is very diminutive. From all that we have been able to learn at present, it appears that about five o'clock the lad, who was respectably dressed, paid the usual charge and ascended to the gallery (from which the ill-fated Miss Moyes plunged) alone. In about 20 minutes afterwards, the person in care of the place was startled by hearing the cries of those persons who had witnessed the catastrophe, and upon rushing into the yard, beheld the youth before mentioned, lying at a distance of fourteen or fifteen feet from the entrance, and near the lamp-post, literally crushed to an almost indistinguishable mass. Of course he was quite dead. The body was immediately conveyed to Bridge Ward watchhouse, to await a coroner's inquest.

The news of the awful tragedy quickly spread, and a great crowd of persons assembled upon the spot, who appeared completely paralysed at the awful occurrence. We cannot of course at the present time give any particulars that might explain the motives that could have induced the poor lad to perpetrate the rash act, but various reports were quickly spread abroad by the busy tongue of gossip, the most popular of which was that the lad was supposed to have lately absconded from his employer with a sum of money, and had committed the dreadful act from a fear of detection and punishment.

At the time that this account goes to press, the excitement is increasing, and vast concourses of persons are congregating in the vicinity of this fatal column, which has lately become identified with two of the most awful calamities that have appalled the minds of the public for many years.

This shocking affair, it is to be hoped, will induce proper authorities to see that all persons are prohibited from ascending the monument until some effectual means have been adopted to prevent the recurrence of such another revolting affair. It reflects the highest discredit upon the persons who have the management of the monument, that any individuals should have been allowed to ascend to the gallery until all danger had been prevented. The means to prevent such disgusting crimes are very simple, viz, by a railing above; and till something of the kind is done, it is shameful to think that such a risk of human life should be run. This is the fifth instance of precipitation from the monument, viz, a man supposed to be a weaver in the 1750, a baker in 1788, Mr. Lyon Levi, a diamond merchant, in 1810, the unfortunate Miss Moyes, and the present ill-fated individual.

FINIS

London:—Published by E. LLOYD, for J. Graves, Printer, 20, Curtain Road, Shoreditch, & MARTIN, Little Prescott Street, Goodman's Fields.

***Above:** A broadsheet report of the suicide of a 15-year-old boy at the Monument, London from the early 19th century.*

Janette Scarborough:
'The Execution of John Charles Tapner'

John Charles Tapner was born in 1823 and originally brought up in Woolwich. He planned to be a chemist, coming as he did from a good family: his grandfather had been a 'gentleman of Chichester', while his father had worked in the pay office at Whitehall before becoming a clerk at His Majesty's Arsenal.

John moved to Guernsey in 1842–3 to work as a clerk in the Royal Engineers Department at Fort George. There he met and married Mary Gahagan and they had three sons. He seemed in every sense a respectable man. However, debt and womanizing were his downfall ...

He fathered an illegitimate child, Eliza Tapner Mollett, in December 1844, and had a child by his sister-in-law, Margaret. In 1854 he was executed for the murder of Elizabeth Saujon. The attack was violent and he attempted to conceal his crime by setting fire to her body, but failed. Yet he managed to get away with many of her valuable belongings. But he was not to escape capture, and when his plea for clemency was turned down, nor did he escape death.

His death was gruesome: the trap door was too small and John only partly fell. As he tried to free himself, one bailiff hung onto his feet and the other pushed down on his shoulders until his struggling ceased. The botched execution led directly to the abolition of capital punishment on Guernsey.

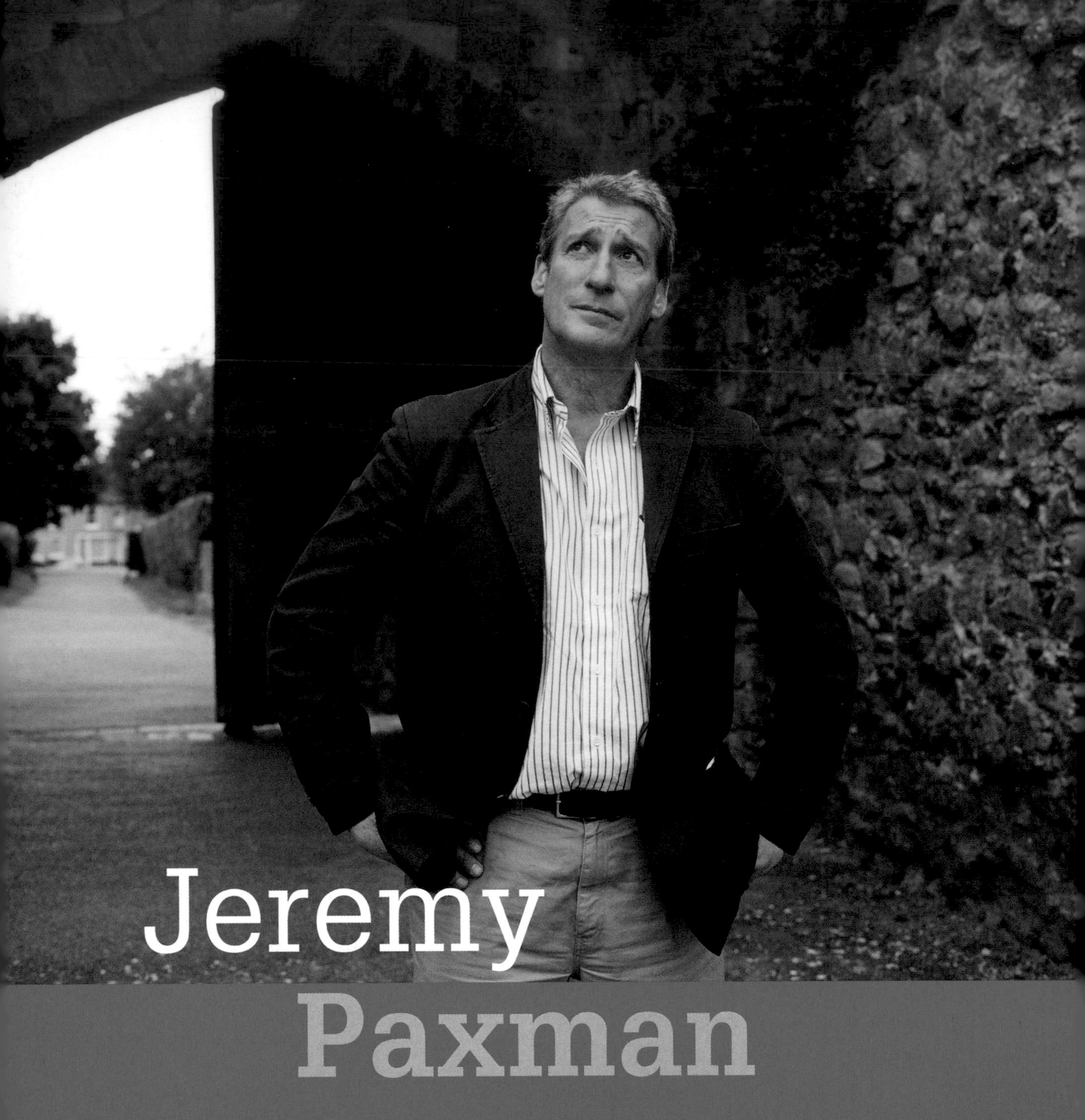

Jeremy Paxman

The research into Jeremy Paxman's ancestral roots is a demonstration of all the facets of family history, from the basic first steps taken to construct a family tree, to more detailed investigations to uncover the hidden secrets surrounding key relatives. As well as offering a snapshot of Jeremy's ancestry, we thought it would be interesting to let you know how the *Who Do You Think You Are?* research team, led by Nick Barratt, who wrote the following piece, pulled together all the rich, colourful strands of our most famous and celebrated political interviewer's family history.

As with all research, the initial stage of work was to build a family tree, and therefore it was essential to speak to Jeremy and various relatives to get an idea of what they knew. In particular, attention was focused on names, dates and places relevant to his ancestors, as well as what they did for a living and any anecdotes about their lives. Armed with this information, research switched to the Family Records Centre in Islington to construct the family tree.

The aim of the exercise was to work back in time to find the biographical details of all Jeremy's direct ancestors. Birth, marriage and – on occasion – death certificates were ordered, and slowly the names of Jeremy's ancestors started to emerge from the records. At first, a simple process of working backwards from known facts was followed – establishing Jeremy's date of birth, verifying the names of his parents, locating their marriage certificate to obtain their ages and fathers' names, and ordering his parents' birth certificates to establish Jeremy's grandparents' names. This process of using marriage data to locate birth records was repeated several times, until relatives born before 1901 were revealed. This is the magic date for family historians, as census returns can then be used to expand the family tree further; in addition to names, ages, occupations and parental information contained in certificates, it is possible to gain an insight into the domestic life of entire families, such as siblings, employment details, places of birth, the size and location of the house, even the nicknames by which people were referred to; in essence it is possible to piece together their identities.

Right: *A new-born Jeremy in the arms of his mother, Joan.*

In this instance, both Jeremy's grandfathers – Arthur Stanley Paxman and Morris Musgrove Dickson – were alive at the time of the 1901 census, which provided an insight into their lives. This also meant that it was much easier to work back in time, and, in combination with certificate data, the family tree was extended further and further into the past through the census records, helped by the fact that the returns between 1861–1901 were available online at Ancestry's website.

With this wealth of information at hand, and the family tree grown to a healthy size, it was possible to step back from the searching and start to see patterns emerging from the records. Most surprising of all were clear indications of poverty on the Paxman branch. A glance at the 1891 census revealed Arthur Stanley Paxman, Jeremy's grandfather, aged only twelve, working as a worsted spinner in Bradford. He was living in a large household with a grandfather, Hugh Sherwin, and a pawnbroker called Rose. We knew from Jeremy's background notes that he had grown up to be a travelling sales representative in textiles, sufficiently prosperous to send his son to a public school, but these early origins were a complete mystery. Above him on the family tree were three generations of Thomas Paxmans, all living in Bradford, and this was where more detailed research was initially focused.

Further digging at the Family Records Centre revealed that tragedy had befallen Arthur at an early age when his father Thomas Paxman died in 1888, aged

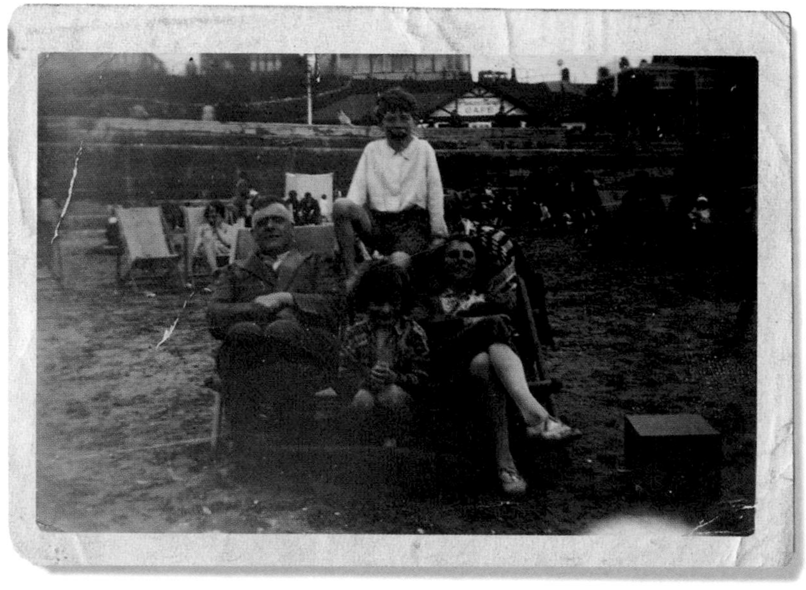

***Above:** A family holiday: Jeremy's grandfather Arthur, his grandmother, Lillian, with their two children, Keith (Jeremy's father) and Margaret on Bridlington Beach.*

Right: *Arthur Paxman (right, with umbrella) in Belfast in the 1930s.*

only thirty-five. The death certificate describes him as a tin-plate worker who died of phthisis pulmonalis, an old medical term for tuberculosis. His widow Mary Jane reported his death, but, within two years, she had also died of the same illness, aged thirty-six. She had worked as a charwoman, and, in addition to the lung complaint, 'exhaustion' was cited as a cause of death. The question of why Arthur and his siblings were scattered to various households by 1891 was quickly made apparent by a further search of the death indexes; two of Thomas's siblings also died young, Louisa in 1892, aged 35, of phthisis and exhaustion, and Benjamin in 1894, aged 44, of bronchitis and heart disease, which meant healthy relatives able to take on additional children were rather thin on the ground. More detailed research in the local Bradford archives lent some perspective to the sorry tale. The mortality rate was high in Victorian Bradford, and tuberculosis a fact of life; yet it is astonishing to reflect that, despite the catalogue of misfortune that befell the Paxmans, contemporary photographs and maps of Bradford reveal that Rosse Street, Arthur's residence in 1881 and 1891, was by no means the worst area in which to live. In a world where it was literally a case of survival of the fittest, families closed ranks and looked after their own, no matter how distant the blood ties; nevertheless, Arthur must have been extremely tenacious to lift himself out of this desperate start to his life.

Yet the Paxman story did not end here. Thomas Paxman was the son of another Thomas, who was married in 1848 when he was employed as a stripper – that is, a worker in the cotton industry, rather than a greased hunk in a posing pouch. Or at least we presume so. But the marriage certificate also provided his father's name – another Thomas – whose occupation was listed as a shoemaker. Thomas senior was located on the 1861 census, and it was rather a surprise to discover that his place of birth was not Bradford – or indeed anywhere nearby – but Framlingham in Suffolk, in 1799. Luckily, parish registers for Framlingham had been included on the International Genealogical Index, an invaluable resource for the period prior to the introduction of civil registration in 1837. Thomas Paxman's baptism in Framlingham was found in 1799, along with his marriage to Jane Pettit in 1820 and

Above: *Jeremy searches the records for his Paxman predecessors.*

the baptisms of their seven children, including Thomas, between 1821 and 1835. The family probably left Framlingham shortly afterwards, as they next popped up in Lancashire in 1837 when their daughter Maria was baptized; with another gap until their appearance in Bradford in the 1851 census.

In an attempt to shed light on the riddle of why a well-established Suffolk family moved from one side of the country to the other, we decided it was time to 'go local' and asked the advice of a Suffolk local historian Clive Paine. Working at the Suffolk Record Office, he found Thomas Paxman, the shoemaker, in the Poor Relief Records of the 1820s and 30s. Clearly this generation also struggled against grinding poverty, as did so many East Anglians following the collapse of the wool trade and the rapid mechanization of farming. Clive uncovered documents and letters from the 1830s detailing a government scheme to relocate people from Suffolk to northern towns – effectively forcible economic migration. The surviving documents specifically mention Thomas Paxman, and reveal that he left Framlingham with his wife and eldest four children on a voyage into the unknown in search of work; the three youngest children eventually joined the family in Bradford once Thomas had found employment and a place to live.

As a footnote to the Paxman quest, a search was made to discover how long the family had resided in East Anglia. The earliest reference to the family in parish records is in 1738 in Great Bradley, with the baptism of yet another Thomas. But a conversation with Professor Andrew Phillips, an expert on the Paxman name, revealed that the Paxmans of East Anglia were descended from a certain Roger Paxman, whose name is first documented in 1367. Professor Phillips thought it likely that Roger initiated the name, 'upgrading' it from Packs-man – 'man with a pack' – to Pax-man – 'man of peace'. Roger Paxman also turned out to be an MP, which provoked a wry reaction from Jeremy. *'So the first Paxman becomes a politician,'* he said. *'I didn't think I could go any lower ...'* Jeremy's long-held belief that he came from a long line of Yorkshire folk had been altered and this stage of the journey ended with the revelation that, instead, his roots lay in rural Suffolk.

Yet there was still another branch of the family to investigate. On the maternal side of Jeremy's family tree, his grandmother Mabel McKay had disappeared from the records at the Family Records Centre. This was quickly resolved; information from Jeremy's family placed her in Glasgow, so research switched to the General Register Office of Scotland in Edinburgh, and local Glasgow archives. Meanwhile, we interviewed Jeremy's mother, Joan, who provided a rich archive of memories and photographs, which allowed us to plot Mabel's life from her childhood in Glasgow to her career in the Salvation Army and marriage to Morris Musgrove Dickson, a bandsman in the Salvation Army. Joan also provided photographs and biographies of Mabel's parents: John, a Royal Artilleryman from Dundee, and his English wife, Mary. She added that several McKays had emigrated to Canada before the First World War. Joan's impression of the family was one of severe poverty.

John McKay's military service history was located at the National Archives, Kew, which revealed he had married Mary Jane Nicholas in Devon in 1877, and retired in March 1891 at the age of thirty-nine. By the time of the 1891 census, the family had moved to Glasgow, where the genealogy reveals a horrific descent into poverty. John McKay does not appear on the 1891 census; perhaps he had not yet arrived in Glasgow following his discharge from the army. But he died in 1894, when his occupation is described as a janitor at Macdonald's School in Rutherglen, where some of his children were being educated. The school log book and register, tracked down at the nearby Mitchell Library, shed light upon his day-to-day duties, the life that he lived following his retirement from the army – and the affection in which he was held.

Mary was left with nine children to feed, and documents at the Mitchell Library Glasgow, show that this was a

Right: *John McKay in his janitor's uniform.*

real struggle. It appears that Mary McKay successfully appealed to the Poor Relief Committee in 1899 for clothes and boots for her dependent children, a situation not uncommon for a poor young widow with so many mouths to feed. But further research unearthed a shocking discovery. A series of anonymous letters informed the authorities that Mary had given birth to an illegitimate child since the death of her husband. The authorities instituted their own search of the records, and discovered that she had indeed given birth to a daughter, Dora. The pauper was to be confronted with the evidence of her 'immorality' and given a stark choice: if she wished to continue receiving financial help, she would have to go into the workhouse. This would mean separation from her children. She declined, preferring to stay with her family. As a result Mary's poor relief was promptly withdrawn – with devastating effect. Local maps and census records showed where Mary lived, and although the exact tenement no longer stands, a National Trust recreation of a similar building in Glasgow provides graphic evidence of the poverty in which Mary was forced to raise her large family. Large families often lived in cramped, single rooms in a filthy environment. Despite a long trawl of the records, no more evidence about Mary came to light and we were left with an apparent dead end.

Above: *Mabel McKay as a young woman, dressed in her Salvation Army uniform.*

It was against this wretched background that Mary's daughter (Jeremy's grandmother) Mabel McKay, and her brother Ernest, joined the Salvation Army. With the help of the Salvation Army, we investigated her life and times through copies of *The War Cry* and other Salvation Army publications, and discovered that Mabel left Glasgow for London, where she trained for nine months in 1905 to become an officer, after which she was posted to different locations around the country. The Salvation Army specifically recruited in the East End of Glasgow, seeking an opportunity to help impoverished families and especially single mothers. The most significant find was located in a warehouse in St Albans, where a vast store of Salvation Army memorabilia has been preserved. Amongst this hoard was an unusual, leather birthday 'card' in the shape of a Cornish pasty, presented to William Booth, the founder of the Salvation Army, in 1909. Inside, the officers working in Cornwall

Right: *The McKay children in their Sunday best.*

had written birthday messages – and there was Mabel's name and photograph! The face in the picture was strikingly similar to that in Joan's photographs; and *The War Cry* confirmed the link, as it recorded that Mabel had been stationed in Cornwall at the time.

As part of her work, Mabel went to America, arriving at Ellis Island with a friend in 1911. Within two years, however, she had returned home and married. Meanwhile, her brother Ernest had emigrated to Ontario shortly before the First World War – a fact confirmed by the Canadian National Archives. Much to our surprise, his mother Mary was listed with him, so with the help of researchers from Ancestry, we started out on a speculative search to trace their movements. The breakthrough came with the discovery of their wills, which revealed that Mary had also been a member of the Salvation Army. In turn, their obituaries were located which showed several of Mary's children had emigrated to the USA and Canada, including the illegitimate Dora. Thanks to the searches of the Ancestry team, Dora's son, James Douglas Rae, was located. 'Doug', aged eighty four, was sufficiently excited by our project to travel from California to England to meet Jeremy Paxman and learn more about Dora's life and family. It was a heart-warming moment to hear Doug cheerfully describe Dora simply as 'a wonderful mother', suggesting that she, too, had overcome the hardship of her youth, giving us a suitably happy end to an amazing journey.

Left: *A studio photograph of Mary McKay as an older woman.*

chapter 2 For Queen and Country

Before the English Civil War there was no such thing as a regular army. If any earls, barons, or indeed kings, wished to wage war then they had to raise a militia, paying men to recruit local people who were willing to fight.

Nearly all of us who delve into our family history will encounter ancestors who served in the armed forces. The two World Wars of the 20th century ensure that. Going back further, however, we may be lucky enough to discover a forebear who fought in the Napoleonic Wars, one of 'The Scum of the Earth' as the Duke of Wellington so charmingly described the common soldier. Maybe they were a Victorian soldier, fighting for Empire on some far-flung field, or an ordinary seaman serving on board one of the ships that were the Empire's lifeblood, defending the seas between the nation's vast and widespread territories.

To discover a military ancestor opens a whole new field of research for family historians; the military's ability to generate detailed records provides a rich seam of genealogical information, which you can use to build a picture of your ancestor's physical appearance as well as discover where and when they served through their service record. Perhaps even more importantly, battles and wars are well-storied and documented, allowing you to discover the conditions in which your forebears fought. This chapter aims to provide you with background information on the lives of your military ancestors.

The Army

Before the English Civil War there was no such thing as a regular army. If any earls, barons, or indeed kings, wished to wage war then they had to raise a militia, paying men to recruit local people who were willing to fight. And while some regiments started life in the 17th century, the concept of a band of regiments fighting as a force only came into being during the campaigns of the Duke of Marlborough. Between 1704 and 1712 Marlborough won a number of victories over the French and their allies with British regiments playing a leading role.

In the 18th century, as the British Empire first spread across the globe, British soldiers were deployed in India and in North America, whilst simultaneously waging a succession of campaigns in continental Europe, usually in coalition with other armies against Britain's arch enemy, France. Yet domestic matters also required military intervention. Throughout the 18th century, resistance to the concept of 'Great Britain' had remained after the Act of Union in 1702, particularly north of the border in Scotland. Jacobite uprisings took place in 1715 and 1745, the quelling of the latter being the last battle fought on mainland British soil when the troops of William, Duke of Cumberland suppressed the army of his cousin, 'Bonnie Prince Charlie', at Culloden in 1746. The Scots forces, Highland clansmen in the main, suffered massive losses and their rebellion was bloodily quashed.

Above: *A request for new recruits to the King's Dragoon Guards from 1800.*

British troops were less successful in their attempts to quash another rebellion, this time in the American colonies which were growing increasingly frustrated by British rule from afar. The disaffected colonists declared independence in 1776 and the

British moved to crush the uprising as quickly as possible, with some initial success until the entry of France, Spain and Holland into the war on the side of the colonists proved decisive. In the face of growing failure on the battlefield and hardened resistance to British domination, Parliament came to the conclusion that the war was proving too expensive and withdrew British troops in recognition of American independence.

There was little opportunity to replenish the coffers before war broke out with France once again in 1793. The French Revolution was a wake-up call for British rulers, and they did not want their own Great Unwashed to get any ideas. The threat of civil unrest, and the possibility of a French invasion to export revolutionary ideas to Britain, made the government realize that substantial garrisons had to be maintained at home, together with reinforcements. Volunteer Units were raised for home defence.

On and off for the next 22 years, British forces were at war with French forces under the command of Napoleon Bonaparte across the globe, wherever the interests of the two great colonial powers clashed. Troops saw service in the West Indies, in the Low Countries, in Egypt, and in Spain and Portugal during the Peninsular War. With help from Spanish and Portuguese allies, the British Army held off superior numbers of French troops, winning a series of crushing victories that drove the French out of Spain, and playing a crucial part in the overthrow of Napoleon. It is from this point that the

Opposite: *A painting by Richard Caton Woodville depicting the British Foot Guards advancing into battle at Waterloo in 1815.*

Parliament came to the conclusion that the war was proving too expensive and withdrew British troops in recognition of American Independence.

British Army gained its reputation as the best fighting force on the planet. The Duke of Wellington, the army's commander, described it as 'the most complete machine for its numbers now existing in Europe'.

This 'complete machine' won Wellington a famous victory at Waterloo in 1815, defeating a band of conscripts and veterans (Napoleon's ill-advised foray into Russia three years earlier cost him hundreds of thousands of his best fighting men), thus sealing the army's reputation and the demise of the French emperor.

By now army life was becoming strictly defined and better organized: there were regiments of infantry, guards and cavalry, and corps for the engineers and artillery. Officers, on the whole, came from the wealthier, landed classes, while the ranks were made up of those from the poorer strata of society, who enlisted for a mammoth 21 years' service (cut to 6 in the 1870s to make signing up more attractive). Officers, for the first part of the 19th century at least, were not well trained and learned the job during Britain's many colonial campaigns, not all of which were a roaring success. In 1839 troops belonging to the British East India Company invaded Afghanistan in aid of the deposed ruler, but were forced to leave three years later in disarray. There was a somewhat dissolute air to the

Above: Members of the 4th Light Dragoons at camp in the Crimea (c.1855).

regiments involved: each officer was allowed ten servants, while two camels were needed to ferry the cigars for the officers of one regiment.

It was 40 years after victory at Waterloo that the British Army fought another European enemy – in the Crimean War. The war was a religious feud, into which the British stepped, in alliance with their traditional enemy France, both supporting Ottoman Turk forces, against the forces of Russia. What is startling about the Crimean conflict is that it was the first 'media' war. Newspaper reporters were on the front line, filing eyewitness reports. William Howard Russell, of *The Times*, was able to use the telegraph to file his reports, though because the military had the monopoly of it, it took three weeks before he could wire his missive. It brought home to those back in England the bloody reality of battle, helping to dispel the romantic view of war that many held.

This report on the Charge of the Light Brigade was published on 14 November 1854:

> **At ten minutes past eleven, our Light Cavalry Brigade advanced . . . As they rushed towards the front, the Russians opened on them from guns in the redoubt on the right, with volleys of**

musketry and rifles. They swept proudly past, glittering in the morning sun in all the pride and splendour of war. We could scarcely believe the evidence of our senses! Surely that handful of men are not going to charge an army in position? Alas! it was but too true – their desperate valour knew no bounds, as far indeed was it removed from its so-called better part – discretion. They advanced in two lines, quickening their pace as they closed towards the enemy. A more fearful spectacle was never witnessed than by those who, without the power to aid, beheld their heroic countrymen rushing to the arms of death. At the distance of 1200 yards the whole line of the enemy belched forth, from thirty iron mouths, a flood of smoke and flame, through which hissed the deadly balls. Their flight was marked by instant gaps in our ranks, by dead men and horses, by steeds flying wounded or riderless across the plain. The first line is broken, it is joined by the second, they never halt or check their speed an instant; with diminished ranks, thinned by those thirty guns, which the Russians had laid with the most deadly accuracy, with a halo of flashing steel above their heads, and with a cheer that was many a noble fellow's death-cry, they flew into the smoke of the batteries, but ere they were lost from view the plain was strewed with their bodies and with the carcasses of horses.

Publicity had a chastening effect on the public. Yet it was not merely reports from the front line that created consternation back home: it was also the thousands of soldiers who died through disease, neglect and, from the point of view of the Victorian age, poor administration. *The Times* ventured a leader, criticizing the situation in the military hospitals (leading to the intervention of Florence Nightingale: see box overleaf).

Calls for reform of the army finally found expression in the 'Cardwell Reforms' of the 1870s and 1880s. In the face of considerable opposition on the part of the army establishment, Edward Cardwell, who was Secretary of State for War (1868–1874), introduced a series of far-reaching measures, attempting to make army service something other than poorly paid penal servitude for the dregs of the nation: the War Department was reorganized; flogging in peacetime was prohibited (though not abolished for active service until 1880); enlistment was shortened to six years; the purchase of commissions by officers was abolished, preventing rich youths buying themselves into positions beyond their talents and intelligence.

Perhaps one of his most lasting reforms was his

Edward Cardwell introduced a series of far-reaching measures, attempting to make army service something other than poorly paid penal servitude.

Florence Nightingale

The Crimean War is etched into popular memory for two things: the Charge of the Light Brigade, immortalized in verse by Lord Alfred Tennyson; and Florence Nightingale, the 'Lady with the Lamp', who treated the wounded. She has become a mythical, almost saintly figure, one of the select few who made it onto the back of a bank note, and the first woman apart from the Queen (on the £10 note, between 1975 and 1993). But who was she and what did she actually do, other than glide around celestially, lamp in hand, saving lives?

What made her remarkable initially was her struggle to achieve 'downward mobility', to slum it, in an age when everyone was seeking to move in the opposite direction. Born to wealthy parents, her desire to become a nurse seemed crazy to her contemporaries, whose summit of ambition was seeking a good husband and building a home. Despite her parents' protestations, Florence eventually managed to train as a nurse and within two years was superintendent at a London hospital for invalided women.

When the Crimean War broke out, she organized 38 other nurses and travelled out to Scutari, the location of the barracks hospital. Usually these were desperate places: filthy, disease-ridden places where mortally wounded men died and the less seriously injured contracted deadly infections. By implementing a sanitary routine and adhering to it in a disciplined way, Nightingale and her band of nurses transformed the concept of military hospitals; for a start, the practices she advocated cut the mortality rate. When she returned, she wrote a book, *Notes on Nursing*, whose ideas about sanitation, nursing practice and military hospitals are still adhered to today.

Lord Kitchener's decision to inter Boers, and their women and children, in concentration camps, where an estimated 20,000 died, caused international outrage.

decision to attach regiments to certain parts of the country. One battalion was to remain at base, while the other was posted overseas. This ensured that new recruits could be trained on home soil before seeing action, while seasoned soldiers saw action. It also rooted regiments in the soil of one region, city or town, gave them local pride and allowed them to build up fearsome reputations. These links exist today and they remain crucial to the army.

The first major campaign since the reforms saw the British Army invade Zululand, South Africa. They suffered a humiliating and bloody massacre at Isandlwana: Zulu warriors, due to blunders by senior army office Lord Chelmsford, killed 1,350 troops. Thankfully for the powers-that-be, the same night a small garrison of 140 men at Rorke's Drift held off the might of 3,000 Zulu warriors (which was celebrated in the 1964 epic film *Zulu*). The heroics of those men allowed military commanders to deflect much of the criticism for the earlier massacre.

The 19th century gave way to the 20th, and it was fitting that a century that would see bloodshed on an unprecedented scale should dawn with Britain at war. In 1899, Britain's wish to annex the Dutch Boer colonies of Transvaal and Orange Free State in South Africa sparked a three-year-long guerrilla war. Working-class volunteers signed up to fight in the war, but as it went on and home forces suffered some setbacks the campaign became increasingly unpopular. It proved to be the greatest test yet for the Victorian army – in one week they lost 3,000 men – and almost every regiment became involved at some stage. Britain eventually achieved what it desired, but at some cost: Lord Kitchener's decision to inter Boers, and their women and children, in concentration camps, where an estimated 20,000 died, caused international outrage and sparked rancour at home.

Above: *Lord Kitchener, taken during the Boer War in 1899.*

The Victorian Soldier

For many, joining the army was a choice made to escape a life of hardship or deprivation. At the beginning of Queen Victoria's reign, conditions for the millions on the bottom rung of the ladder were brutal, harsh and acutely miserable. Each day was an act of survival, a hard slog to earn enough money to buy bread. If you had a job, then you survived; if you didn't, and many didn't, then you had problems. One way you might solve them was by joining the army to 'take the Queen's shilling'. The reality is that many men who joined the army did not do it out of love for Queen and country, but because they wanted to eat.

FORWARD!
Forward to Victory
ENLIST NOW

The food was rationed and poor in quality; barracks were squalid and overcrowded, and sanitation was primitive. Recruits sought solace in drink and rare were the soldiers whose records did not contain some form of punishment for drunkenness. Neither did they win many popularity contests with civilians; the army were often called in to deal with civil disturbances, which were viciously quashed. Most people preferred to hear or read about romantic Imperial exploits on foreign fields, rather than witness them up close cracking skulls. Despite these privations, life in the army was infinitely preferable to life outside, which is why conscription was not necessary until well into the First World War.

The First World War

Not much can be written about this murderous and bloody conflict that has not been said before. The facts alone tell the story: in four years the war claimed 15 million lives worldwide and wounded and maimed millions of others. The psychological scars ran deep: 80,000 British soldiers were treated for shellshock. One in seven of the British population saw military service, which means almost all of us will have an ancestor who saw service: many survived, but it is likely that we have a relative who was one of the 1,663,000 wounded, or 723,000 who were killed.

What was unique about the war, other than the size and ferocity of the slaughter, was that it required the mobilization of an entire population and the recruitment of an army of civilians. There were no problems in encouraging the young men of Britain to sign up in the lead-up to war. It is poignant to consider the mood in the country: men, chests bursting with patriotic fervour, in search of adventure, enlisted in their thousands to fight the Germans. Groups of friends, work colleagues, sporting teams, all joined en masse to do their bit for King and country. What that 'bit' would involve they did not know, but being able to wander around in uniform, getting free rides on buses, admiring looks from women, and the respect and approval of their peers was very seductive. But of course those that signed up in droves died in droves in the mud and blood of Flanders. A generation was destroyed; those that did not die crept home, wounded or crippled or shocked beyond help, pitiless figures seen selling matches or begging on corners for a few pennies.

Just to read some of the dispatches from the front line is heartrending. Malcolm Brown collected some of the spirit and courage of the British solider in his book *Tommy Goes to War*, an uncensored collection of letters and diaries of those who fought. One new recruit captured the spirit of excitement and adventure that lured many into vowing to fight for their country, and their motivation for doing so:

Above: *Female labour was crucial to the industrial health of the nation during the war years.*

We had been brought up to believe that Britain was the best country in the world

and we wanted to defend her. The history taught us at school showed that we were better than other people (didn't we always win the last war?) and now all the news was that Germany was the aggressor and we wanted to show the Germans what we could do.

(Private George Morgan, 16th Battalion West Yorks Regiment (1st Bradford Pals))

'Pals', such as the regiment Private Morgan was a member of, were bands of locally raised troops; groups of friends, or men from the same street, usually in the industrial cities and then accepted into regiments. Of course, one consequence of this was to deprive those streets and towns of males in their twenties and their thirties when the slaughter reached its peak. Private Morgan was lucky: he received a 'Blighty' in 1917 – a piece of shrapnel

hit him in the leg and caused him to be shipped back home, hence the name of the type of injury.

The image of the war in the popular imagination is a grim one, quite understandably. However, while conditions at the front bore unimaginable horrors, many soldiers underwent long periods of training and rest and only experienced active service on the front line for a short time. Some very lucky souls never fired a shot in anger, though one can imagine that a detail like that went unreported to the grandchildren at their knee, or their friends at the local pub.

Above: *New World War I recruits from the Derby Scheme lining up at Whitehall: a pre-cursor to conscription, the Scheme was launched by the Earl of Derby to increase voluntary enlistment.*

Walter Towers

William Towers might have died, but his children lived on. One of them, Walter, enlisted to fight in the First World War and through his service records we can track his career. He signed up to fight on 20 April 1915 in Whitehall. He was 21, five feet nine inches tall, and a little over nine and a half stone in weight; his physical development was described as 'good', and the only defect noted on his medical report was 'a slight deformity, little toes, both feet'.

Interestingly he had broken away from the family trade, bricklaying, and become employed in a new profession, as a chauffeur (elsewhere, on other records, he is more prosaically described as 'motor car driver'). This skill was much sought after, which is why Walter was enlisted in the Army Service Corps (which received the Royal Warrant in 1918 and became the Royal Army Service Corps). It seems safe to assume his role was driving trucks or ambulances, ferrying men and vital supplies.

We know from his service record that he was sent to France and served from 27 July 1915 until 2 November of the same year; then he was on leave until June 1916, when he set sail for Salonika, where he arrived in July 1916 and where he served for the rest of the war.

A closer inspection of the records reveal why he was sent home from France and spent a relatively substantial amount of time on leave.

A closer inspection of the records reveal why he was sent home from France and spent a relatively substantial amount of time on leave: he was diagnosed with tuberculosis, and he continued to receive treatment for that on his return. He had spent the best part of a month being ill before being sent home: first with myalgia (muscle pain), then several bouts of rheumatism, and finally with TB. (In a medical report four years later, Walter himself refers to the illness as 'Double Pneumonia', which might have been the diagnosis when he returned to England.) Whatever the actual illness was, it was a testimony, perhaps, to the mud and damp that seeped into soldiers' bones during their stints near the front.

Salonika (now known as Thessalonika), where Walter Towers spent most of his war, is among the less celebrated and storied fronts of the First World War. Allied forces were called in at the request of the Greek Prime Minister to help Serb forces in their fight against the Bulgarians. The Allies set up an entrenchment camp around the town known as the 'Birdcage', and waited for a Bulgarian attack that never came. The British continued to build up their forces throughout 1916, when Walter Towers arrived. The Allies advanced towards the Serbian frontier and trench warfare began. In 1917 the Allies launched an offensive but failed to break through. However, in September 1918, they attacked again and within two weeks had forced Bulgaria to surrender unconditionally.

Back home, life in Salonika was viewed as an easy alternative to the mud and guts of France. It was anything but. It was hot and the soldiers had to contend with disease, in particular malaria. For every one who died in battle, three died of malaria or other diseases. Bearing that in mind, Walter Towers can count himself lucky that when he contracted malaria, as the medical forms showed he did in September 1916, he was lucky to survive. On his statement as to disability, filled in by Walter himself after he was discharged in 1919, he also reveals that he suffered from diarrhoea in 1917 (the month after he was promoted to Lt Corporal); in fact, on the form it can be seen that Walter wrote 'dysentery' at first, but then changed it to diarrhoea, perhaps trying to downplay the illness.

His disability claim was accepted and Walter returned to life as a chauffeur driving the streets of London, a less hazardous experience than driving supply trucks in Salonika.

By 1919 he had not yet suffered any relapses from his malaria, but when he was demobilized he put in a claim for disability for having had the illness and the chances that somewhere down the line it would return, as it did for thousands of veterans. His disability claim was accepted and Walter returned to life as a chauffeur driving the streets of London, a less hazardous experience than driving supply trucks in Salonika. He had survived the Great War, but the illnesses he suffered would have consequences for the years to come and probably afflicted him for the rest of his life.

Simon Bennett: 'An Unfortunate Call of Nature'

My great-uncle Arthur Woodworth was a First World War hero. He joined the Royal Scots Fusiliers and was stationed in India from 1905 to 1914. As a full-time soldier he returned home in 1914 and set out to fight in a war they said would not last beyond Christmas.

He was present at many battles: Le Château; first Battle of the Marne; first Battle of Aisne; second Battle of Ypres (which witnessed the first German use of poisonous gas); Battle of the Ancre; third Battle of Ypres; and the Battle of Lys. How he managed to survive all those ferocious battles and remain sane, I don't know.

In 1919 his battalion had to renew the old regimental experience of duty in Ireland during the troubles there. He was stationed there until 1921. Later he left the army and returned to Bristol.

It was no surprise come the outbreak of the Second World War in 1939 that Arthur wanted to do his bit. He joined up with the Auxiliary Fire Service as a firewatcher. One cold November evening in 1940, while not on duty, Arthur paid a visit to the Greenway Bush pub, Southville, for a beer with a few mates. I can only imagine that the pub was busy, and the recent bombings of Bristol and the progress of the war were the main topics of conversation. Late in the evening the dreaded air-raid siren sounded and people started evacuating for the local air-raid shelter. Arthur, however, needed the toilet.

A German bomb destroyed the pub: the only casualty was Arthur. He had got through some of the First World War's bloodiest conflicts, yet had been killed because of an unfortunate call of nature.

The Second World War

The Second World War, for the forces involved, was less static, less relentlessly gruesome than the First; much of the fighting was waged in the air, and there was far more action at sea, so less onus fell on the army. The army was a much smaller body than it had previously been; many soldiers were used to support infantry, rather than actually take part in the fighting themselves. Churchill described them as the 'fluff and flummery' behind the fighting troops.

In 1940, nearly 200,000 British troops were evacuated from Dunkirk's beaches by hundreds of naval and civilian vessels; they did not return to France until four years later. Yet the successful withdrawal of so many men, even though many left their weapons behind, buoyed the nation in what was a dark period for the allies. The 'Dunkirk Spirit' might have boosted the war effort, but it is an illustration of how technology rendered the overwhelming use of infantry a thing of the past.

Above: Troops wading out to rescue vessels from the beaches of Dunkirk in the summer of 1940.

The Navy

Britain's supremacy as an industrial and imperial power was guaranteed by its dominance of the sea throughout the 19th century. Without that power, the nation's ability to export goods and democracy would have been restricted. By the end of the Victorian era, half the ships on the high seas were British registered. Britannia truly did rule the waves.

This naval dominance can be traced back to Trafalgar, whose facts are known to most of us. Napoleon had plans to invade Britain from 1798, and to do that he needed to win the war at sea. Until the Spanish entered the war in 1804 he did not have the naval firepower to beat the British blockade, which had kept the French ships pinned down. But, when Spain joined France as an ally, Napoleon had the ships and ports he needed to

By the end of the Victorian era, half the ships on the high seas were British registered. Britannia truly did rule the waves.

Above: *A Royal Navy press gang during the late 18th century, when Britain ruled the seas.*

execute his plans. However, his admirals rather jumped the gun and sallied forth too early, allowing the British navy to engage them in a sea battle off the coast of Portugal in which 33 French and Spanish ships lined up against 22 British vessels. Yet while Napoleon's forces had the numbers, the British fleet were under the charge of Admiral Nelson, a tactical genius who engineered a stunning victory and assured Britain's global domination of the seas for a century.

What accounts of these glorious victories do not tell is the life of the ordinary sailor. It was not much better than life in the army at the time. Until the 1850s there was no permanent structure to a naval career: men signed on for specific voyages, which means that while they served on a Royal Navy ship, they frequently spent time on merchant vessels as well. Even officers spent much of their time ashore awaiting a posting.

Life on board in the first half of the 18th century was hard. Rations were grim: salted beef and pork that may have been up to a year old, or boiled beef or pork, and hard tack (a form of biscuit), the only perk being a daily ration of grog (rum diluted with water) and because the water on board was foul, men were allowed to drink beer. Of course, this often led to drunkenness and fighting, though discipline was maintained by clamping down hard on miscreant behaviour. Floggings, which took place on deck in full view of the crew, were common, as were court martials for those guilty of serious offences.

Those on board were drawn from all parts of working life: there were committed seamen who had worked for the merchant navy, as well as those who had worked in dockyards – shipwrights, coopers, anchorsmiths – who performed similar tasks on board. Others often had no previous experience of the sea. They might be fleeing a crime of some sort, or displaced labourers unable to find work on land, those with jobs affected by seasonal differences, or simply young men seeking adventure.

The 19th century saw a huge change in the way the Royal Navy operated. For a start, rations improved. The introduction of lime and lemon juice, and then fresh vegetables, saw scurvy becoming increasingly rare – though on long voyages it could still pose a problem. Steam gradually replaced wind power, the propeller replaced the sail, weaponry grew more advanced and the wireless telegraph transformed communications.

The use of impressment, or the 'press gang' as it was more commonly known, was less prevalent during the early 19th century. Though the image of the press gang was of a ruthless bunch who co-opted poor, unwitting unfortunates into the navy, whisking them away from wives, sweethearts and children, and while such incidents did occur, the reality was that the gangs targeted coastal towns and tried to press experienced seamen into signing up for a voyage. They might also intercept merchant ships coming into shore and coerce some of the men on board into enlisting. Of course, it was universally unpopular among sailors and even officers did not favour it, on the basis that a willing volunteer was worth twice as much as a man forced on board under sufferance. The practice was eventually ended by law in 1815.

Prior to the Crimean War, Britain's naval supremacy had been asserted using wooden ships. Britain led the way in the building, development and maintenance of those ships. Yet in the second half of the 19th century things changed: new designs, new guns, new armour, all these innovations rendered certain types of ships obsolete, and the race was on to build the biggest and best ships. Most of these were built at the Royal Navy dockyard at Portsmouth, the centre of British naval power. In 1801 the town had a population of more than 33,000, large for the time; by the end of the 19th century, when it was churning out increasingly larger ships, it had risen to more than 188,000.

Given the absence of naval battles, the main role for the Royal Navy throughout the 19th century was in extending Britain's Empire and protecting its trade. Many of our ancestors who worked and lived at sea, during the 19th century in particular, might not have seen any military action at all. Instead they would have played a part in maintaining Britain's dominance of global trade, as part of the burgeoning merchant navy. Many more people earned a living through the sea than we might think conceivable now. Due to the far-flung nature of the Empire, merchant shipping played an essential part right up to the outbreak of the Second World War. By 1939 the British Merchant Marine employed more than 190,000 seafarers from across the Commonwealth. And as we will see, they had a major role to play in wartime.

Above: *British sailors lowering a lifeboat from HMS Lord Nelson during World War I.*

The introduction of lime and lemon juice, and then fresh vegetables, saw scurvy becoming increasingly rare – though on long voyages it could still pose a problem.

Above: *In a naval engagement off Heligoland, the 'Lion' sinks a German cruiser.*

The First World War

When the First World War broke out there was little doubt that the Royal Navy was the most powerful naval force in the world. But between 1914 and 1918 it saw little meaningful action; its main role as the war wore on was to protect vital supplies that were being shipped to England from the United States.

The one naval battle of substance from the conflict was the Battle of Jutland. Controversy and debate still rages about who came out the best from the only major fleet action of the war. The Royal Navy lost more men and ships in the battle, while Germany no longer possessed a viable fighting fleet afterwards. Both sides, with some justification, claimed victory. The British public, convinced of their naval infallibility, were dismayed by the lack of a decisive victory; they had hoped for a second Trafalgar, a pivotal moment that could swing things their way once and for all.

The Second World War

The navy played a crucial role in the successes of the Second World War. Had the German naval forces, in particular the U-boats that Churchill described as the only thing that ever really frightened him during the war, been able to prevent vital supplies reaching the UK from America, then Britain might have been starved into submission and its armies prevented from being replenished with US-built equipment.

The navy did sterling if unglamorous work in escorting these merchant ships across the Atlantic under threat from submarines, and in escorting and landing troops for offensives such as the one at Normandy. The convoys originally consisted of up to 30 or 40 merchant ships in lines or columns (though later in the war, Atlantic convoys became much larger, often exceeding 70 ships). At the outbreak of war the navy was short of ships suitable for convoy-escort work. But in September 1940 50 old American destroyers were transferred to the British Navy. These old but sturdy ships did vital work escorting the convoys. Yet thousands of British and Commonwealth sailors lost their lives – 8,400 in 1942 alone. By May 1945, 30,000 merchant seamen had died. The battle for control of the Atlantic was among the fiercest of the war, as the Allies attempted to tackle the vexing problem of the

U-boats. Thankfully, cracking the Enigma code – the means by which German U-boats communicated and tracked British shipping – and, perhaps more significantly, the entrance of American forces after the Japanese attack on Pearl Harbour, proved decisive in the naval battle.

Royal Air Force

The First World War

The RAF was formed in 1918 out of the Royal Flying Corps – an army regiment – and the Royal Naval Air Service. Both played a part in the First World War, despite flying being in its infancy. At the outbreak of the war, aeroplanes were used almost exclusively for reconnaissance; one man flew the plane while the other took pictures. At the beginning of the war, France possessed 132 aircraft and Germany 246 (including 5 Zeppelins), while the RFC boasted 84 and the RNAS 71, plus seven airships. None of the British aircraft were equipped with guns, though crew were given revolvers in case of crash landing.

In 1915 the RFC conducted its first bombing raid, and fighter squadrons were formed the same year. Slowly but surely the new aircraft were proving more adept in wartime, providing support for infantry as well as vital reconnaissance. Flying was a perilous activity, however: the average life expectancy of a pilot in April 1917 was two months. Perhaps it was as a result of this danger that pilots became the most heroic members of the armed forces in the public mind, or perhaps it was because their daredevil exploits made a pleasant, romantic contrast to the slaughter and deadlock

At the outbreak of the war, aeroplanes were used almost exclusively for reconnaissance; one man flew the plane while the other took pictures.

Above: *A spitfire in flight during World War II: the role of the Supermarine Spitfire in the Battle of Britain made it one of the most famous and best-loved fighter aircraft in history.*

Jenny Morley: 'Desertion and Redemption'

My grandfather was a mystery to us. Grandma hardly mentioned him and we didn't think to ask. An old photograph of him in uniform the year before he was killed fired my interest; I became determined to unravel his story.

His name was David Brandon, a Lancashire lad working as a boilermaker on the docks at Bootle when WW1 broke out. He volunteered but was turned away; his was a protected trade. Undeterred, he simply turned up at another recruitment station in Salford with a new identity. He was taken on and became Private John Smith, 3rd Battalion, Lancashire Fusiliers.

He was sent to a training camp in the Hull area. There he met Ethel Ward. She soon discovered she was pregnant. David/John requested leave, which was denied, so he went AWOL. He didn't get far. On 28 April 1916 in a court martial at Padrington, he was charged with desertion, for which the punishment was six months' imprisonment. It was later commuted to a charge of absence, and a period of detention.

When he married Ethel on 24 July 1916, when she was eight months pregnant, he gave his address as Wakefield prison, where he was serving his detention. He must either have just completed his sentence, or been let out for the day to get married.

In March 1917 he was sent to Belgium to join the 1st/7th Battalion Lancashire Fusiliers. As far as we know he never returned. On 6 September he was killed in action at Passchendaele; his baby son, my dad, was one year old.

It came into its own at the Battle of Britain, where Hitler's ambition to invade Britain was thwarted by the inability of the Luftwaffe to defeat the RAF in the skies.

on the land below. Their role became increasingly influential in breaking that stalemate. The numbers of men fighting in the air continued to swell: by March 1918 the RFC had 579 aircraft in the field, 261 of which were fighters.

On 1 April 1918, the RAF was formed. At a stroke this resolved the tension and rivalry that existed between the RFC and RNAS and recognized the growing importance of aerial warfare. Their merging under one command made sense, and for the remaining months of the war the RAF and Allied aircraft dominated the skies, providing invaluable support to ground troops in forcing the surrender of German forces.

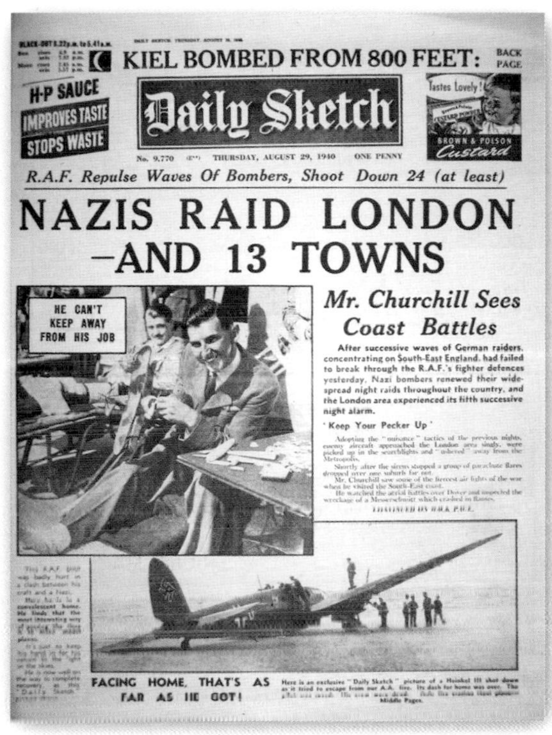

KIEL BOMBED FROM 800 FEET: BACK PAGE

Daily Sketch

No. 9,770 THURSDAY, AUGUST 29, 1940 ONE PENNY

H-P SAUCE IMPROVES TASTE STOPS WASTE

Tastes Lovely! BROWN & POLSON Custard

R.A.F. Repulse Waves Of Bombers, Shoot Down 24 (at least)

NAZIS RAID LONDON —AND 13 TOWNS

HE CAN'T KEEP AWAY FROM HIS JOB

Mr. Churchill Sees Coast Battles

After successive waves of German raiders, concentrating on South-East England, had failed to break through the R.A.F.'s fighter defences yesterday, Nazi bombers renewed their wide-spread night raids throughout the country, and the London area experienced its fifth successive night alarm.

'Keep Your Pecker Up'

Adopting the "nuisance" tactics of the previous nights, enemy aircraft approached the London area singly, were picked up in the searchlights and "ushered" away from the Metropolis.

Shortly after the sirens stopped a group of parachute flares dropped over one suburb for not.

Mr. Churchill saw some of the fiercest air fights of the war when he visited the South-East coast.

He watched the aerial battles over Dover and inspected the wreckage of a Messerschmitt which crashed in flames.

FACING HOME, THAT'S AS FAR AS HE GOT!

Here is an exclusive "Daily Sketch" picture of a Heinkel III shot down as it tried to escape from our A.A. fire. Its dash for home was over.

Middle Pages.

Above: *The front page of The Daily Sketch from August 1944.*

The Second World War

Despite these successes, the reputation of the RAF was forged in the white heat of battle during the Second World War. It came into its own at the Battle of Britain, where Hitler's ambition to invade Britain was thwarted by the inability of the Luftwaffe to defeat the RAF in the skies. The fighting was intense, though reading the daily reports of the battle does not give much indication of how fierce it was. In fact, the effect is to make a massive aerial assault sound mundane, though of course it was anything but. Here is an extract from the daily report of 14 August, around the time when the Luftwaffe intensified and increased their attacks, concerning the action in the skies above the South and South East coast:

> ***A hostile reconnaissance of the Thames Estuary was followed at 100 hours by two reconnaissances of the Dover Downs area. No contact was effected. At 1100 hours, about 100 aircraft attacked Hawkinge aerodrome. RAF wireless stations in this area were out of action for a time owing to the electric mains having been cut by enemy***

Above: *World War II RAF Hawker Hurricane pilots resting at-the-ready between combat missions.*

bombs. At about 1430 hours, some 200 enemy aircraft concentrated in the Calais–Boulogne area and at 1500 hours simultaneously attacked the RAF station at Martlesham, RAF establishments at Bawdsey, Dover, Deal and Lympne, but with comparatively little success. Eight squadrons met this attack and 15 enemy were destroyed.

At about 1800 hours, four raids of 70+ aircraft crossed the coast at Dungeness and attacked targets at Rochester and RAF stations at West Malling and Croydon. Seven squadrons intercepted and destroyed about 17 enemy aircraft.

At about 2100 hours, eight raids came in from the Dutch Islands, penetrated inland to the North Weald area and are reported to have bombed Harwich.

Once Hitler realized he could not achieve air supremacy he switched tactics, deciding to drop bombs on Britain's cities in the hope of weakening its resolve. Between July and October, more than 1,700 German planes were shot down, while the RAF lost only 915. Of course, tons of explosives were still dropped by German planes, but for the valour and heroism of RAF pilots, it might have been worse. Once Germany's power in the skies had been resisted, the RAF went on to play a major part in ending the war with the strategic bombing campaign of Germany.

Once Hitler realized he could not achieve air supremacy he switched tactics, deciding to drop bombs on Britain's cities in the hope of weakening its resolve.

The East India Company

Britain dominated world trade throughout the 19th century and its cornerstone was the East India Company. Initially the company was formed for the sole purpose of trade, but given the competition it received from the rival Dutch and French Empires, it soon became necessary for it to secure and protect trading posts and routes. To that end, it established its own army and navy. It was the sole aim of those troops, ships and seamen to do all they could to guarantee and protect British trade. As a result, Britain dominated in India.

The posts and routes set up by the East India Company brought in a whole new variety of goods that had a dramatic impact on British cultural life, none more so than tea, from China, one of the company's biggest legacies. It was also instrumental in bringing spices and porcelain from Asia to these shores.

During the Indian Rebellion of 1857 many Indians took up arms against the British. The introduction of so-called Western practices by the company – child marriage was abolished for example – caused a mutiny among sections of the army, a rebellion that lasted for 10 months causing thousands of deaths. The result was that the East India Company became unsustainable and it was dissolved in 1858. The Crown took responsibility for the administration of India.

The result was that the East India Company became unsustainable and it was dissolved in 1858.

Julian Clary

Best known as one of the more flamboyant and colourful entertainers on our screens, Julian Clary guards his privacy very carefully. Throwing open the door to his family history was not a decision he took lightly, particularly as there was much he didn't know about his family's past. The few details he did possess came from having written out a sketchy family tree when he was a child, though he knew little or nothing about most of the names on his list. Julian was keen to flesh out the stories of these mysterious relatives who existed only as a childish scrawl on a yellowing piece of card.

Above: Flight Sergeant Jack Clary stands on the left of the picture; a chief mechanic in the RAF, Julian's grandfather served in both World Wars.

The first ancestor Julian wanted to discover more about was his grandfather, Jack Clary. Jack died relatively young, before Julian was born. 'I wonder what he would have made of me,' Julian wondered. 'He'd have been horrified, probably.'

Julian's father Peter remembered his father Jack fondly, though he was frequently away from home for long periods, partly due to illness and later as a result of military postings away from home. Jack Clary had served in both World Wars, joining the Royal Flying Corps in 1916 (a body which later became the Royal Air Force) and rejoining the RAF during the Second World War, returning to his old rank of Flight Sergeant. As a young child, Peter had believed that his father was part of an aircrew, flying daring missions against the Germans. It was only later that he realised, to his disappointment, that he had actually been an engineer.

Julian's research took him to the Imperial War Museum at Duxford, where he learned more about his grandfather's role in World War One, as chief mechanic for the Bristol fighters of 48 Squadron. While arguably a less glamorous role than that of the men who

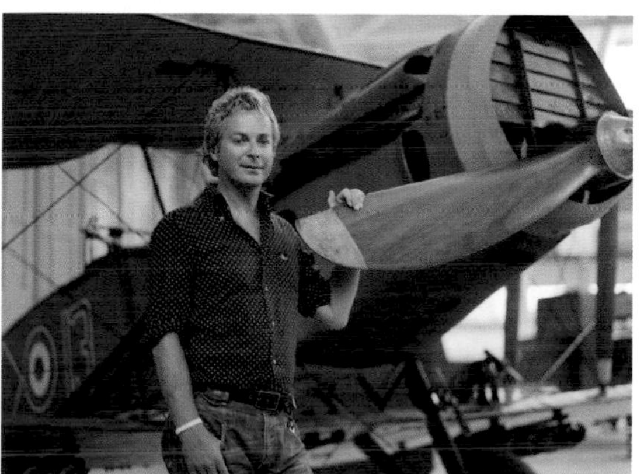

Left: Julian poses beside the exact make of aircraft that his grandfather once maintained.

Above: *The wedding of Jack Clary and Victoria Tiedemann in 1925.*

fought in the skies over the trenches, the engineer's job was nonetheless vital. Early aeroplanes such as the Bristol were unreliable machines at the best of times, and it took no little skill to keep them running, allowing the men in the cockpit to complete their missions. Jack worked fourteen-hour days in all weather conditions, living in basic accommodation, often under canvas, and under constant threat from enemy air attacks. It was preferable to the mud and blood of the front line, but hard, backbreaking work all the same.

After the First World War, Jack was employed as a skilled wood turner, making pipes for the famous Dunhill firm. In 1925 he married Victoria Tiedemann, Julian's grandmother, and the couple had two children, but it appears that Jack had gone through some difficult times in the interwar years. Julian's father, Peter, dimly recalled having visited his father in a psychiatric hospital some time in the 1930s, but couldn't remember, or

Right: *The happy couple pictured together in the 1930s.*

Right: *Julian's great-grandfather, Herman Tiedmann. 'Herman the German', as he was known, emigrated to England, leaving his German homeland in the 1870s.*

hadn't been told, why Jack had been admitted. Perhaps he had suffered some sort of nervous breakdown?

Julian managed to find out that the hospital in question was located in Napsbury in Hertfordshire and indeed the hospital records contained a certificate confirming his grandfather's admission. In fact, Jack Clary had attended Napsbury voluntarily, and chose to stay there between August 1926 and April 1938, free to discharge himself at any time. Attitudes towards mental health had changed dramatically since the end of the First World War. Napsbury hospital had treated many patients with shellshock during the conflict, and as a result employed relatively progressive techniques. By the time Jack Clary attended in the 1930s, voluntary admissions had been introduced and treatments included modern innovations such as occupational and art therapy. The peace and tranquillity of the hospital's grounds were thought to aid patient recovery and Jack would have been encouraged to spend as much time outdoors as possible. Whatever personal demons had led Julian's grandfather to Napsbury, he finally felt well enough to leave the hospital in 1938. He died in 1951, eight years before Julian was born.

Next on Julian's list of interesting ancestors to investigate was his German great-grandfather or, to use Julian's nickname for him, 'Herman the German'. Herman Tiedemann was the father of Julian's paternal grandmother, and he left Germany to emigrate to England in the 1870s. At that time, Germans made up one of the biggest groups of foreign immigrants to this country, most of them settling in and around London. Herman and his compatriots will have assimilated relatively easily into London society – that is, until the outbreak of the First World War. Foreign workers who had been made welcome just a few short decades before were suddenly eyed with suspicion, vilified by the media and derided as fifth columnists, and Julian had heard a rumour from his father that Herman had been interned during World War One. Through his research, Julian discovered that over 30,000 civilian German men were interned during the war – a number of them at Alexandra Palace, where they lived much like prisoners. The families of these men were often shunned by neighbours and left to fend for themselves in the absence of their main breadwinner, and the end of the war offered little respite; many were simply repatriated.

Still not certain whether the rumour that Herman had been interned was true, Julian went to visit his Great Aunt Ivy, the youngest child of Herman and his English wife, Louisa. Ivy had almost no memory of her father – she was only three when he died – but she was able to tell Julian that Herman had been deemed too ill to be interned. He had died from consumption – now more commonly known as TB – in 1917, and Herman's death left his wife Louisa to bring up their seven children on her own. Ivy remembered the bitter struggles her mother had faced, trying to find enough work to put food on the table for seven hungry mouths even as her own health began to fail. To make matters worse, it appears that the young family received little help from Louisa's family. Ivy was convinced it was because they disapproved of Louisa having married a German.

Julian puzzled over this apparent disapproval of his great-grandfather. The idea that Louisa's family didn't like Herman simply because he was German didn't quite ring true – after all, Julian had learnt that until the outbreak of war in 1914, Germans were known to have assimilated well into British society. Was there another, more fundamental reason for their disapproval? As a relatively poor immigrant looking for work, perhaps Louisa's family felt that she was marrying beneath herself? In search of a possible explanation, Julian stumbled across a closely-guarded family secret: Louisa had been six months pregnant when the couple married. Perhaps this was the real explanation for her family's reluctance to help when Louisa hit hard times in 1917.

__Above:__ Julian with his Great-Aunt Ivy – the youngest of Herman's seven children.

Having gained a taste for family history, Julian turned his attention to his other great-grandmother, Theresa. Julian's mother, Brenda, remembers her grandmother as fussy and particular, but believes that it was Theresa's side of the family that carried the artistic gene. 'Thanks goodness,' Julian exclaimed, 'because there's just rough, vulgar poverty on the other side.'

Theresa Long's background was something of a mystery. Julian ordered her marriage certificate and discovered that young Theresa Walter, the daughter of a hair merchant, was twenty when she married the professional photographer Charles Edmond Long. The certificate listed her profession as 'artist'. In 1881, the year of their marriage, there were few professions a woman could take on which met with societal approval, but this was one. Julian visited the house in

Above: *Julian flanked by his two older sisters, Frances and Beverley.*

Marylebone where Theresa lived just before she got married and was delighted to discover it was in a relatively respectable area – 'I feel very at home here!'

Julian and his sister Frances were curious to find out more about Theresa's background. They looked for the family on the 1881 census, and were amazed to discover that Theresa Walter, Julian's great-grandmother on his mother's side, was born in Trier, Germany – yet more German blood! Apparently, dear old 'Herman the German' was in good company. Julian and his sister wondered if their grandmother knew this secret, but decided that this was unlikely, given that Frances remembers their grandmother being outraged when the family bought a German dog. 'I hope the BBC is going to pay for our counselling,' Julian added.

This new discovery inspired Julian to journey to Trier to find out more. Finding Theresa's birth certificate and a record of her parents' marriage, it became clear that Theresa's family had come to Britain some time in the early 1860s – a period of economic depression in southern Germany, when thousands left their homes in search of work in the booming economies of Britain or the USA.

Julian returned to England to inform his mother of her unknown German ancestry. He didn't think she would be upset. 'It's not like saying, "Mother, I'm afraid I'm heterosexual." It's not nearly that bad, is it?'

chapter 3

Shipping In, Shipping Out

Throughout the 18th century and the early part of the 19th, people kept arriving, from mainland Europe on the whole, unable to resist the mercantile and industrial pull of London, or fleeing turmoil and upset in their homelands.

Britain has a justifiably proud tradition of letting in and integrating migrants, refugees and those seeking asylum, and has, on the whole, adopted them with a relaxed and liberal attitude. But while people came here in their droves, it is estimated that 10 million people left the British Isles in the 19th century alone. They emigrated to the United States, Australia or Canada – though many of those 10 million had little say in the matter, as we will see later.

Moving Here

Ever since the Middle Ages, Britain has attracted immigrants. After 1066 there was a steady flow of migrants as the ruling elite bolstered their numbers from across the Channel, mainly Normans but increasingly from the southern lands around Gascony and Poitou. Yet large numbers of foreign merchants lived in England throughout the Middle Ages, particularly Italian bankers and trading blocks

The 1841 census reveals there were 289,404 people living in England and Wales who were born in Ireland.

from what is now modern Germany. The flow of immigrants quickened during the 16th century, when groups such as the Protestants in the Low Countries and France fled persecution to the relative safety of Elizabethan England, a country that had embraced the Reformation. These refugees were welcomed for their skills and the new crafts they brought with them. When the Huguenots found themselves maltreated by Louis XIV in France towards the end of the 17th century, a number sought sanctuary across this side of the Channel. Many of us, though we will struggle to prove it given the absence of records, have Huguenot blood (such as Nick Barratt) – so those of you who fell asleep during school history lessons about the siege of La Rochelle might wish you'd paid more attention! Throughout the 18th century and the early part of the 19th, people kept arriving, from mainland Europe on the whole, unable to resist the mercantile and industrial pull of London, or fleeing turmoil and upset in their homelands. It may come as a surprise to know that until the late 19th century, the largest immigrant community was German. But in the last 200 years, the time when most of our immigrant ancestors will have entered the country, there have been four distinct groups who have settled in this country. This section deals with those.

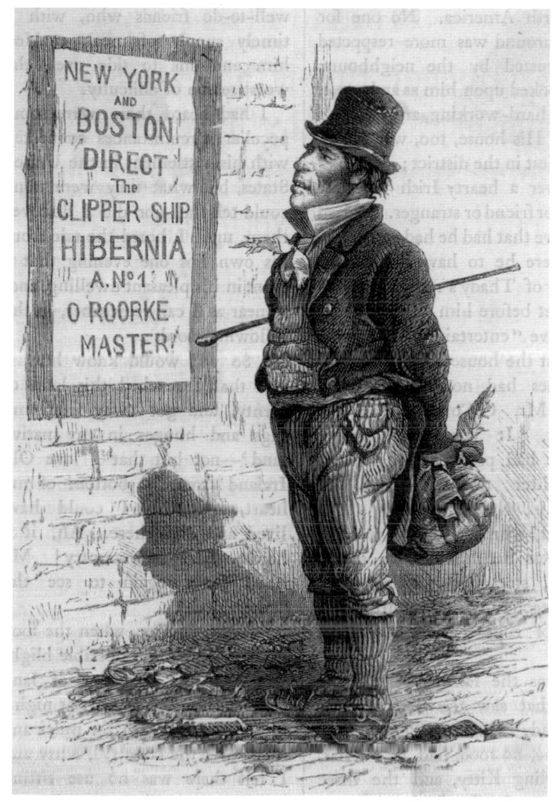

***Above:** An Irish Farmer contemplates the prospect of a new life in America (1873).*

Irish Immigration

The Irish have moved back and forth across the Irish Sea for centuries. The country was effectively a colonial possession of England going back hundreds of years to the 1160s, but only became part of the United Kingdom following the Act of Union in 1801. But before and after the Act the Irish emigrated to England, Scotland and Wales in large numbers. The 1841 census, for example, reveals there were 289,404 people living in England and Wales who were born in Ireland. They spread themselves across the British Isles: those from Ulster tended to favour

Scotland, while those from the South favoured the English cities. London was a popular destination, as was Liverpool, not surprisingly given its closeness to Ireland. The 1851 census disclosed that 22 per cent of the city's residents were born in Ireland.

In the first half of the 19th century, Ireland was a poor, rural land entirely dependent on agriculture. The potato was the staple of their diet (an adult male, it has been estimated, consumed 14lb of potatoes a day). The effects of the potato famine of the 1840s were intensified because potatoes were cash crops; not only was there less to eat, but there was also less to sell.

Above: *Irish farmhands leave for England to find harvest work following the famine of the 1840s.*

The consequence of the potato famine was disastrous: people were starving, and to survive they were forced to flee. During 1841–51, the population of Ireland fell by 1.5 million: dispersing across the world, crammed onto wooden ships ('coffin ships' as they were known) destined for the United States, Canada and the United Kingdom.

Wherever they alighted, the Irish tended to live in clusters, forming tight-knit communities. Many of them were originally peasants, poor and unskilled, which meant they often lived in the worst quality of housing in the less desirable parts of the city. In the industrial slums, their native neighbours viewed them with suspicion and downright hostility. But employers were more welcoming: the Irish were willing to do jobs the natives were reluctant to carry out, and willing to do it for less money. (A pattern familiar to most immigrants to this country, and one that leads to the cry of, 'They're taking our jobs.' Nothing much changes.) In 1836 a royal commission into the state of the poor in Ireland examined the plight of Irish immigrants in England. The report states that, 'The kind of work at which they (Irish immigrants) are employed is usually of the coarsest and most repulsive description, and requiring the least skill and practice; and their mode of life is in general on a par with that of the native population, if not inferior to it.'

By 1861, there were more than 600,000 Irishmen and women living in England and Wales (though this does not take into account children born in England to Irish parents, which swelled numbers in Irish communities). From that point on the rate of immigration dipped, though until 1890 the Irish were still the biggest – and most visible – minority group in the country, and while their numbers in the 1901 census had fallen to around 425,000, there were vast numbers of second- and third-generation Irish immigrants in London, Liverpool and Glasgow. The perception of Irish immigrants had altered over time, and the stereotypical view of them being drunkards and violent abated – though that may have been because the influx of Russian Jews into England in the 1890s created a new minority for the press and public to mistrust and malign. The view of the Irish as feckless, violent drunks was common still – and not always unfounded. Charles Booth noted this in his description of the Irish living in the streets between Gale Street and Furze Street in the East End:

> ***This block sends more police to hospital than any other in London. 'These are not human, these are wild beasts.' You take a man or a woman, a rescue is always organised. They fling brickbats, iron, any thing they can lay their hands on. Not an Englishman or Scotchman would live among them.***

The United States became an increasingly popular destination for those who emigrated, particularly from the western counties of Ireland, but the Great Depression, which gripped America in the 1930s, made England, by necessity, the choice for those who had to leave. Many single, pregnant women, for example, fled Ireland in the 1920s to escape the censure of what was a strict Catholic country: it was easier to get an abortion in England and the adoption provision was years ahead of that back home. Of course, life in modern Ireland is more liberal these days, and its economy is one of the most impressive in Europe, so the urge to leave has decreased as the years have gone by.

The consequence of the potato famine was disastrous: people were starving, and to survive they were forced to flee. During 1841–51, the population of Ireland fell by 1.5 million.

Navvies – the Men Who Built the Railways

The origin of the term 'navvy' comes from 'navigator', based on the original crews who cut out the canal systems across England. The railway explosion of the 19th century required an entire new workforce to build it: digging the cuttings, laying the lines and packing the ballast. It was back-breaking, dangerous work, involving shifting and moving thousands of tons of earth, all done with picks, shovels and wheelbarrows. By 1845 there were 200,000 men building 3,000 miles of new railway line, and many of them were Irish immigrants. The railway-building boom of the 1840s coincided closely with an agricultural crisis in Ireland, and navvying provided a means of subsistence that would otherwise have been lacking. Many Irish navvies sent their earnings home and lived in makeshift huts by the railway line, which accommodated up to 20 men, for which they paid one-and-a-half pennies a night for a bed. Those who slept on the floor paid a lot less. Five nights of floor sleeping cost one penny.

The Irish presence was not welcome among the English and Scottish navvies. The latter hated them, while the English had a reputation for fighting anyone but especially the Irish. Navvies, often quite justifiably, were known as hard-drinking men, and conflict was not uncommon, particularly after a drinking spree of several days. The native navvies viewed the Irish as inferior colonials with strange religious practices. Harmonious relations were not helped by the willingness of the Irish navvies to work for less money, thereby lowering wages generally. It was an itinerant life; they moved to wherever the work was, arousing the ire of the locals but a welcome from the landlords when they moved into town.

***Left:** Navvies working on the canal system: the demand for experienced navvies led to the creation of a migrant workforce which moved with canal- and railway-building projects around the country.*

***Opposite:** An engineer instructs navvies.*

L. ATLAS
COLD DRINKS
½ Glass
WATERS

Jewish Immigration

Records of Jewish people arriving in Britain date back to the Norman Conquest, but they were expelled by Edward I in 1290 and only allowed back into Britain in 1654. For most of us who discover Jewish ancestors, we will find they arrived from Russia and Eastern Europe between the late 1880s and the beginning of the Second World War. Some left out of economic necessity, others because of persecution. Tsar Alexander II of Russia was assassinated in 1881, and his successor, Alexander III, in an attempt to ensure only one religion existed throughout the Russian Empire, began to persecute the Jews.

Being Jewish in Russia and places such as Poland and Romania was not much fun in the second half of the 19th century. They were often made scapegoats for ills affecting the local population, and became seen as a group upon which unwarranted blame could be attached. 'Pogrom', a seemingly unthreatening word with a sinister meaning – the organized massacre of a minority ethnic group – was a reality for many Jews, as were attacks on their property, restrictions of movement and laws that discriminated against them. Unsurprisingly, some chose to leave and the United Kingdom was a popular destination.

The Jews settled in London, the East End in particular, Manchester, Leeds and other large cities. They were soon disabused of the view that they had turned their back on hatred and prejudice, however. The arrival of thousands of immigrants – the 1901 census revealed that more than 50,000 Jews had

***Left:** A Jewish fruiterer in Manchester, c.1900.*

settled in the East End of London – gave vigour to the debate that there should be some form of restriction on immigrants. Not all of the clamour came from little Englanders or the press; many liberal commentators and politicians believed quotas might be a good thing because of the cluttered state of some of the Jewish communities, and the appalling conditions of some of the sweatshops they worked in. It was not uncommon, especially in the tailoring industry which employed many newly arrived Jewish men, women and children, to work 16- or 17-hour days in dusty rooms as hot as saunas, the air choked with wool particles. Lung diseases were rife. (These conditions, of course, were not exclusive to Jewish workers. Many other workers, even after the various Factory Acts were implemented to improve working conditions, had to suffer similar environments.)

Above: *Jewish men in Whitechapel, London march against the killing of Jews in Poland in 1919.*

By 1905, unease over the number of people entering the country led to the 1905 Aliens Act, the first piece of legislation in this county to restrict the amount of immigrants.

The plight of the Jews attracted the attention of Charles Booth on one of his walks around London. He noted the police impression of them, which was favourable given their public sobriety, a stark contrast to the 'Irish Cockneys' mentioned above:

> ***Jews drink very little in the public houses; the police cannot understand them at all. They shut themselves up in their clubs and there is no getting near them. He (Inspector Reid) has not seen more than 6 Jews in the whole of his 3 years at this place brought to the station drunk.***

Much of the suspicion of the Jewish newcomers stemmed from how alien they seemed; their command of English was often poor, while their dress and religion was markedly different in a way that was perhaps more unsettling than either the Irish or German immigrants that preceded them. In each place they settled one of the first things they did was to build a synagogue (in the meantime they met in attics and back rooms.) But these new

They were often made scapegoats for ills affecting the local population, and became seen as a group upon which unwarranted blame could be attached.

The 1930s saw an increase, however, as a result of the rise of the Nazis in Germany. Between 1933 and 1939 50,000 Jews arrived in the country,

buildings were not the only contribution the Jews made to British life. They forged new trades and new habits: retail giants Burton and Marks & Spencer (see box overleaf) were both built by Jewish immigrants.

The Aliens Act had a deterrent effect on Jewish emigration – the United States became a much more attractive option – and the rate of immigration from Eastern Europe slowed to a trickle. The 1930s saw an increase, however, as a result of the rise of the Nazis in Germany. Between 1933 and 1939 50,000 Jews arrived in the country, though many thousands more tried and failed to get permission to either leave or gain entry. Many Eastern European immigrants did not intend to stay in Britain; their aim was the USA. In fact, some became confused, mistaking the UK for the US. In Hull there is a pub called The Statue of Liberty: some immigrants thought it was the real thing!

Afro-Caribbean Ancestors

The first African immigrants to these shores arrived as Roman legionaries about 2,000 years ago. The first recorded black face in Great British documents in the National Archives is a portrait of a black man in the abbreviation of the Domesday Book in the 13th century. He was probably a royal minstrel.

Since then, people of African descent have lived

Marks & Spencer

No one person epitomizes the eventual assimilation and success of Jewish immigrants better than Michael Marks. He emigrated from Slonim, Russia when he was a young man. Without a trade and unable to speak English, he, like many other Jewish immigrants, moved to Leeds. In 1884 Marks met warehouse owner Isaac Dewhurst. Marks agreed to purchase goods from Dewhurst and to sell them in the numerous villages around Leeds. The venture was a success; Marks soon raised enough money to establish a stall in Leeds market.

Not content to rest on his laurels, Marks rented stalls at the new covered market in Leeds. At one, he sold goods that cost just one penny. Next to the stall was a big poster with the words: 'Don't Ask the Price, It's a Penny.' It was a huge success. During the next few years he opened similar stalls in markets all over Yorkshire and Lancashire.

But still, Marks was not satisfied; he wanted to expand even further. In 1894 Marks decided he needed a partner to help him expand the business. He needed investment. He asked Dewhurst, who politely refused, but suggested that his cashier, Tom Spencer, might be interested. Spencer agreed – he was an admirer of Marks – and stumped up £300 for a half-share of the business.

Above: An early Marks and Spencer's Penny stall in 1901.

Spencer managed the office and warehouse, while Marks ran the stalls. The partnership worked perfectly: the pair opened stores in Manchester, Birmingham, Liverpool, Middlesbrough, Sheffield, Bristol, Hull, Sunderland and Cardiff. Other branches followed, including seven in London. In 1903 Marks & Spencer became a limited company: Spencer's £300 investment was now worth £15,000. Spencer retired but Michael Marks continued to develop the business. 1906 was a record year for the company, but Marks was unable to enjoy the success: on 31 December, aged 48, he collapsed and died, though his shop was to go on and become a British institution, its fortunes and fluctuations the subject of front-page news for the next century.

in Britain for hundreds of years. In the 19th century some of these were celebrated personalities, such as Walter Tull, professional football player for Spurs, who was later killed in the First World War.

Mention must be made here of Britain's part in the slave trade. The trade in humans was established by the Elizabethans, and it was not until 1807 that it was abolished in this country and, thanks to the efforts of William Wilberforce, it was finally ended throughout the Empire in 1834. Many plantation owners brought black slaves back to this country and used them in domestic service, in reward for their freedom. Black faces were a regular sight in 18th-century England.

About the time of the outbreak of the First World War, the black community began to grow mainly around Britain's ports, made up primarily of seamen from colonial outposts. London, as the home of the Empire, and the point where all routes led, was home to many. A West Indian regiment fought in Europe during the Second World War, while this conflict swelled numbers further: ranks of colonists joined the armed forces and fought for the Allies, then chose to stay and make their lives in Britain come the peace.

Post 1948, the era of mass immigration began. The arrival of the *Empire Windrush* was a momentous moment in the history of both the United Kingdom and the islands of the Caribbean. On 24 May of that year the boat left Jamaica with 300 passengers below deck, 192 above. Most of the travellers were women or ex-servicemen, unaware of the fate that awaited them in the UK. Some had prospects, jobs awaiting them in the RAF for example, others did not. As the ship neared these

Above: *London's Notting Hill Carnival stems from the Carribean tradition of carnivals and originated in the 1950s with the influx of West Indian immigrants.*

shores, national newspapers formented disquiet and discontent about the arrival of those on board, raising spectres of rising crime, job and housing shortages. As a result, questions were asked in Parliament.

As most of the settlers had nowhere to go, they were eventually housed in the Clapham Common Deep Shelter, a disused air-raid bunker, until they were able to find a place to live. Many of the settlers decided to live nearby, in Brixton, which remains the heart of London's black community to this day.

The arrival of the *Windrush* did not introduce a huge surge of immigrants from the Caribbean. A few more boats did arrive, but the influx was not to begin until the period between 1955 and 1962.

Aspiring West Indians had always favoured emigration to the USA rather than Great Britain, but an act of 1952 limited the number of migrants allowed into America from the Caribbean so the UK became the preferred destination. This upswell caused a hullabaloo in the English press: there were no barriers to colonial migration and it was claimed that the authorities could not provide an accurate answer as to how many people were entering the country from the Caribbean. It became obvious that the government would introduce some form of system to restrict immigration. This encouraged more people to make the journey from the Caribbean, before the loophole was closed. Between 1955 and 1962, a quarter of a million people arrived here from the Caribbean.

In 1962, as a consequence of mounting pressure in the press, which had warned of the prospect of civil unrest, the Commonwealth Immigrants Bill was passed, ushering in the era of managed immigration. Colonists were granted entry on the offer of a job. There were some firms or industries that actively sought to recruit colonists. In 1956 the London Transport Executive agreed with the Barbadian Immigrants Liaison Service to loan Barbadians their fares to Britain – to be repaid as part of their wages.

Life in 1950s Britain was bewildering for many of the new arrivals. It seemed a cold, often hostile place. In 1958 gangs of white youths rampaged around Notting Hill attacking and injuring individual black men. They prowled the streets beating up any West Indian in their path; and for a week in August 1958 the violence escalated. The immigrants attempted to fight back, but thankfully before the situation deteriorated into an out-and-out race war, the police were able to intervene. However, at the trial of some of the white rioters, they were told their conduct had 'set the clock back 300 years'. Inflammatory situations like these precipitated the 1962 act, but also fostered spirit and action among the immigrant communities which were not prepared to allow themselves to be victimized. The Notting Hill Carnival, an annual colourful celebration of Anglo-Caribbean life, is the most popular street parade in Europe, but it began as an act of defiance following the murder of a Jamaican man in the late 1950s.

Asian Ancestors

The roots of the Indian, Pakistani and Bangladeshi presence in this country were laid down long before the subcontinent gained its independence in 1947. Indians, as British subjects, had been free to enter the UK. As a result, a small number of professionals – doctors, businessmen or lawyers – had established themselves in Britain from the mid-19th century onwards, and, similarly to Caribbean immigrants, there was an Asian presence at many ports.

Post 1947, there was more to attract immigrants to this country. The 1948 British Nationality Act redefined the authorities' attitude to British nationality; the aim was to attract colonists to come to Britain and help in its reconstruction

The roots of the Indian, Pakistani and Bangladeshi presence in this country were laid down long before the subcontinent gained its independence in 1947.

Chris Hanson-Khan:
'Political, Economic and Religious Migrants from across the World'

The broad sweep of world events has shaped my family history and origins. My father was born in Shanghai, China, in 1922. His family was part of the 1930s, English-speaking mixed race bureaucracy that ran the British colonies. That's why the Japanese imprisoned them during the Second World War, and why they had to flee China when Mao's Communists took over in 1948.

At some point in our family's colonial past, our family name was changed from Hassan Khan to Hanson-Khan. My father and his siblings went to a public school in Shanghai (Thomas Hanbury Public School), while his father Joseph (anglicized from Yussef) was a local-government official and an auxillary policeman. In the prisoner-of war-camp, my grandfather died, while my father almost starved. My father eventually made it to the UK.

In 1950 he met my mother at GCHQ in Cheltenham. My mother's father was a third-generation Irish immigrant tailor from Cork, James Kearney. His youngest son John married Mary Bataille, who was descended from French Huguenots fleeing religious persecution in late 18th-century France. Meanwhile, my grandfather Henry Kearney married Annie Gelbfarb, whose family were Polish Jews who fled Warsaw and arrived in London in 1900.

Above: A shopping arcade in Brixton, London during the post-war immigrant boom.

following the Second World War. This economic boom attracted a number of migrants, and more migrant workers from India, Pakistan and, later, Bangladesh arrived here. While economics were a motivating factor, there were other reasons for the influx of Asians – political expulsion being one. By 1961 over 100,000 Indian and Pakistani nationals had taken up residence.

Most of the post-war immigrants settled in urban areas: London, the Midlands and other industrial areas in the north, working in factories and foundries. Those that arrived first would then bring over their families and dependants once they had established themselves, often after years of sending the vast majority of their pay home (which was a boon to the economies of the countries they left, a reason why the governments of many countries did not prevent their residents from emigrating). Apart from their families, the early immigrants who had found accommodation and employment in England then sponsored other men, usually from the same family group or village, to join them – so-called 'Chain Migration'. Because of this, many Asian immigrants from the same region would congregate in the same English suburb. Up to 90 per cent of Pakistanis in Bradford and Birmingham come from the area of Mirpur; Southall

> **Most of the post-war immigrants settled in urban areas: London, the Midlands and other industrial areas in the north, working in factories and foundries.**

in London is home to a large Punjabi Sikh community, while in 1991 Bangladeshis made up 22.9 per cent of the population of Tower Hamlets.

Shipping Out

People have always left the British Isles, for a variety of reasons. Some have gone voluntarily, in search of new beginnings, a better life elsewhere; others have been taken abroad by their jobs, to colonial outposts of the British Empire. Others had no say in the matter; they were sentenced and, as part of their punishment, were transported to live in a penal colony, often for life but usually for a period of seven or fourteen years. The harsh conditions on the long journey meant that many never made it home again. In one of the darker episodes of this nation's history, not only criminals were transported involuntarily but innocents, such as orphans, were too.

Altogether, since the 17th century, it has been estimated that Great Britain and Ireland dispatched more than 10 million migrants to the USA; 4 million more to Canada; 1.5 million to Australia and New Zealand; and 17 million in total. Not only that, Britain has always been a port of transit, a place where migrating Europeans, often on the way to the United States, caught their onward journeys.

Below: *A group of emigrant families waiting for their ship at Liverpool in the 1880s.*

Above: *A prison ship docked at Portsmouth harbour in 1828: often prison ships were used to confine the excess convicted offenders ahead of transportation to the colonies.*

Transportation

To 21st-century sensibilities, transportation seems an appalling way to treat criminals: sentenced to years of back-breaking hard labour, thousands of miles from their families, with little prospect of return once their sentence was served, often for offences that would be categorized under 'petty' in this day and age. Yet our ancestors actually believed it was an efficient and humane way to deal with offenders. One can see why they might believe it was efficient: criminals were sent to another country where they would become somebody else's problem, and not cluttering up crowded jails or re-offending on their release. The idea it was humane is more difficult to comprehend, given the arduous journeys convicts undertook to the colonies, though care was taken to select the youngest, fittest criminals because they would be able to work hard and be most productive in the outposts to which they were sent.

From 1614 criminals were sent to the 'New World', America and the West Indies. Most of these were the poorest criminals, shipped to work on sugar and tobacco plantations alongside slaves captured from Africa. Under the existing legal

But once America had gained its independence in 1776 the authorities had a problem – an increasing amount of criminals but nowhere to send them.

system in 17th-century Britain, the only course of action for dealing with criminals who had committed a capital offence was execution. Therefore transportation to a penal colony offered the authorities some form of manoeuvre, allowing them to punish a criminal without actually having to kill him, yet generating some benefits in return. The convict would be offered a pardon on condition of transportation. In effect, after 1718 transportation was to America only, and set at fourteen years for those who had been pardoned. Transportation for seven years was introduced as punishment for some non-capital offences.

But once America had gained its independence in 1776 the authorities had a problem – an increasing number of criminals but nowhere to send them. They experimented with prison ships on the Thames known as 'hulks', but it became clear that they needed a land, some godforsaken, far-flung place where they could rid themselves of thieves and murderers. The answer was provided in the form of a newly claimed territory, now known as Australia.

On 13 May 1787 the first fleet set sail for Australia, consisting of six transport ships, two warships and three store-ships, carrying a total of 717 convicts. By the time they arrived, in Port Jackson in January 1788, 48 of them had died. A second fleet of ships left in 1789 and this crossing proved even more arduous: 278 convicts died before reaching dry land. The estimates are that more than a thousand ships sailed to Australia, ferrying around 165,000 men and women – and some children – to New South Wales (until 1840), Van Diemen's Land (renamed Tasmania in 1856) and Western Australia until transportation was abolished in 1868.

So who was sent to Australia? The answer is a wide range of criminals, from the petty to the serious. A scan of the passenger lists for any of the voyages reveals a wide range of offences: arson, burglary, larceny, theft, rape, robbery and manslaughter were all quite common; less so, but still represented, were offences such as firing a haystack, buggery, bestiality and sheep stealing. One Amos Bradshaw, 14, found himself transported for life (a longer sentence than for those who raped humans) to Western Australia on the *Runnymede* in 1856 for combining two of those less common offences: buggery *with* a sheep. Records kept for that ship revealed him to be, unsurprisingly, a farm labourer.

Those transported were mainly working class or poor, though a few unlikely men found themselves whisked away down under. On the same ship as the sheep-loving Mr Bradshaw was a chemist and druggist, a commercial agent and a schoolmaster, George Wilkins, convicted of 'feloniously forging an acceptance of a bill of exchange with intent to defraud'.

Of course life on these ships was hardly a picnic. Former soldiers, known as pensioner guards, taking the opportunity to live and work in Australia, guarded the convicts. Many of them had their families with them on board, making for a curious mix of convicts, wives and children. All of which meant strict rules had to be observed. Gambling was forbidden, as was speaking to the crew or guards. Obscene language and 'immoral songs' were outlawed too, and prisoners had to be in bed and asleep by 8.30 at night, and up the next morning at 5am. During the day, the prisoners were kept below decks, often in disgraceful conditions, apart from the occasional bout of fresh air and exercise. Disease was rife: dysentery, scurvy and fever claimed scores of lives, though conditions improved as the years passed.

Once they arrived at their colony, the convicts were put to work, often with settlers who had applied for a convict farm hand or servant. Hardened, dangerous criminals were bypassed and assigned to chain gangs, building roads and railways and other civic necessities. Convicts who worked hard and behaved themselves were often rewarded by having their families shipped from England to join them. Single men and women often met and married free settlers or other convict settlers. By 1840 New South Wales had had its fill of convicts, and the free settlers and their governor politely requested that the mother country should find another home for its unwanted. In 1850 Western Australia's economy was becoming increasingly moribund, so they applied for convict labour to reverse that trend.

While some recidivists caused trouble and returned to a life of crime, others, particularly those sentenced for their one and only offence, sought to rehabilitate themselves. 'Tickets of Leave' were granted to convicts to allow them to work or become self-employed in a district within a colony prior to them serving the whole of their sentence. Like parole, it came with certain conditions attached: the convict had to attend church, appear before a magistrate when required and gain permission to move to another district. Conditional pardons were granted to those willing to stay, live and work in the district, while those wanting to return to England were granted Absolute Pardons. Most, grateful for the chance of a fresh start in a new land of opportunity, and not wishing to risk their lives on another mammoth sea journey, chose to stay and live alongside the free settlers and pensioner guards, all helping to build the vibrant young country that is modern Australia.

In 1868 transportation was abolished, though in practice it had been used increasingly sparingly for more than a decade.

Child Emigration

While convicts were no longer dispatched to Australia, Britain's habit of getting rid of its unwanted did not end. Between 1618 and the late 1960s, an estimated 130,000 British children were removed from orphanages and institutions and transported to Australia, New Zealand, South Africa, Canada and other outposts of the British Empire. The 'peak' of this scheme was from the 1870s until the outbreak of the First World War, when an estimated 80,000 children were sent to Canada alone.

This scheme is not elucidated in many textbooks, and is considered among the more harmful, misguided acts conducted by the British authorities. It was not done with any malice; the charities and religious institutions involved with the scheme honestly believed they were doing what was best for the children, taking them out of orphanages and institutions and placing them with good Christian families who would offer them a prospect of a future.

__Above:__ Miner's sons aboard the Montcalm emigrating to Canada in 1928.

During late Victorian Britain, there is no doubt that social conditions and mores played a part in so many children being deported. The common view was that children of broken homes, or unwanted children, were potential nuisances, criminals in waiting. Meanwhile, there was Canada, vast and untapped, with a small colonial population in desperate need of young males to help work the land and young women to help in the house.

Between the wars, given the awful death tolls on the battlefield of the First World War, Britain was reluctant to allow any of its children to leave, whatever the scheme. But after the Second World War thousands of children were transported to Australia. It was part of a plan to populate Australia with 'good, white British stock', to plant the 'seeds of Empire'. 'If you want to go, put your hands up' was the instruction used for selecting children by institutions such as Dr Barnardo's. The fact is, of course, that many of the children were unaware of what lay waiting for them, and had little say in the matter. They were often put to work as labourers on farms and building sites, without pay or proper supervision. Many of these men and women, now in their sixties and seventies, claimed their lives were ruined by this crude piece of social engineering, and

> **The fact is, of course, that many of the children were unaware of what lay waiting for them, and had little say in the matter.**

are only now able to discover families that they never knew existed. The British government has since accepted that the schemes were ill-advised and, following a report from a House of Commons select committee, it announced in 1999 a raft of measures to help those who suffered under the scheme, including allowing them access to records to enable them to be reunited with close family members they were forced to leave behind – siblings, aunts, even parents – when they were dispatched to Australia.

Emigration

British people have not simply left this country on the say-so of the courts, or through the misguided intentions of a charitable or religious institution; they have left to seek new opportunities elsewhere. The size and scope of the British Empire, which reached its zenith during the Victorian era, offered a host of destinations in which the poor, the ambitious or the plain desperate could seek a better life for themselves and their families. Estimates suggest 1.7 million people left these shores for the colonies in the 17th and 18th centuries, while a whopping 10 million left during the 19th and 20th.

While America was a colony until 1776, the vast majority of people did not emigrate there from the UK until it had achieved independence. A fifth of modern-day Americans can trace their ancestry to England, a fraction more than to Ireland. The attraction for many working-class artisans, during the 19th century especially, was the opportunity to own land, which was virtually impossible at home. Men and women who had lived their lives in manufacturing towns, working in factories and mills, became farmers who lived off the land in their new homes in the New World.

Once the United States became industrialized, increasing numbers of workers were attracted to it. Displaced tin miners for example, before the boom in coal mining, went in droves, while the American textile industry lapped up the expertise and experience British workers could offer. The agricultural depression of the 1870s forced a number of people to leave their rural homes in search of good fortune in the rural states of the US. Estimates claim that more than half a million emigrants lived in the US by 1850, and 2 million by 1890, while millions more arrived between then and 1920, though Germany, Italy, Ireland and Austro-Hungary were providing more emigrants in those years.

While much has been made of the Irish diaspora, few other European nations have had to contend with the amount of emigration as Scotland. The first three decades of the 20th century, for example, saw a massive exodus: around 600,000 Scots left the home of their birth for North America and England. Canada had long been a destination for displaced Scots, ever since the Highland Clearances of the late 18th and 19th centuries, in which thousands of people were forced from their homes and lives in search of new beginnings.

Opposite: *Emigrants aboard the Royal Edward on its first voyage from Avonmouth dock in 1910.*

As the 19th century wore on, Canada proved to be immensely popular, for Englishmen as well as Scots. Since the beginning of the 19th century it had always been the second most popular destination behind the US, but when gold was discovered in Australia it was briefly eclipsed. As land ran out in the US, and the opportunities for skilled workers decreased, Canada became a more attractive option for those seeking a new life and a chance to make some money.

In recent years, Australia has become the destination of choice for young emigrants, though in nothing like the numbers that made the long, perilous journey by boat during the 19th century. However, it was not just convicts who went there in the first part of the 19th century. The government actively encouraged settlers to go there, offering land grants and cheap passages – sometimes the government would pay the cost of someone's passage if they could prove themselves to be of good character – to deter people from going to the United States instead. Again, the prospect of cheap land and a new start attracted increasing numbers of emigrants, to New Zealand as well as Australia. The discovery of gold spiked interest in the mid-19th century, while sheep-farming provided another lure for those gripped by the rural depression.

The other colony that attracted British emigrants was South Africa, once it was reclaimed from the Dutch in 1806 and formally became part of the Empire in 1814. Natal became a colony in 1843,

In recent years, Australia has become the destination of choice for young emigrants, though in nothing like the numbers that made the long, perilous journey by boat during the 19th century.

while Transvaal and the Orange Free State followed in 1902. All the provinces attracted British settlers.

Sometimes, the British settled in places you would least expect them to. Somewhere in Argentina are Latin Americans running around with Welsh roots, after a group of Welsh settlers left their homeland in 1865, dissatisfied with life as an adjunct to England, and fled to Patagonia in search of new horizons. The chapels they built still stand.

Along with all those who left these shores permanently, the maintenance, regulation and control of the British Empire, which in 1901 covered approximately 12 million square miles of the globe, caused millions of Britons to live abroad for substantial chunks of their working lives. Soldiers, sailors, merchant seamen, consular staff and civil servants were involved in protecting and running the colonies. Millions of children were born to British families overseas and were educated in schools for expatriate children before returning to Britain. Thankfully, records of many British families whose work took them to the colonies still exist to allow people to trace their family's path, wherever it took them.

Lyn Fry:
'New Zealand Zealots'

What would motivate four families to leave England and head on a challenging 12,000-mile journey to New Zealand? Health, economic need, adventure and class freedom …

Health … The McKillops left Enfield in 1879. My great-grandfather, Alexander, was a Scot, recruited to work at the Royal Small Arms Factory. This factory sought skilled workers from all over the British Isles. Sadly, Alexander developed tuberculosis. He left England on a long sea journey to New Zealand hoping the sea air and the wide-open spaces of his new home would restore his health.

Economic need … The Mills family emigrated from Waterford, Ireland, in 1880. Thomas was a Londoner who had left England originally to go to Ireland to work on the railways, at a time when many were going in the opposite direction. He met Mary Ann, got married and stayed. They survived the ravages of the famine, but with a growing family and the scarcity of jobs, their prospects looked poor. A favourite son died in an accident, and a baby passed away too. They turned their back on Ireland and left for New Zealand, where Mary's brother had already settled.

Adventure … Bert Badcock was at school in Hornsey when he was seduced by tales of heroism from the Boer War. He signed up with the Royal Horse Artillery, serving eight years in India, but when he was discharged found himself unable to adapt to life outside the army. In 1909 he signed up as a steward in the merchant navy. Legend has it that he jumped ship in Auckland and never came back.

Class freedom … My grandmother, Ethel, was brought up in poverty, in Bournemouth mainly. At 14 she got a job as a maid in Twickenham. She became engaged but it was broken off in 1909, and it became clear she would never better herself in England; her class would for ever hold her back. She left later that year for a new life of respect and success in New Zealand.

Jane Horrocks

Jane Horrocks was eighteen when she left the small Lancashire town in which she had grown up, to work as an actress in London. And yet Rawtenstall, nestled among the rolling hills of the Rossendale Valley near Bolton, is very much still a part of her, most noticeably in her distinctively strong Lancastrian accent. Now an unassuming northern backwater, Rawtenstall once lay at the very heart of the British textile industry, a thriving cog in the industrial revolution that transformed the landscape of the county and the lives of the people who lived and worked there. Jane's ancestors were bound up in that transformation, and successive generations of her family watched the slow decline of Rawtenstall that followed, once the white heat of the revolution had dissipated and the factories and mills began to close. The town Jane knew as a child, the quiet community from which she had escaped, was a far different one to that which her ancestors knew.

Jane focused her research on the women of her family. She wanted to know more about the long line of strong, working-class women who preceded her, and in particular her great-grandmother, Sarah Cunliffe. Sarah completes a trio of women, alongside Jane's mother Barbara and grandmother Doris, from whom Jane believes

Above: *Jane's grandmother, Doris (left of picture), at the slipper factory where she worked in Rawtenstall.*

Above: *Jane's Aunt Molly, who proved to be a rich source of information during Jane's search.*

she derives many of her characteristics. Doris worked in the local slipper factory, the town's lifeblood since the initial decline of the cotton industry in the 1870s. Despite the long hours, working in the slipper factory was sociable work: friends and families worked together, an arrangement that gave the community a strong sense of cohesion.

Jane's journey started with her Aunt Molly, her mother's sister, from whom she learned the remarkable fact that her mother, grandmother and great-grandmother had all lived on the same cobbled street in Rawtenstall. Through conversations with Molly, the first picture of her great-grandmother, Sarah Cunliffe, began to emerge. A tough woman, Sarah was forced to raise her two brothers following the death of their parents – and as a consequence, put her own life on hold. As far as Molly knew, Sarah was just twelve years old when she was shouldered with this enormous responsibility.

The truth turned out to be different, but no less illuminating. Sarah's parents Jane and John Cunliffe did both die of unrelated illnesses within eighteen months of each other, and Sarah did indeed become head of the family – but she was a grown woman of thirty-two at the time. And while Sarah did look after her two youngest brothers, Fred and William, Jane discovered that Sarah had many other siblings who had either gone unmentioned, or been forgotten – most poignantly of all, a young boy named Thomas who had tragically died of scarlet fever, aged just three. Thomas died during the height of the cotton famine of 1861–64, when the northern states of the USA blockaded the export of slave-picked cotton from the South – cotton on which Lancashire mills were utterly reliant. Without it, those mills closed, and mass unemployment, hardship and hunger stalked the county. Entire families suffered, and the Cunliffes were no exception. With the death of her little brother Thomas, and the subsequent passing of her parents, Sarah Cunliffe was no stranger to grief and suffering.

One fact that particularly interested Jane was Sarah's age when she assumed care of the family; surely to have been unmarried in your early thirties during the mid-Victorian period must have been rare? Perhaps surprisingly, that wasn't necessarily the case. Much like today, the fashion for many women at that time was not to get married until later, and Sarah continued to work, supporting the family as a cotton weaver, a tough job characterised by long hours and low pay. It was an industry in which women made up most of the workforce: at the turn of the century in Rawtenstall, sixty-two per cent of cotton workers were female.

Right *Great-grandmother Sarah, with her husband John; Molly is standing between them.*

At one stage of her journey into her family's history, Jane was given a tantalising glimpse of what life might have been like for her family. The name Horrocks was at one time synonymous with mills, since a family of that name had built one of the largest cotton empires in the world, living a life of luxury to match. Could they be related? The answer was: sort of. Jane's branch of the Horrocks and the factory-owning, cotton-goods-producing, money-making Horrocks did share a common ancestor, but the family lines split way back in the seventeenth century, thus preventing Jane from laying claim to any share of the Horrocks empire. She did, however, manage to find the valley in which, before the various strands of the family went their separate ways, Horrocks' had farmed, lived and loved for centuries; her true ancestral home. But while one part of the Horrocks family went on to build a cotton empire, Jane's branch remained at the opposite end of the industrial scale, working as 'bleachers', a hard, dirty job which involved cleaning

Above: *Sarah, John Taylor (senior), Doris (in pigtails) and John, leaning against the pillar, all pose together for a family photo.*

Above: *The Taylor family stand together outside their family business.*

newly-woven cloth with strong chemicals in poorly ventilated rooms. It was not an occupation that guaranteed long-term health.

Now that Jane knew more about her great-grandmother, Sarah Cunliffe, she was itching to find out more. When *did* Sarah eventually marry? Back on the paper trail, Jane found that at the age of thirty-seven, Sarah had finally found a husband: John Taylor, a local postman and the postmaster's son. Aunt Molly remembers the Taylors as strict Methodists, devout and unwavering in their faith, and Sarah's marriage to John lifted her out of a life of manual work, enabling her to swap the grind of life in the cotton mills for the relative comforts of the postal industry. From the date of their marriage, Jane worked out that Sarah had had her first and only child – Jane's grandmother, Doris – when she was forty-two, which would have carried with it tremendous health risks to both mother and baby in Victorian Britain. It goes without saying, of course, that had Sarah not run those risks, then Jane would not have been here today.

In her conversations with Molly, Jane came to learn of another of the mysterious, 'forgotten' siblings of her great-grandmother Sarah: a brother named Ernest, who had somehow ended up in Australia and who had, so the story went, sent a precious opal to Jane's grandmother Doris on her 21st birthday – an opal which Molly now wears in a ring. Jane discovered that in 1910, Ernest Cunliffe had left England for Australia, one of some 10 million people to have emigrated to the colonies between 1870 and 1913. Ernest died in 1937 at the age of 63 in Toowomba, a centre for the opal-mining trade. That seemed to solve the mystery of where he had found such a precious stone, but it came no nearer to answering why he had sent the gem to the other side of the world as a gift to his niece.

Jane instantly felt an emotional bond with Ernest: here was a man who, for some reason, had found life in Rawtenstall too constricting, who had chosen to leave small-town Lancashire life behind and strike out in search of adventure. Even more intriguingly, his profession was recorded as 'billiard marker', that is, a professional referee in snooker and billiards clubs. Some games would no doubt have been played for money, and it is tempting to imagine Ernest as a charismatic 'hustler', making the odd bit of money on the side by fleecing unwitting opponents, saving up to buy an opal for his young niece back home.

Ernest turns out to be that archetype of family history, the black sheep. It's likely that he had been living with Sarah, his elder sister, but when she married the local postman, a strict Methodist, the regime changed. Billiard-loving Ernest, we can speculate, may not have thought much of his new life and after living with the couple for a short while decided it wasn't for him. Despite getting married he needed to escape, and finally made for the long voyage to Australia, his wife following a year later. And the opal that Doris received on her twenty-first birthday from a man she barely knew? Perhaps he had grown close to young Doris before he left? Maybe the gift was an effort at reconciliation after the breakdown of his relationship with his sister Sarah? Those are the sorts of questions that only personal letters – which are so easily lost or destroyed – can answer, to add meat to the tantalizing hints preserved by public documents, archives and indexes. But at least Jane now knows she was not the first member of her family to feel they had outgrown their hometown, and that, in order to grow, knew they had to leave.

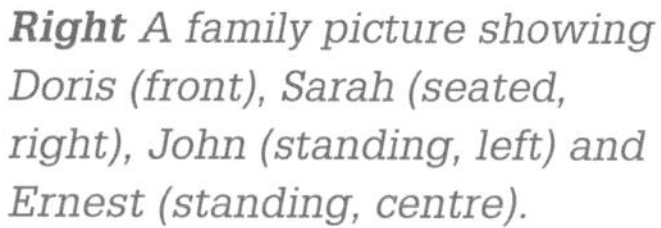

Right *A family picture showing Doris (front), Sarah (seated, right), John (standing, left) and Ernest (standing, centre).*

chapter 4
Earning a Crust

Our ancestors spent more time at work than anywhere else: in general, during the 19th century and beyond, working hours were long and punishing, particularly for members of the urban industrial working classes.

The world of work in this country can be split into two distinct eras: pre- and post-Industrial Revolution. Before the early to mid-19th century, Britain was largely an agrarian, rural society and people predominantly worked on the land. The census of 1851 was a turning point, however, marking the first time that more people were deemed to be living in urban areas than rural. From that point the nation became increasingly urban, as cities and towns grew and spread. Of course the main reason for this was growing industrialization, as people left the country and headed for the town in search of work (a phenomenon that will be dealt with in the next chapter, 'Moving Around'). Given that Britain's current manufacturing industry has been decimated, some people might find it difficult to believe that it was once the envy of the world. All of us will have ancestors affected by the Industrial Revolution, directly or indirectly (in the same way our descendants will study the

effects of the IT revolution on our lives; they may well ask 'What's a call centre?' in the same way people now ask 'What's a mill?').

The jobs people performed were affected by several factors, among them the social class to which they belonged and the region where they lived. Our ancestors spent more time at work than anywhere else: in general, during the 19th century and beyond, working hours were long and punishing, particularly for members of the urban industrial working classes. Yet an occupation, listed freely on census returns and civil registration certificates, is an easy way into finding out the sort of life your ancestor led. Perhaps he or she was born into money, living a life of leisure, or they might have been part of the rise of the professions, one of the emerging middle class; or were they manual workers, performing back breaking monotonous work, or even members of the poor, those unfortunates who fell through the many gaps in society and were caught only by the net cast by the Poor Laws.

Of course, our ancestors, as we do now, earned their livings in a vast array of trades and occupations: brickmakers and blacksmiths, tanners and teachers, cab drivers and clockmakers. It would be impossible to offer a description of the conditions of each and every job here, but we hope to offer a flavour of the environment in those industries and trades that occupied the mass of working men and women, and the events, regulations and acts that shaped their working lives.

Dark Satanic Mills

For the majority of our ancestors, during the early 19th century in particular, their lives would have been one of simply working to survive. Work was essential to feeding and clothing your family and often this meant punishing hours, much of it done by the young. In 1821 for example, 49 per cent of the workforce was under the age of 20. At the turn of the 19th century Britain was still a predominantly rural country and most people found their work in the fields. But creeping industrialization was changing that: cotton and woollen textile mills sprouted up, and there was no legislation to govern them. It was common for children to work from 5am to 9pm at night, and child workers were often beaten should they turn up late for work or lose concentration as a result of exhaustion.

Right: *A government inspector visits a factory which employs children (1881).*

The 1802 Factory Health and Morals Act was the first act to attempt to leaven the harsh conditions that existed within the nation's first factories. It compelled the factory owners to observe the law, provide two outfits for its apprentices, limit hours of work for children to 12 hours a day, to educate them rudimentarily for the first years of their apprenticeship and to offer them religious instruction on a Sunday. It was not much but it was a start.

What little good that act brought was largely negated by the gathering pace of industrialization and the hundreds and thousands of factories that began to spring up in its wake. In Leeds, for example, there were only 20 factories in 1801 and not all those were textile mills. By 1838, however, there were 106 woollen mills alone, employing around 10,000 people. As a consequence the city was transformed into a teeming metropolis.

In order to survive, families and clans were forced to leave the villages of rural and semi-rural England in their thousands, to turn their backs on labouring jobs on the land or small-scale manufacturing from home, known as cottage industries, in search of mill and factory work in the cities, living cheek by jowl in poor living conditions – slum housing, basically – with others displaced by the changing fabric of the country. In the face of this stampede, and the growth in factory work, the 1802 act was impotent, like stopping a tidal wave with a single sandbag.

In response to this rapid industrialization, the 1833 Factory Act went further, particularly in

Left: *A weaver at work in a Lancashire cotton mill in the 1890s.*

> **No factory was to be allowed to employ a child under nine years old, while children between nine and thirteen were prevented from working more than nine hours a day.**

attempting to prevent children from working appalling hours in atrocious conditions. The new machines were often dangerous, and dozing on the job could lead to the loss of a limb or death. In one dire case at a Leeds mill in 1832, a child died after being prevented from stopping work to visit the toilet.

Factory owners, fearful of rising costs and eager to maintain their liberty to make as much money as possible while treating their workforce as they wished, were resistant to any legislation, but Parliament still acted. No factory was to be allowed to employ a child under nine years old, while children between nine and 13 were prevented from working more than nine hours a day (those aged 13 to 18 could work no more than twelve). Children were forbidden from working the night shift and the factory was bound to provide them with two hours of schooling every day. To ensure those regulations were not broken, the act set up an inspectorate: unfortunately, there were to be only four inspectors tasked with checking up on every factory in the country, which meant unscrupulous factory owners were not too troubled by fear of punishment if they flouted the regulations. Conditions remained appalling. Acts in 1844 and 1850 went further, the latter restricting women and all young people to no more than ten-and-a-half hours' work a day. Men were given no such protection, though.

There is some justification in the argument that says that in the short term these steps were not entirely in the workers' interests. Many families were more than happy that their children were working because it maximized their income; when they could no longer work, their income fell. Young girls who could no longer work in the factories often sought work elsewhere; many turned to prostitution. Social reform did not always have an immediate benefit for those it was meant to help.

From 1850 onwards, England was the major industrial power in the world. First in textiles, only for that industry to be superseded by steel, iron, shipbuilding and railway construction. Another massive industry was coal.

King Coal

The major industries that flourished in Victorian England needed fuel on which to thrive; the railways, steel and iron industries in particular required a cheap source of energy. This was supplied by coal, which was in plentiful supply in England and Wales. The rising price of wood made it even more attractive. At first coal mines were small affairs, rarely employing more than fifty men. But by the time Queen Victoria had assumed the throne, deep mines had been sunk across a lot of the North East and other parts of the country, employing hundreds of people. The second half of the 19th century saw a huge increase in mining: the 1901 census counted more than 640,000 people who worked in the pits, compared to only 183,000 in 1851. Though the population had increased greatly in that period, the figures still show

how important the coal industry was to Victorian and Edwardian England. The country could not function without it; and whole communities sprung up and flourished in and around coalfields. Cardiff, for example, went from being a small Welsh village at the beginning of the 19th century to the leading coal-exporting port in the world by the 1890s.

The practice of sending children to work down

The Commission, after hearing evidence from scores of children who worked in mines, made it law that no child under 10 could work down the mine.

Above: *A small boy – maybe only 5 – holds a trapdoor open for a young boy and girl to push their wagon through (1843).*

the mines was halted in 1842 by a Royal Commission report. Prior to that date, six- or seven-year-old boys worked underground for 12 hours a day. The Commission, after hearing evidence from scores of children who worked in mines, made it law that no child under 10 could work down the mine, which was later raised to 12. There is evidence, however, that a lack of inspectors to enforce the new legislation meant it was flouted until into the 1860s.

The increase in scale of the industry did not change the nature of the job, which involved back-

Rita Bailey:
'The Fearless Mailman'

My grandfather, William Bailey, was born in Bishop's Castle, Shropshire, on 30 March 1882, the son of a local farmer turned butcher. Having decided to seek his first job away from the family bosom, Will tried the post office, where the postmaster at the time was named Alfred Bore.

Most of my family are small, so it is likely that Will looked even younger than he was, so might not have been thought capable of doing the job, though he was given the chance to prove himself by being asked to put a bridle on a stabled horse. While attempting to do this, Will was crushed against the stable wall by this huge brute of a horse. Will thought quickly on his feet; he gave the beast a few good clouts with a curry comb, to show it who was master. He then put the bridle on and calmly led the horse out, much to the amazement of his intended employer. He walked up to Mr Bore and said, 'I hope I've got the job or I will tell my brother that you sent me in with a dangerous horse.' This is how he came to be employed, as the 1901 census confirms, as a mail cart driver between Bishop's Castle and Craven Arms.

Above: 'Colliery lasses' in Wigan in 1900.

breaking, physical work with picks and shovels way below ground, in intense heat, without natural light and amongst clouds of dust and dirt. The men who worked at the face performed perhaps the most arduous jobs that existed in 19th- and early 20th-century England. They worked by the light of a lamp attached to their helmets, with pads on their knees to guard against injury, a reflection of how long they spent kneeling, bending and crouching while they hacked away. Rarely were they able to stand up. Their hours were less than those of factory workers, but they needed to be. And they worked in constant danger.

One of the worst disasters to afflict the mining industry was the West Stanley Pit disaster of 1909, in which 168 lives were lost at a Durham mine.

Mining disasters were regular occurrences, death and serious injury an everyday hazard. One of the worst disasters to afflict the mining industry was the West Stanley Pit disaster of 1909, in which 168 lives were lost at a Durham mine. Residents were first alerted to the tragedy by a muffled bang, followed by a loud roar from Burns Pit, West Stanley, at 3.45pm on 16 February 1909. Eyewitnesses said that flames shot more than 1,500 feet into the air, and thousands of men, women and children rushed to the colliery. But there existed no trained rescue team, and there was no suitable equipment to remove the wreckage. To worsen matters, no one knew where the trapped miners were located and it was 14 hours before the first survivors were brought to the surface. Meanwhile 168 miners lay dead underground, killed by the force of the explosion, from burns or carbon-monoxide poisoning. One street of 14 houses lost 12 men, while the final death toll included 59 under the age of 21. A whole community was devastated.

Trade Unions

Perhaps as a consequence of the difficult working conditions imposed upon the working class during the Industrial Revolution – though there had always been a history of protest among the workers of England – it was no surprise, with mineworkers at their forefront, that the nation's trade-union movement gathered pace in the Victorian era. Prior to 1868 most industrial towns had formed trade councils, but in that year their leaders took a further step and agreed to form a Trades Union Congress and met for the first time in Manchester.

By 1874 the unions had more than one million members, all striving for better pay and working conditions. The late 19th century and the early part of the 20th century saw the unions gather in strength and ambition. The upper and middle classes saw them as seething hotbeds of rampant socialism, but in many regards they were wrong. The evolution of many of the unions stemmed back several decades, from well before the concept of international socialism, and most members remained ignorant and resistant afterwards. Friendly societies of all kinds had been set up in response to the Industrial Revolution and the privations of the urban poor. They embraced a wide range of activity, building societies, co-operative societies, savings banks and welfare clubs. All existed to help alleviate

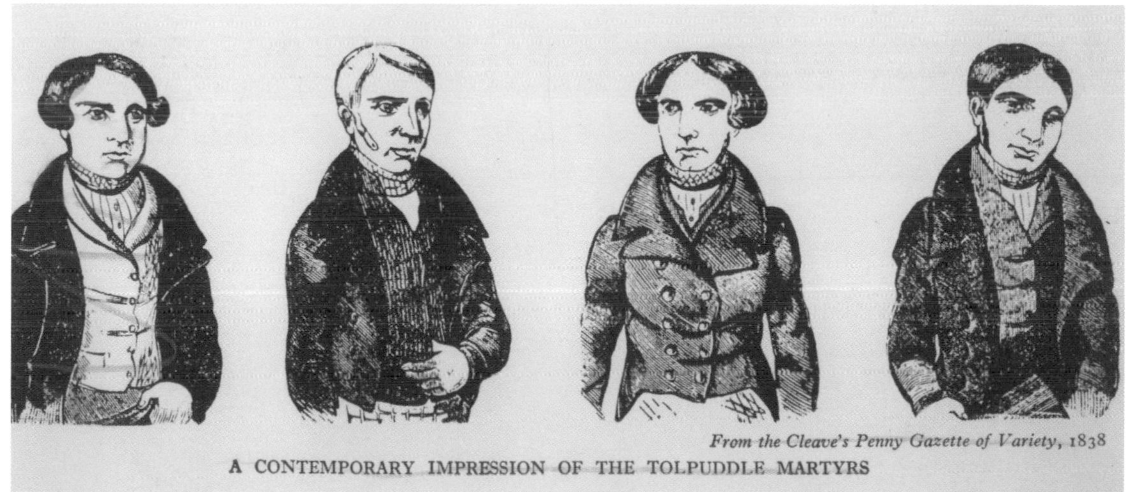

From the Cleave's Penny Gazette of Variety, 1838

A CONTEMPORARY IMPRESSION OF THE TOLPUDDLE MARTYRS

the burden of the poor, and this type of collective action contributed to the growth of the trade-union movement. One such Friendly Society were the Tolpuddle Martyrs. The Reform Act of 1832 had made unions legal, so that year six men from Tolpuddle in Dorset founded the Friendly Society of Agricultural Labourers to protest against the gradual lowering of wages. They refused to work for less than 10 shillings a week, although by this time wages were as low as 6 shillings a week. A local landowner wrote to the Prime Minister, Lord Melbourne, complaining about the union, invoking an obscure law from 1797 prohibiting people from swearing oaths to each other, which the Friendly Society had done. James Brine, James Hammett, George Loveless, George's brother James, George's brother in-law Thomas Standfield and Thomas's son John Standfield were arrested, found guilty, and transported to Australia. The move backfired. The group were celebrated, turned into popular heroes and were released in 1836. They are seen as early pioneers of the trade-union movement.

On the whole, the aims of the first trade unions were not revolution or overthrowing the status quo, but simply to guarantee better conditions for the working man. It was not until 1888 that unskilled workers held their first strike, seeking better conditions at the Bryant & May match factory – while this may seem an unlikely source of unrest, given that most of the workers were teenage girls, the match industry was one of the most perilous in Britain, and there had been real pressure to clean it up; phosphorus was a dangerous material with

Left: *Police and demonstrators struggle during the General Strike of 1926.*

which to work, and accidents were frequent and horrible; even daily work could lead to sterility. Charles Booth on one of his walks around London in the 1890s noticed the defiant aspect of the Bryant & May workers:

> ***Bryant & May have a rough set of girls. There are 200 of them when they are busy. Rough and rowdy but not bad morally. They fight with their fists to settle their differences, not in the factory for that is forbidden, but in the streets when they leave work for the evening. A ring is formed, they fight like men and are not interfered with by police.***

On an early July afternoon, 200 workers, females between 12 and 15, walked out after three of their colleagues had been fired, accused of lying to a freelance journalist about their working conditions. They stayed out for three weeks, and eventually returned when their employers agreed to most of their demands. This apparent victory by a group of vociferous, fearless teenage girls inspired the movement and accelerated its power. The following year, the dockers' strike for sixpence an hour pay ended in victory, too.

Employers in Britain's staple industries launched a concerted effort to increase productivity without increasing wages for workers.

The zenith of collective trade-union action in this country was the General Strike of 1926. Following the First World War, employers in Britain's staple industries launched a concerted effort to increase productivity without increasing wages for workers. The miners bore the brunt of this attack. A Royal Commission set up in 1926 approved wage reductions for the coal industry, a decision not met with equanimity by the miners. They called a strike, which was backed by the Trades Union Congress, crippling key industries such as shipbuilding, electricity and the railways, and causing strife across the country, as strikers attempted to prevent non-strikers from going into work, and the ruling class sought to undermine the strikers' action at every turn. A group of Cambridge students arrived at Dover docks in chauffeured cars offering to load ships, a gesture that was not exactly appreciated by those strikers present. The strike lasted for nine days, until TUC leaders accepted a settlement.

Sons of Toil

Agriculture dominated Britain until well into the 19th century, and it was the land that provided employment for most of our ancestors until that time. The enclosure movement was the cause of one of the greatest changes in the landscape of rural England. It was the process whereby the use and regulation of the arable land, open pastures, meadows and uncultivated land by the community that lived on and around it was gradually substituted by a system of private land management. It involved both legal and physical change.

Individual landowners and tenants took over separate private control of defined areas of land, often common fields, superseding the rights the community once had over it, such as grazing. The poorest suffered most as a result; many people were dispossessed, forced to leave the land they had lived and worked on all their lives. Wide open fields, unfenced and unhedged meadows and pastures, and the expanses of fen, moor, common and heath were divided up into hedged, fenced or walled fields by acts of Parliament or private agreements between manorial lords and their tenants.

Many of us who locate ancestors in the 19th century will discover that they worked on the land, particularly those who lived in the first part of the century. Some will have been farmers, the vast majority 'agricultural labourers', a catch-all term for people who performed a variety of jobs. Poverty, or a state of near poverty, was taken for granted as the usual state of the labouring poor, those employed to work the land at the mercy of harvests and the vagaries of the English weather. Life was tough and people accepted it. Millions of agrarian workers lived in this way, and their lives went unrecorded. Much has been written about the struggles of the urban poor, less of the rural. Outside a Thomas Hardy novel, it is difficult to find any description of the life of an average farm labourer. Suffice to say, the hours were as punishing as those in the factories, basic farm machinery did not make it much less dangerous and wages were often as low, if not more so. About the only thing going for it was that you worked outdoors rather than in.

Above: *The 'gang' system – whereby farmwork was contracted out to those who ran their own workforce of manual labourers – encouraged tough working conditions.*

The number of people who worked in agriculture decreased as the century wore one, but despite being eclipsed by the rapid increase of urban living, farming and labouring did not die out overnight. Far from it. In 1851 more than 23 per cent of the available male workforce still worked on the land (though this had fallen to 9 per cent by 1901). While industrialization had altered dramatically the way our ancestors worked, agriculture was still a mass employer and vital component of the national economy.

The land and the people who worked it dominated great swathes of the country, away from the growing new cities. In the early part of the 19th

Karen Reeve:
'Upstairs, Downstairs'

Lillian Mary Lucas was born in 1879, and addresses on census returns between 1881 and 1901 reveal that she never lived more than 200 metres away from Buckingham Palace. In her twenties, like so many women of that time, she became a servant and worked as a cook for Lord and Lady Londonderry.

She became seriously ill, and required what we would now call a mastectomy. The Londonderrys paid for this operation, which saved her life, and while it was hardly a perk of the job, their kindness dispels the myth that the gentry always separated themselves emotionally and financially from those 'downstairs'.

Her sister Millie worked alongside her, though when the Lord and Lady moved to a mansion, Plas Machynlleth in Wales, they decided against moving with them and left to marry their husbands.

The family connection does not end there, however. Their sister Ada joined the Londonderrys and lived with them in Wales. She was said to have died 'in service' many years later, one evening alone in the mansion when the Lord and Lady and their staff were away. A local policeman passing the house recognized Ada through the window and tapped on it to attract her attention: she is said to have died there and then – he literally gave her the fright of her life. She is buried in the local cemetery.

> **By 1885 the amount of British land under wheat had shrunk by a million acres and Britain became increasingly dependent on foreign cereals.**

century it was common for farm labourers to move around the countryside searching for work, particularly in the South, where, unlike the North, farmers were less likely to be competing with nearby industrial cities for labour. However, the agricultural industry suffered a severe depression in the second half of the 19th century. Until that point British agriculture still led the world, but an influx of cheap American wheat changed all that, allied with the Repeal of the Corn Laws in 1846.

By 1885 the amount of British land under wheat had shrunk by a million acres and Britain became increasingly dependent on foreign cereals. The labour market was decimated: labourers headed for the cities in search of work, quite often being forced to live in slum housing and take whatever job they could; while some fled the country – between 1870 and 1880, the first decade of the agricultural depression, more than a million people left the country. Young and enterprising people who would previously have become involved in working the land

***Below:** A painting: On The Fens, by Robert Walker Macbeth (1878).*

realized the only rational decision they could make was to get out of it. The 1815 Corn Laws had protected the agricultural industry from cheap foreign imports, but the Repeal of 1846 ended that protectionism. Britain had taken a giant step towards becoming a free-trading nation, but the consequence was a slump in the agricultural industry and the effects were long-lasting.

Another slump in the early 1890s prevented any chance of recovery. Those farming families who had managed to avoid the first depression succumbed to the second. The 'defeat' of the countryside by the town was assured: in 1901 77 per cent of the population lived in urban areas, only 23 per cent remained in rural villages. The problem was that many of the new towns could not support those fleeing the country, and consequently there would be those unfortunates unable to find work, who fell through the many cracks in Georgian and Victorian society. What happened to them?

The Poor

Until the Poor Law Amendment Act of 1834, the help offered to the most vulnerable members of society varied according to the region in which they lived. A 1601 act obliged each parish to offer relief to the aged and helpless, put abandoned children to work and provide some form of work for those capable of performing it. An act of 1662 allowed for parishes to 'resettle' – evict, basically – any newcomer who they thought would end up costing them money. While a 1697 act required the dubious practice of

Below: *A satirical cartoon: the wealthy view the care of the poor through rose-tinted spectacles.*

'badging' the poor – literally branding those who received poor relief with a huge badge with the letter 'P' on it, preceded by a letter identifying their parish.

In 1722 an act allowed parishes to set up workhouses, in which their poor could be settled. Like a prison, the belief behind these institutions was that they would act as a deterrent; they boasted harsh regimes that only the desperate would accept, while the idle and workshy would eventually get on their bikes and find some form of employment. It was as a result of this approach that the workhouse gained its Dickensian reputation as a place of depravity and ill-repute.

In 1834 the system was shaken up. A nationwide policy was imposed on the poor, rather than the piecemeal local approach. Newly created unions instead of parishes were set up to administer the law, which was underpinned by the belief that the deserving and undeserving poor could be differentiated by one test: the latter would never take a place in the workhouse because the conditions were so repugnant. The deserving, meanwhile, had no choice. It was not quite on a par with 'If she drowns she's innocent, if she doesn't she's a witch', but not far off. The new law also made it clear that the workhouse conditions should never be better than those of a labourer of the lowest class.

Workhouses became places to be avoided at all costs, which may have been the authorities' intention, though the regime was often repellent, with beatings and sickness common. Many workhouses segregated their dormitories into male and female only, so that families forced to enter were often split up. Many illegitimate and abandoned children, whose mothers were unable to afford to keep them, or had

Workhouses became places to be avoided at all costs, which may have been the authorities' intention, though the regime was often repellent, with beatings and sickness common.

fled, were dispatched to the workhouse, hence *Oliver Twist*. The old and the infirm, who were without any other form of support, were also sent there. However, it was not a one-way ticket: people could leave and find work if they wished. Inside, the routine was deliberately monotonous: inmates woke at 6am in the summer (7am in the winter), said prayers, ate breakfast and started work at 7am (8am in the winter). They worked until midday, ate lunch and then worked until 6pm when supper was served. At 8pm they went to bed.

One of the most notorious scandals of the time, and one that highlighted the harshness of workhouse conditions, occurred at Andover in 1845. One of the jobs given to inmates at several institutions was bone crushing: smashing the bones of dead dogs, horses and other animals to provide fertilizer for local farms. The work was back-breaking and dangerous: the inmates, some as young as eight, had to manually lift the solid iron 'rammer' that crushed the bones, and the danger of flying shards causing injury was ever present. That was not the source of the scandal, however. Rumours spread around the neighbourhood that the inmates were so starved that they were seizing on bones to which gristle was still attached and eating them. Some even resorted to sucking the marrow from the rotten bones. There was an

investigation, which discovered the rumours to be true, there was uproar in the press and a change of regime was installed.

Due to scandals like the one at Andover and pressure from campaigners, workhouse conditions did improve but the shame and calumny visited upon those forced to enter them did not abate. At the beginning of the 20th century, change was on the way. A 1905 Royal Commission spent four years investigating the Poor Law and the plight of the unemployed, agreeing that the 1834 act was out of date and out of time. Yet its members failed to reach agreement on what should be done: a majority advocated replacing workhouses with more specialized institutions for the sick, the elderly and mentally ill; a minority were more radical, favouring a system that prevented destitution rather than offered relief from it. That classic political solution, the 'fudge', was employed, followed swiftly by the outbreak of the First World War.

From 1913, the term 'workhouse' was abandoned in favour of 'Poor Law Institution', but regardless of name, the institution was to live on for several decades. In 1929 – twenty years after

Above: *Dinner time at the Marylebone Workhouse; there would usually be separate male and female dining halls in the larger workhouses as well as separate sleeping areas (1900).*

the Commission had reported – control was transferred to county and county borough councils. The Second World War and the subsequent creation of the National Health Service and the welfare state gradually reduced the need for these institutions.

> **The Victorian era saw an increase in the role of the state and so a rise in bureaucracy, creating jobs for civil servants, doctors, lawyers and teachers.**

The Rise of the Professions

The reason this chapter has so far concentrated on the working lives of the working class is simple: most of us will discover our ancestors were drawn from what were once called the 'lower orders'. Even by the 1901 census, 75–80 per cent of the population were described as working class, those whose work involved getting their hands dirty. The rapid growth of managerial and professional positions, which increased the number of people deemed to be middle class, was still some way off.

The middle class did not appear from nowhere. The term arose around the middle of the 18th century to describe those who did not fit into the two traditional groups of English society: those who worked in the professions, namely the Church, law and medicine, who were deemed to be below the aristocracy and landed gentry, but above the craftsmen, merchants, traders and labourers who comprised the working population.

The 19th century and the Victorian era saw their numbers swell: businessmen who made good during the Industrial Revolution; shopkeepers and merchants who sold the fruits of that industrial change; clerks and managers who worked in the proliferation of banks and financial institutions that handled the increase in trade and wealth; and the growth in transport, the railways in particular, created a number of job opportunities. The Victorian era saw an increase in the role of the state and so a rise in bureaucracy, creating jobs for civil servants, doctors, lawyers and teachers. All in all, the opportunities for social mobility – climbing the social ladder – increased. For example, on the railways men were able to start as porters and over the years work their way up to the lofty position of station master. Of course, the amount of money

Right: *The Doctor by Arthur Miles (1860). The status of the doctor was rising at this time; traditionally lower than the clergy or legal professionals, growing social changes were to greatly increase their standing in the community.*

Above: A clerk, albeit to the Deputy Speaker at the House of Commons (1919).

these different professions earned varied widely; some accumulated a lot of money and went on to become wealthy, while others earned marginally more than the working classes. A small business might offer someone the chance to accumulate capital and join the middle classes.

But the growth of this class was self-perpetuating. A typical story involved a man, the aforementioned railway porter for example, rising through the ranks to become station master. He might move away from the slum areas in the town, towards what we now know as the suburbs. He might even hire a servant or maid. His vow would be to provide a better education for his children than the one he endured. His children would then leave school better educated and better suited for a job in one of the professions, and so on. The railway porter had lifted his family out of the working class, and altered the path of his family's fortunes, but often this yielded small incomes for enormous amounts of work. White-collar jobs in banking and public administration offered better chances for upward mobility. One group that was discouraged from enjoying this relative prosperity was women: while, by the turn of the 20th century, women held jobs such as teachers or clerks, few entered the better-paid professions. Doctors, lawyers, journalists and bank managers were almost exclusively male.

One group that was discouraged from enjoying this relative prosperity was women: while, by the turn of the 20th century, women held jobs such as teachers or clerks, few entered the better-paid professions.

The censuses of 1891 and 1901 confirmed this amplification of the middle class. The number of barristers and solicitors rose more than 5 per cent in that time, while the number of surgeons and doctors rose by almost 20 per cent.

Salt of the Earth

The stereotypical image of the Victorian factory or mill owner is of a belt-and-braces, no-nonsense northern industrialist, with the single aim of making as much money as possible by working his staff into the ground, every hour of the day. While the conditions many of our ancestors found themselves working in were abhorrent, and many industrialists cared little for the welfare of their workers, there were many other exceptions too.

Probably the best example of these enlightened capitalists was a Yorkshire mill owner, the evocatively named Titus Salt. Salt owned five textile mills in Bradford, back then a grim industrial town with a swelling population but problems with pollution and disease. An environmentalist at least a century before anyone had dreamt of the concept, never mind the word, Salt discovered that the Rodda Smoke Burner produced little pollution and in 1842 he arranged for these burners to be used in all his factories.

In 1848 Salt became Mayor of Bradford, using his power to try and persuade the council to pass a by law that would force all factory owners in the town to use these new smoke burners. The other factory owners in Bradford did not take too kindly to this plan, refusing to accept that smoke was injurious to health.

Like any stubborn Yorkshireman, Salt took his bat home. In 1850 he built a brand new industrial community, named Saltaire, on the banks of the River Aire. Saltaire took 20 years to build. The focus of the village was a textile mill, the largest and most modern in Europe. Many of the machine mechanisms were located underground, drastically reducing noise; large flues removed the dust and dirt from the factory floor; to avoid pollution, the mill chimney was fitted with Rodda Smoke Burners.

Salt built a village with 850 homes to house his 3,500 workers. He also built a park, a school, church and hospital for them, as well as shops and wash-houses. Each house had an outside lavatory, and fresh water piped into their home, and gas to provide light and heating. At work, Salt was among the first to introduce a ten-hour day, so allowing families to spend more time together.

Salt was not perfect: he did not agree with laws preventing children from working in the mill, and he was no supporter of trade unions. A strict moralist, he did not allow pubs or pawnshops to be built in the village (ironically, there is a modern pub named after him in Bradford). He was a philanthropist, though, as his family discovered upon his death in 1876. His fortune had gone: it was estimated that he had given away over £500,000 to good causes, a reason why 100,000 lined the streets for his funeral. But his legacy lives on: Saltaire still stands, and is a UNESCO World Heritage site.

Strange Occupations

During your trawl through your family tree, there is every chance you may encounter an occupation that has since become obsolete, or has become known as something else. Here are some of the oddest jobs, or oddest job titles, you may encounter:

Acciptitrary: One who worked with hawks, falcons and other birds of prey.

Acreman/Ackerman: A Ploughman.

Back washer: Person who cleaned wool in the worsted industry.

Boilermaker: Originally a person who made boilers, but came to include anyone who worked with metal in a factory or manufacturing.

Bottom Knocker: Assistant to a Sagger Maker (see below).

Clodhopper: A Ploughman.

Collier: Coal Miner.

Costermonger: A person who sold goods, especially fruit and vegetables, from a cart in the street.

Faker: A photographer's assistant who touched up black and white photos in the days before colour.

Finisher: Person who operated a machine that put the finishing touches to various objects made by the manufacturing industry.

Haberdasher: A seller of clothing and sewing goods.

Hewer: A miner who cut coal from the seam.

Knacker: Person who disposed of dead or unwanted animals, as in 'knacker's yard'.

Lamplighter: Person whose job was to ignite and extinguish gas street lamps.

Mudlark: Person, often a child, who searched for detritus, coins and jewellery in mudflats during low tide.

Ostler: Person employed to look after horses.

Paperhanger: Person who decorated with wallpaper.

Ponderator: An inspector of weights and measures.

Sagger Maker: Person in pottery industry who made fireclay containers in which stoneware was placed for firing.

Scrivener: A clerk, scribe or notary.

Stevedore: Labourer who loaded and unloaded ships' cargo.

Tanner: Person who made leather.

Tosher: Someone who went down the sewers in search of detritus that had been washed away, from the River Thames in particular – some got rich, but their stench made them few friends.

Wheel Tapper: Railway worker whose job was to check for cracked wheels.

Jacqui Hellowell: **'Upward Mobility'**

My ancestor Bentley Wrigglesworth had an interesting life, and worked in a wide range of occupations, climbing the social ladder. He was born in 1837/38 in Birstall, West Yorkshire, the younger of two brothers; the family also had three girls. The 1851 census shows him to be living at Flatt Lane, Cleckheaton, Yorkshire; he was 13 and he was working as a labourer (dyer) at the dyehouse at Hunsworth Mills.

By the 1861 census he was 23, living at Flatt Lane with his widowed father, his widowed sister Martha, and his niece; he was still a labourer, at a chemical works. From trade directories of 1871, 1875 and 1881 I discovered he was listed as a manufacturing chemist at Whitechapel Lane, Cleckheaton. On 27 June 1877, he married Sarah Rose at the late age of 39; he was now living in Tong, another part of Bradford, but he was a farmer. However, in the 1901 census, he was listed as a retired manufacturing chemist aged 63, living in Shipley.

He died in 1912. But here is the intriguing part. His death certificate records him of being of 'independent means', which means he had some money. I managed to find an obituary of him in the *Cleckheaton Guardian*: it made fascinating reading. He was described as a 'shrewd businessman who also acquired property in Windhill, Bradford and other places'. He had no children but he left a 'considerable fortune' of £30,000 to his nephews and nieces, one of whom was my great-grandfather, John Wrigglesworth.

Stephen Fry

Stephen Fry is a man of many talents: comedian, actor, director, wit and novelist. To most people, he would appear to be as English as tweed, silver toast racks and the London black cab he can be seen proudly driving around the streets of the capital, and one might expect his family history to reflect this: a quintessentially English story of a comfortable middle or upper-middle class family; perhaps an illustrious ancestor or two, and the odd dashing tale of derring-do.

The reality, however, is somewhat different, as Stephen himself discovered on a moving journey into his past. Genealogy had always been of interest to him, a curiosity shared with one of his ancestors, George Samuel Fry (1853–1938). George, a keen amateur genealogist, compiled an impressive record not only of the history of his branch of the Fry family, but also of a whole host of other, unrelated Frys. His collected research, completed without recourse to records offices, censuses and the vast resources of the Internet upon which modern family historians rely, was deposited with the Society of Genealogists following his death and is a treasure trove of information on a whole host of historical Frys. George's work helped to dispel a few family myths that even Stephen believed might be true; sadly, the prison reformer Elizabeth Fry and the Quaker chocolate makers of Bristol who bore the name were not related to Stephen's family.

The truth, as it often is, was even more fascinating. The first mystery Stephen set out to solve was the story of his beloved maternal grandfather, Martin Newman. Martin's actual name was Neumann, and he was a Jew of eastern European descent. By the time of his death, when Stephen was just eleven years old, he had already made an indelible mark on his grandson. Stephen remembers a flamboyant man in stark contrast to the parents or grandparents of his school friends. He had long wondered what Martin's story was, and this was his chance to get to know more.

The Neumanns lived in Surany, a small town in what is now Slovakia. In 1927 Martin and his wife, Rosa, whom he had met in Vienna after

Right: *Stephen's beloved grandfather Martin Neumann (c. 1920).*

Above: *A photograph taken on the day of Martin's marriage to Rosa Braun.*

the First World War, left the family home with their daughter Gertrude and settled in England, in the unlikely setting of Bury St Edmunds. Why there? The answer, perhaps surprisingly, lay with sugar. During the 1920s, Britain was keen to develop a home-grown sugar beet industry that would prevent the nation from having to rely on foreign imports, as it had been forced to during the First World War. The Government began to scout for possible sites with the right soil and climate for growing sugar beet, and in the end chose Bury St Edmunds. In Surany, meanwhile, Martin was working as an agricultural advisor in the largest sugar beet factory in Europe, and Martin and his friend Dr Robert Jorisch were soon hired to come and teach the Brits a thing or two about the cultivation of sugar beet. Their legacy is a lasting one, since the sugar factory still dominates the town of Bury St Edmunds to this day.

Of course, Stephen was both proud and amused to discover that his grandfather had blessed Bury St Edmunds with a sugar beet factory. But he was also interested in discovering more about Martin and his family's life prior to their move to East Anglia. And what of the other branches of the Neumann family? By the late 1920s, with the spectre of Nazism beginning to loom in Germany, widespread anti-Semitism was already affecting the lives of millions of Jews across mainland Europe. What had been the fate of those Neumanns who had stayed behind when Martin came to England?

Martin served in the Austro-Hungarian army in the First World War, fighting against allies of the nation he would call home little more than a decade later. Despite being just eighteen years old when he volunteered, he won a medal on the Eastern Front – where millions of men lost their lives – in the battle for Romania, and worked his way from the rank of private to that of corporal. When the war was over, he took the opportunity to visit some distant cousins in Vienna, the Brauns, and a member of the Braun family, Rosa, would eventually become his wife. Stephen's grandmother Rosa remembers Martin arriving at her house laden with food, a scarcity in post-war Vienna.

The Brauns were members of Vienna's 200,000-strong Jewish community. Stephen paid an emotional visit to the house in which they lived, and was startled to see a plaque commemorating the house's inhabitants, among them Rosa's parents, his great-grandfather and great-grandmother, Berta and Samuel. They had

Above: *Rosa and daughters at Bury St Edmunds*

remained there until 1942, at the height of the Nazi terror, when they were deported to a ghetto in Riga, Latvia, along with 65,000 other Viennese Jews. Only a small number of those sent to Riga survived; the others, Berta and Samuel among them, were killed.

Stephen's next stop was Surany where Martin and Rosa had moved in 1924, to live with Martin's extended family. At the time, Surany boasted both a thriving Jewish community and a flourishing sugar beet plant. The Neumanns had strong ties to the factory: Martin's father, Leopold, worked there as a guard, and like much of the town's population, the family lived in factory accommodation, though Martin's managerial post afforded him better standards of living than most. Now, only one survivor of the Holocaust remains in Surany, and the town's factory has closed.

Right: *Stephen's mother as a two-year-old standing in the gardens of the family house. The picture was taken in 1934, Gertrude stands to the left and Margaret stands to the right of their father Martin.*

Above: Stephen's mother, the youngest of the three girls, sits on the wall of the family house in Bury St Edmunds.

Leopold died in 1929, but what became of the other Neumanns who remained in Surany? The answer is as tragic as it is inevitable. Located in what was then Hungary, there was no resistance in Surany to the Nazi's anti-Semitic policies; the lives of the town's Jews were ruined, property ransacked or burgled, people deported or murdered. In all, more than 600 Jews from Surany were killed in the Holocaust. The government sent 400 policemen to the town, who closed all access roads and corralled the Jewish population into a small ghetto around the synagogue. There they were forced to live, malnourished and in unsanitary conditions, until they could be transported away to their deaths.

Martin's sister Reska was one of the many who chose to stay through that terrifying time, marrying a man called Tobias Lamm. The couple had children but during the Second World War the whole family was sent to concentration camps. Some disappeared en route; most died or were murdered in Auschwitz. Had fate not intervened, in the form of a humble sugar beet factory in Bury St Edmunds, that awful destiny may have befallen Martin Neumann and his family.

On his father's side, there had always been a mystery surrounding Stephen's paternal grandmother, Ella. Stephen's father, Alan, said that no one knew much about her beyond her maiden name: Ella Constance Dunthorne Pring. Her side of the family was never spoken of by the well-to-do Frys, but what was the source of this mysterious family taboo? With only her name as a lead, Stephen headed to the Family Records Centre to see if he could bring the Prings back to life.

To his delight, he discovered that Ella's father, Albert, was a humble hairdresser. Perhaps that explained why her in-laws did not approve of her? Stephen was even more startled to discover that in the 1881 census,

Right: Stephen's mother Marianne, and father Alan. This picture was taken soon after their wedding.

Above: *Stephen sleeping in the lap of his Hungarian grandfather Martin. Martin was to die soon after, when Stephen was just eleven years old*

Albert's father, Henry – Stephen's great-great grandfather – was in the Lewisham workhouse. Albert, meanwhile, together with his brothers Ernest and Christopher, was in the Metropolitan Infirmary for Children in Margate. Why Margate? At the time, it was believed that sea air was beneficial to patients suffering from respiratory diseases, and it seems that the infirmary in Margate had close ties with the Lewisham Union. Many children who had contracted illnesses such as tuberculosis were sent to Margate to recuperate, including the Pring brothers. Happily, young Albert went on to live for another forty-two years, though it was, nonetheless, TB that brought about his death in 1923.

According to the public records, the Prings were in and out of the workhouse for much of the nineteenth century. Henry Pring died in there, while one of his sons, Ernest, took to crime and served time in Knutsford Prison, in Cheshire. Discovering this almost Dickensian past of poverty and petty crime, Stephen exclaimed, 'Well, I'm beginning to wonder how much further down the social scale my family are going to tumble.' Albert fared better, plying his trade in a small hairdresser's on the Old Kent Road – though the poverty that blighted his family probably explains both the Frys', and Ella's, reluctance to discuss the Pring dynasty in any great detail.

chapter 5
Moving Around

For many people, the new promised land of opportunity and work turned out to be a Dickensian reality of disease, poverty and slum housing but still people flocked to the urban centres in search of work.

While our society has never been more fluid or more mobile than it is currently, it is a myth that most of our ancestors tended to live their lives in the same town. It is true that prior to the onset of industrialization, families often remained in the same area for centuries, but many others for one reason or another have felt the need to uproot and move elsewhere. Of course, the advent of transport made this easier and more attractive, the birth of the railways and canals in particular. Where once travel was an arduous task, it became possible to move around in relative comfort. This chapter looks at why our ancestors migrated.

Rural Migration

The fashion or necessity for moving from country to town has not ceased since the beginning of the Industrial Revolution. Only three years ago a local authority in Wales, backed by the Welsh Assembly, set up a scheme to try and encourage its young people to stay rather than migrate to the city. How successful the 'Get On in Gwynedd' campaign actually is remains to be seen, but it highlighted a trend in the United Kingdom that has stretched back two centuries: the flight from the country to the city in search of work and wealth.

As has been mentioned earlier, the 1851 census marked a watershed in this country's history, because for the first time it was revealed that more people lived in the emerging towns and cities than in rural areas. This internal migration increased in speed during the agricultural depression, which blighted rural areas during the second half of the 19th century from which they have never recovered. Since then towns and cities have expanded, gobbling up ever more agricultural land. The changes to society were highlighted sharply in the arts. The early 19th century was marked by literature about English country life and its manners; then came Dickens who wrote about urban hardship and deprivation in the teeming metropolis. Artists found new inspiration for their pictures in urban landscapes and the 'dark satanic mills' immortalized in Blake's stirring poem 'Jerusalem'.

Before the Industrial Revolution, those who migrated from rural areas would have moved only to another rural area, usually nearby, in search of work. In this sense, the migrant agricultural labourer has been a feature of the English landscape since Elizabethan times, when fields were first enclosed, forcing people onto the roads to find work. But that seasonal work in the fields was declining: the introduction of steam changed everything. Horsepower became a thing of the past; instead new technology such as traction engines proved to be more efficient and 20 times faster, and fewer people were required to undertake the back-breaking work in the fields. Elsewhere, factories appeared with a modern infrastructure to support them. Workers realized their labour was more in demand

Horsepower became a thing of the past; instead new technology such as traction engines proved to be more efficient and 20 times faster, and fewer people were required to undertake the back-breaking work in the fields.

Right: *Villagers forced to leave their homes due to enclosures in the 18th century.*

from these new employers than was the case on the land.

In his report on the 1871 census the Registrar-General made this observation:

> ***The improved roads, the facilities offered under the railway system, the wonderful development of the mercantile marine, the habit of travelling about and the increasing knowledge of workmen have all tended to facilitate the flow of people from spots where they are not wanted in the fields where their labour is in demand. The establishment of manufacture or the opening of a new mine rallies men to it, not only from the vicinity but also from the remote parts of the kingdom.***

Rather than working for a pittance in a declining industry, or facing the ever-growing threat of unemployment, farm labourers chose instead to head for the Elysian fields of the city. For many people, the new promised land of opportunity and work turned out to be a Dickensian reality of disease, poverty and slum housing but still people flocked to the urban centres in search of work. Most of these people, particularly in places such as Lancashire, which witnessed such rapid industrialization, will have moved only short distances, from the outlying villages to burgeoning towns such as Blackburn, Bolton and Preston. Sometimes the whole family might have made the move: grandparents, siblings, aunts and uncles. Urban populations exploded: by 1851 Manchester and Sheffield had grown to four times their size in 1801, while Bradford and Glasgow were eight times bigger.

Take Middlesbrough, the growth of which is a perfect illustration of migratory trends in the 19th century. In 1801 it boasted 25 inhabitants; by 1901 it contained more than 91,000. In 1801 it was a farm and tiny hamlet, based on the banks of the Tees. In 1830 a railway at nearby Port Darlington linked it to the rest of North Yorkshire. A group of businessmen saw the potential of the site; a few houses were built, though by 1831 the population was still only a princely 134. Ten years later the 'town' boasted an iron works, which would be the catalyst for its growth in the 1850s and 1860s. The discovery of iron ore in the nearby Easton Hills triggered the boom: iron and steel industries, heavy engineering and shipbuilding companies moved into the area. Workers flooded in from the surrounding countryside, from the North East and Yorkshire, and from Ireland. William Gladstone visited the city and described it as an 'infant Hercules'. Its population continued to grow well into the 20th century. Boundary changes meant it swallowed increasing amounts of the surrounding countryside, changing the face of Teesside, once an area dominated by agriculture, now a thriving industrial region.

Once settled in the cities and towns, it has to be noted that very few people moved on (as we will see below, workers such as coal miners were a major exception). Instead they settled in that community for several generations. You might find

Opposite: *Farm Labourers at Wellesbourne, Warwickshire hold a strike meeting in 1872.*

by scanning census returns that some of your distant ancestors were born in rural areas but at some point moved to an urban centre where the family remained for many years. Travel was easier, cheaper and more comfortable, but that does not mean people became itinerant. The urban working class in Victorian/Edwardian England remained as attached to their communities and localities as the rural workers of a century before were attached to their villages. If they had jobs, their family around them, a role in the community, they tended to stay put, fearing change unless it was thrust upon them. It was only when public transport became affordable in the later decades of the 19th century, with the introduction of trams and the omnibus, that people moved further out from the cities and further away from their place of work, heralding the birth of the suburbs.

But for the adventurous minority, usually young men in search of a change in fortune, the ability to migrate from one town to another was too tempting to ignore. The advent of the railways made town-to-town migration possible.

Steam and Speed

The railways had an emphatic impact on the migratory habits of the United Kingdom. Journeys that had taken days now only took hours, and they were far more comfortable to undertake. Reduced travel times shrank the country and broadened people's horizons. Trade was revolutionized, the concept of travel democratized and extended beyond the domain of the rich. This development

The railways had an emphatic impact on the migratory habits of the United Kingdom. Journeys that had taken days now only took hours.

was not to everyone's liking: the Duke of Wellington was concerned over the consequences, fearing 'they [the railways] would encourage the lower classes to move about'.

The first major railway line – wooden railways had been employed in mines since the mid-18th century, but they were often worked by horses and no more than a couple of miles in length – was opened in 1825: the Stockton and Darlington Railway, built ostensibly to carry coal from Durham to the port at Stockton. Its main innovation was steam-powered trains, built to transport large amounts of coal at speeds of little more than 10 miles per hour. It might not sound much to us now, but it was a revelation at the time and palpably superior to horses. But it was no more than a tantalizing glimpse of the possibilities and potential of the new technology.

The increase in trade was the main driver behind the growth of the railways. As industry flourished and grew, new methods of transport were urgently required to ferry goods to other parts of the country and to ports for exportation. Roads and canals were struggling to cope. This was the case in Manchester, where the cotton industry was booming and the existing infrastructure between city and the port in Liverpool was proving inadequate. Local businessmen began clamouring for a railway and

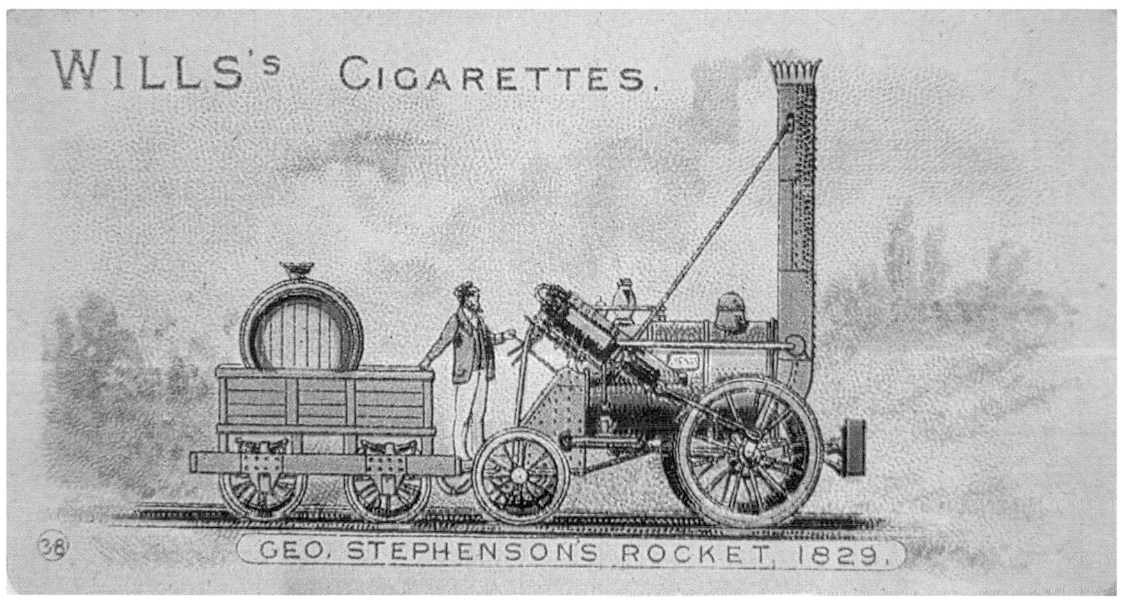

Above: A cigarette card depicting Stephenson's Rocket.

got their wish in 1830. The big question was: what type of train would run on it? A trial was held – the first day of which was watched by 15,000 people – and won by George Stephenson's infamous *Rocket*: the age of the steam locomotive had arrived.

The Liverpool and Manchester railway, the first to carry passengers, opened on 15 September 1830, a day that has entered British history, for more reasons than one. William Huskisson, the MP for Liverpool, fell into the path of the *Rocket* on its maiden journey. The onrushing engine was unable to stop and it ran over his leg, crushing it. Huskisson was heard to mutter the immortal words, 'This is the death of me.' He was right; he died that evening, the first ever railway fatality. Despite that setback, two days later the first passenger service was launched and the country was changed irrevocably.

Between 1829 and 1851 6,800 miles of track were built in England, creating an entire workforce: by 1845 200,000 men were employed building the new track. A semblance of a national network emerged, though more by accident than design because the new railway lines were built and owned by private companies. Manchester and Liverpool had been linked, and London had links with Birmingham, Leeds, Manchester and several other towns and cities, while Isambard Kingdom Brunel was working on the first London to Bristol route as part of his vision to open up a seamless trade and passenger route to America. Connections between provincial towns and cities sprang up too, and in some cases competing lines were built as people attempted to cash in on the boom.

At first, the public were not universally impressed; landowners resented the fact that the tracks had to

pass over their land and strongly opposed the multitude of railway bills that were put before Parliament for approval by the companies. Some farmers, for example, harboured the impression that the new trains would cause their worried cattle to miscarry, and the adherence of many parts of the country to local time (as opposed to GMT – some places were as much as 20 minutes different) wreaked havoc with the timetables. Many towns and cities changed their public timekeeping to tally with

Above: *The first railway line at Edgehill, Liverpool opens in 1830.*

that in London, but the result was many trains arriving and departing at times different from those shown. By 1855 the problem had been solved and almost all public clocks were set to GMT. By that year railways were well on their way to becoming the main means of movement for the masses; people moved between towns simply because it had become much easier. Acts of Parliament ensured standards of

Those living at the edges of Britain, who would never have considered moving because the prospect was too demanding, were now connected to the centre.

comfort and that fares were affordable to most. It even became the favoured method of transport for royalty: Queen Victoria made her first journey in 1842 and never looked back, enjoying not only the comfort but also the opportunity it gave her to show herself to her subjects en route. The boom continued: by 1900 almost 19,000 miles of track were in use and millions of passengers used the system, which also ferried huge quantities of freight. In the 1860s the first toilets were installed on trains, the first sleeper cars followed in the 1870s and dining cars came into use in 1879.

Those living at the edges of Britain, who would never have considered moving because the prospect was too demanding, were now connected to the centre. Suddenly a life of quiet, rural poverty was not enough for some. Word spread of the new cities and towns; perhaps the adventurous few left first and returned with glowing paeans to urban life. Not all of it would have been positive – the streets invariably turned out not to be paved with gold – but rumour would wind its way back with stories of someone making good, getting on. More and more would then leave villages and hamlets, where work was scarce, get on a train and go and seek a new future elsewhere.

The huge commercial changes instigated by the railways were another key agent in encouraging people to move and migrate. Ferrying vast quantities of goods to ports such as Liverpool created wealth and employment in those places, which in turn generated more and more labour, so attracting increasing amounts of newcomers, and so on. Previously insignificant coastal towns became thriving international ports – places such as Whitehaven in Cumbria, for example. At one point during the mid-18th century it was the third largest port in the country, thanks to the Whitehaven Junction Railway, exporting goods, coal in particular, across the world (the town's grid system was said to be the inspiration for the layout of New York). The line was engineered by George Stephenson and for decades the town flourished. When the railway boom ended, however, and under competition from other, less far-flung ports, the town's fortunes crumbled.

Above: *Whitehaven harbour during its heyday as a busy port.*

Dawn McIntyre: 'Migrant Families'

Ancestors from my mother's side of the family originated in rural areas, but in the late 19th century they moved to industrial Manchester and Salford. Frederick Vickers, her great-grandfather, moved to Salford with his young bride; within one week of the birth of their son William she died of meningitis. Frederick later set up a successful milk business and remarried.

My mother's great-great-grandfather George Hart worked at Punchard's Farm, Diss, Norfolk, before moving to Salford in 1877. The reason? To work in the mines. He brought his family with him: his sons followed him into mining; his daughters went into domestic service. George moved to Trimdon Colliery, Durham, working as a screeman, dying at the mine in 1895.

Mining and Migration

If you discover, or already know, that your ancestors were one of the many hundreds of thousands who made a living working down the mines then it is probable they migrated to various parts of the country to ply their trade. While most of our ancestors would have migrated only short distances, from the country to the nearest city for example, miners tended to cross the country in search of work – or even emigrate. The poet Herbert Thomas wrote these words in 1896:

Some say of the Cornish miner
His home is the wide, wide world,
For his pick is always ringing
Where the Union Jack's unfurled.

As a consequence, you can find miners with Cornish roots on census returns living hundreds of miles from home in the mining counties of Kent, Nottingham, Durham, Northumberland and throughout Wales.

When the country's coalfields were discovered and opened en masse during the 19th century, it offered an unprecedented opportunity for men to gain stable employment and they travelled long distances to obtain it. The opening of a new colliery was a siren call; miners would pack their picks and head for it, often taking their families with them, occasionally leaving them behind, returning to them between jobs. Often these collieries would be opened in remote areas, creating a new community in an instant.

The sanitary conditions of these new communities, sort of jerry-built villages put up quickly by the colliery to house as many people as possible as quickly as they could, were a cause of concern for many. The following extract is taken from *The History, Topography and Directory of the County Palatine of Durham* by Francis Whellan (1894):

> *A colliery village usually consists of houses built in pairs, which are placed in rows. The space between the fronts of the houses, forming the street, is unpaved and undrained; but that between the backs of the houses not unfrequently exhibits a jointstock dust-heap and dung-hill running along the avenue, flanked here and there by pig-sties and heaps of coal. The pitmen's houses are erected either by the coal-owners, or by certain petty companies, who speculate in the building and letting of them to the proprietors of the colliery, at rates varying from three to four pounds per annum. As these houses are erected for the convenience of the men employed in the pits, in the neighbourhood of which they are situated, it follows as a necessary consequence that when the pits are abandoned the villages are abandoned also, and in such cases they present a most desolate appearance. The houses may be divided into three classes: the first, or best class, possesses only two rooms on the ground-floor, with a kind of loft above; the next class have only one room on the ground-floor, with a loft above; while the third possesses only a single room.*
>
> *Some of these dwellings are allowed to remain in very dilapidated condition, the lofts or attics being scarcely fit for human beings to sleep in. It is no uncommon occurrence in winter to find on waking that Dame Nature has put on a counterpane in addition to those put on by the 'auld wife' the night before. It is pleasing to note that the colliery owners of the present day are doing their best to make up for the shortcomings of their predecessors; houses built within the last ten years are models of comfort and convenience, with ample outdoor accommodation. To most of these gardens are attached, and in some instances even hothouses and*

greenhouses. In some districts much of the available land adjoining the villages is utilized as kitchen gardens. Many of the pitmen take great pride in the cultivation of their gardens, and display an extensive knowledge of horticulture.

As the extract suggests, conditions in these pit villages improved. Dan's grandfather, who came from a long line of miners, was provided with a house in a pit village called Lynemouth Colliery in Northumberland, after retiring from his job at Ellington Colliery where he spent 48 years working beneath the surface. The village was built in 1926, and it contained a school, a church, shops, a pub and a miners' institute. Most people living there, until the colliery at Lynemouth was closed, worked or had worked down the mine, providing a strong sense of community and social cohesion. The pit was the focus point of the community, and when it closed a couple of decades ago the effect on the village was devastating: male unemployment in the village rose to 90 per cent.

The building of villages with amenities such as Lynemouth meant that miners became increasingly less migratory as the 20th century dawned. They would move with their families, or young men working at the mine would marry and settle down, often with the daughters of their fellow miners. It was not until the second half of the 20th century and the beginning of the industry's decline that miners were forced to leave their communities in search of work, from the coalfields of the North East of England to the Midlands for example.

Below: *Local people gather at the pithead at colliery village Wingate Grange, Durham, following an explosion which killed 26 miners in 1906.*

> **Unmarried mothers were often banished from the family bosom and forced to fend for themselves, while the young men who impregnated them often headed for the hills to avoid facing up to their responsibilities.**

Miners were not the only people who moved around the country during the 19th century in search of work. Those who made their living from the sea often moved as ports grew and shrank; not only merchant seamen, shipbuilders, stevedores and fishermen, but those who manufactured anchors, timber merchants, dockyard labourers, ships' carpenters and other craftsmen. If your ancestors worked in one of the coastal trades then more than likely they would have moved around regularly in search of work, though less so than the miners.

Shame

Not all the reasons for our ancestors to move around were economic. As we saw in the chapter on skeletons, scandal was a key motivation in forcing people to leave their homes and families. If you can't see an occupational, economic or fiscal reason for why your ancestor was born in one part of the country, yet crops up on census returns in another, then you might want to consider this possibility. Unmarried mothers were often banished from the family bosom and forced to fend for themselves, while the young men who impregnated them often headed for the hills to avoid facing up to their responsibilities. Bigamous spouses often went as far away as they could from the scene of their first betrothal to avoid detection, while those who were responsible for administering the Poor Laws often 'encouraged' people to leave the area so they wouldn't have to support them. Government schemes were introduced to relocate the rural poor into towns and cities where work could be found. But there are no shortage of personal problems and events that could have persuaded someone to start a new life elsewhere, even if only in the next parish or borough.

Take William Towers, for example. We know from his birth certificate and census returns that he was born in Richmond, Surrey, in 1861, then a village outside London, and that his family were still living there in 1871. In 1881, however, the census tells us that the family was living in Battersea, a borough of London. Why did they move? Perhaps William Towers senior, a bricklayer, could not find enough work in sleepy Richmond and the growth of a place like Battersea offered the opportunity of more, better paid work. But could there be another reason? In 1872, as we know, young William and his friend were sentenced to a month's hard labour for stealing two rabbits. It is possible that the family, consumed by shame at William's larceny, simply decided to move out of the area to avoid disapproving looks and tutting neighbours. (Ironically, William junior was to live the second half of his life in Wandsworth, not far from the prison. Perhaps he enjoyed the air, or needed a constant reminder of his youthful folly.)

Of course it is impossible to ever nail down the reasons. But there is much fun to be had speculating. Occasionally people do weed out the reasons behind a peripatetic ancestor's need to move.

London

London has always attracted migrants. It still does. People come from all over the country, Europe and the world to live in London. Sit down on a tube train and in one carriage you will witness people from almost every region of the country. No city on earth has proved such a magnet for people of all nationalities, backgrounds and religious faiths. People have moved to London for a vast array of reasons: to find work, to find fortune, to escape, to avoid being found, or simply to be in the thick of it. All human life could and can be found there.

In the 16th and 17th centuries London went from being the capital of England to becoming the world's centre of commerce and trade. It was the gateway to the Empire: all human life was attracted to it, passing through, stopping off, some people staying. Because of that status it provided unrivalled opportunity for trade, drawing in merchants and salesmen from across the country. With this influx it began to grow in size, swallowing up land to house its swelling population. The growth continued steadily during the 18th century before it exploded in the 19th, prompted by the Industrial Revolution. It became a vast, teeming metropolis, embracing extremes of wealth and poverty. People flocked in their thousands, brought in by the newly constructed railway system. Euston station was built in 1837; Waterloo, Paddington, Victoria and the rest all followed shortly afterwards. All lines led towards the capital. Stations such as Fenchurch Street were built too, allowing clerks and other white-collar workers to travel in and out of work in the city from their houses in the 'sticks'.

By the end of the 19th century the population of London was more than four million, while those living in Greater London – the new suburbs – had increased five-fold between 1861 and 1901. The city was cramped, bursting at the seams; in 1870 a person died every eight minutes, though someone was born every five minutes, which explains why the population continued to explode – on average in the 19th century it increased by around 36,000 annually. People arrived in London on trains, boats and on foot. They were immigrants and refugees from abroad, and the ambitious or the just plain desperate from the rest of the country. In the 18th and 19th centuries, the influx of people to the capital was predominantly from the rest

The city was cramped, bursting at the seams; in 1870 a person died every eight minutes, though someone was born every five minutes, which explains why the population continued to explode.

of the country; the same goes for the 20th century too. But during that last century, as we saw in an earlier chapter, migrants from overseas began to arrive in increasingly large numbers. It was famously yet appositely said that 'London is not in England. England is in London'. Now it is the case that the world is in London, because no city, not even New York, can compete with the combination of different nationalities that live in the capital.

Below: *A London Homeless Mission in 1895.*

Gurinder Chadha

Gurinder Chadha is best known as the writer and director of *Bend It Like Beckham,* the feel-good story of a young Sikh girl who rebels against the traditional values of her parents by dreaming of playing football. The film's humour and charm delighted audiences around the world, but the process of making it was touched by sorrow: while Gurinder was writing the screenplay, her beloved father Bhajan passed away. As with many people who have lost a parent, the death of Gurinder's father moved her to take more of an interest in her family's background, and to learn more about her own place within that story.

Some of Gurinder's recent family history was already known, her father having written a memoir of his life. Gurinder was born in 1960 in Kenya, where her parents lived amid the Sikh community until Bhajan took the decision to leave Kenya in 1961 to make a new life for his family in Britain. A well-educated man who had worked in a bank in Kenya, Bhajan instinctively went in search of white-collar work in the UK, only to encounter a surprisingly hostile reception. At a time when immigrants to Britain were not necessarily afforded a warm welcome, Bhajan's beard and turban immediately marked him out as different in Shepherds Bush, earning him the distrust of locals and even making it difficult to find somewhere to live. Eventually he was advised to take a 207 bus to Southall, in west London; he would know when he arrived, he was told, when he began to see other Indian faces from the bus window. Bhajan took the advice and, once settled in Southall, went in search of work. The best job he could find was as a postman, and even to be accepted for that he was forced into the ignominy of shaving off his beard and discarding his turban, though his faith remained undimmed.

***Above:** Gurinder's grandparents Bishen (left) and Takar Devi (right).*

***Left:** Gurinder's parents Bhajan (left) and Balwant (right).*

Left: In the late 1930s Gurinder's grandfather, Bishen, built this parade of shops in Kericho, Kenya.

In 1962 Gurinder's mother Balwant followed Bhajan to London from east Africa. The culture shock was, she said, enormous. She was used to a community in which everyone knew each other, where the women sat out on verandas preparing food together and talking, customs which seemed a world away from cold, wet, lonely west London. The couple lived within a largely Indian community, but even then their African roots marked them out as different to their neighbours. They struggled to fit in, and it was against the backdrop of these tensions and trials that Gurinder grew up. She was born in Kenya, and her family retains strong ties to that country, but nonetheless Gurinder feels unequivocably British, a theme she tries to reflect in her work. And yet Gurinder takes delight in the knowledge that, while it was imperial Britain that forcibly exported its culture to the colonies in the past, in the twenty-first century it is the culture of the colonies, or at least the children of those colonists, which is now really making itself heard.

This theme of cultural exchange and movement, inextricably linked to the rise and fall of the British Empire, lay behind Gurinder's journey to find out more about her family's origins. As that once-great empire began its slow decline, the Chadha family was uprooted, dislocated and scattered to the four winds. But where did they originally come from, and why did they choose – or why were they forced – to leave?

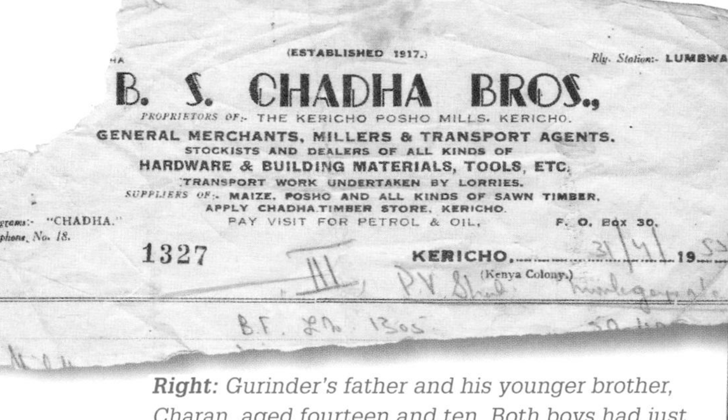

(ESTABLISHED 1917.)

Rly. Station:- LUMBWA.

B. S. CHADHA BROS.,

PROPRIETORS OF:- THE KERICHO POSHO MILLS. KERICHO.

GENERAL MERCHANTS, MILLERS & TRANSPORT AGENTS.

STOCKISTS AND DEALERS OF ALL KINDS OF

HARDWARE & BUILDING MATERIALS, TOOLS, ETC.

TRANSPORT WORK UNDERTAKEN BY LORRIES.

SUPPLIERS OF:- MAIZE, POSHO AND ALL KINDS OF SAWN TIMBER.

APPLY CHADHA TIMBER STORE, KERICHO.

PAY VISIT FOR PETROL & OIL.

Telegrams:- "CHADHA."
Telephone, No. 18.

P. O. Box 30.

1327

KERICHO, 31/4/ 19 53
(Kenya Colony.)

Right: Gurinder's father and his younger brother, Charan, aged fourteen and ten. Both boys had just been sent to boarding school in Nairobi.

Right: *Bhajan and Balwant (left), along with Gurinder's uncles, Charan (middle) and Kulwant (right).*

The trail started in the Kenyan town of Kericho, where Gurinder's father Bhajan was born, along with no fewer than five brothers and six sisters. What was an Indian family doing in an African country in the first place? At the end of the nineteenth century, Britain took control of Kenya and set about developing the new colony using cheap labour from other, more established regions of the British Empire such as India. Bhajan's father Bishen and his brothers were among the first to make the move; Bhajan's uncle Ladha had left India in 1886, answering a recruitment drive seeking policemen for the nascent colony. Ladha sponsored his brother Bishen's education and brought him over to Kenya in 1907. Bishen became a shipping clerk. The middle brother, Lakha, served in the British army on the disputed border of British Somaliland. His regiment was deployed in crushing a rebellion against the British expansion into Africa. In 1917, Ladha retired from the police force and persuaded his brothers to join him in setting up a family business in Kericho.

In 1917, the brothers decided to go into business together. Since they were legally unable to buy land in the nascent colony – only white settlers were afforded that right – they instead set up a general trading store named BS Chadha and sons, which catered for the needs of a steady influx of white tea-farmers and their predominantly black workforce. Ladha returned to India in 1920, while Lakha, who did not take to the business in Kericho, instead set up a mill in a quiet, remote area of the country called Lumbwa. Only Gurinder's grandfather Bishen decided to stay and take his chances with the family shop, scenting the business opportunities that were beginning to open up in colonial Kenya. He married an Indian woman called Takar Devi in a traditional arranged marriage, and the couple thrived as Bishen's business grew. In 1929, Takar Devi gave birth to their fifth child, Bhajan – Gurinder's father.

In time, Bishen became a successful businessman, able to send his children to boarding school in Nairobi, and the first Indian in Kenya, so the family anecdote goes, to have owned a Model T Ford car. Hungry for more information about the lives of her wealthy grandfather and his brothers, Gurinder ventured back to Kericho and made contact with her Uncle Charan, who still lives there. Charan gave her a guided tour of the town where her grandfather had built his thriving business, the place where her father had raised his family and where she herself had been born. She

Above: A Chadha family picture, showing Gurinder (left), her father, mother, grandmother and sister (right).

learned that Lakha had died in 1936, after which Bishen had added his brother's mill to his business, helped out by his sons Mohinder and Bhajan when they had completed their studies.

According to a family rumour, Lakha had at one stage lived with an African woman, and had fathered two children with her. At the time this would have been regarded as deeply shameful, since colonial Kenya was bound by a rigid class system, with whites at the top, Indians in the middle and native blacks at the bottom of the heap. Such a deeply ingrained sense of taboo about mixed-race relationships would explain Gurinder's belief that the family had tried to suppress the truth about Lakha's children, and she certainly found few people back in Kenya who were willing to talk about it. Eventually, however, her persistence paid off. She tracked down Lakha's old house, spoke to some of the locals and managed to find the Chadha brothers' old driver. From him, Gurinder learned that there had indeed been a child of mixed race, who was known by the nickname 'Sheli-Sheli', a term used to describe someone who was not from a recognisable tribe. Despite her best efforts, the fact that nobody remembered the man's real name meant that Gurinder was never able to track down this enigmatic relative. She was disappointed – to have located this secret, unacknowledged branch of the family would have given her great satisfaction – but she took consolation from the knowledge that, according to the locals who knew him, he had lived a good life

The next step on Gurinder's journey was to travel to India itself, searching for clues about her family's history before her grandfather and his brothers had moved to Kenya. In Delhi, Gurinder met with one of her uncles, Kulwant, who was able to fill in some of the gaps. Bishen, her grandfather, was born in Dariala Jalib, a village about two hours drive from Jhelum, formerly a part of northern India but now part of Pakistan. The division of India along religious lines in 1947, which led to the creation of Pakistan, was to play a significant part in the shaping of Gurinder's family, as it had so

Right: A rare picture of Gurinder's mysterious great uncle Lakha. The middle of three brothers, Lakha, went to Kenya to serve in the British Army.

many families across the country following independence from the British. Pakistan, with its predominantly Muslim population, became an Islamic republic during Partition, as the political process was called, while India's Hindu majority ensured that it remained a secular state. During the events of 1947, some 12 million people were uprooted from their homes and more than a million people killed in fierce rioting between Hindus, Sikhs and Muslims. Bishen, now comfortably settled in Kenya, frequently visited his family back in northern India in the 1940s, and was not, presumably, worried when his wife Takar Devi journeyed to Dariala Jalib in 1947 with five of their children to find suitable marriages for her daughters. In fact, as Sikhs, Thakar Devi and the rest of the Chadhas, found themselves on the 'wrong' side of the newly created border. In constant danger and fearing for their lives, they were forced to travel for several days until they reached Panipat, to the north of Delhi. For six months they remained as virtual refugees, surviving on pitiful amounts of food and water. Tragically, their youngest daughter died. Bishen scoured the country for his family and when he found them could not believe his eyes, so pale and thin had they all become.

Gurinder's travels finally took her to Haridwar, where the ashes of several members of her family are scattered. Haridwar is an important religious site for both Sikhs and Hindus, where a family priest records each relative's pilgrimage to the site, and each relative's death. From the meticulously kept public records there, Gurinder discovered that her great-great grandfather, Amir Singh, and his brother Wazir Singh, had served in Maharaja Ranjit Singh's army in the early 1800s. Ranjit Singh was the ruler of an independent Sikh kingdom in the Punjab, the last region in India to be annexed by the British in 1839. It was in Haridwar that Gurinder also discovered that her ancestral home was not Jhelum, as she had thought, but the tiny village of Dariala Jalib, where her ancestors had lived for generations, back to the time when India was invaded by Alexander the Great in 327BC. To finally reach that place was a humbling moment.

This set the seal on Gurinder's investigation. She can trace her family line from the last independent Sikh kingdom through the Raj, the Imperial acquisition of East Africa, Indian independence and Partition, through to Kenyan independence and the wave of Asian immigration that propped up post-war Britain. Her family history encompasses much of Britain's colonial history, and knowing where she has come from only serves to reinforce Gurinder's sense of being British.

Right: *Gurinder (left) together with her sister.*

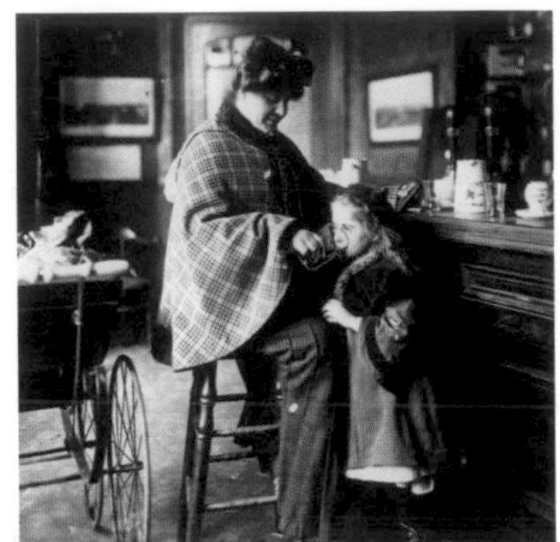

chapter 6

Everyday Life

The good news for the genealogist is that tracing our ancestors using civil registration and census forms is relatively straightforward because family units were more united and stable, in contrast to today's trend towards fractured and isolated families.

Our ancestors were primarily concerned with the daily struggle to survive, and so the focus of their lives was the local community in which they resided. Very few would have been preoccupied with national issues or institutions, either because they were illiterate and unable to read the newspapers in circulation, or because such issues played no role in their daily lives. For the masses, life revolved around several dependable institutions: the home, the church, schools (if they were lucky), the workplace, and for those fond of a drink, the pub. To understand how our ancestors lived, it is essential to develop an understanding of how these institutions worked, and the role they played in the daily routine of life.

The Family

The good news for the genealogist is that tracing our ancestors using civil registration and census forms is relatively straightforward because family units were more united and stable, in contrast to today's trend towards fractured and isolated families. Married couples were far less likely to separate or divorce; they generally would have several children who would live with them until they married, and families usually cared for their elderly relatives. Furthermore, it was likely that extended family lived in the surrounding area: brothers, sisters, cousins, aunts and uncles might be in the same town or village.

Married couples were far less likely to separate or divorce; they generally would have several children who would live with them until they married.

One striking thing many novice family historians notice is the size of the families they research, particularly when combing through civil registration and census documents from the middle of the 19th century. In early Victorian times the average number of children born to a family was six, though the statistics showed that one in every ten children would die in infancy, and one in every six would die before they reached adulthood. By 1901 this was falling,

Below: *A mother and her eight children stand in a line for a family portrait c1905.*

Above: *During the Victorian period, contraception was almost universally condemned for religious and moral reasons, but practised by the different classes of society nonetheless.*

accounted for by people marrying later and increased celibacy. The condom was introduced in the late 19th century, which may explain the declining birth rate, but the sheath was never the contraceptive of choice for the working classes, who had other ideas about birth control.

For some couples having a child was an annual event. In an entertaining article about our ancestors' family planning, published in the ninth edition of *The Family and Local History Handbook* (Robert Blatchford Publishing), Colin R. Chapman outlines some of the more bizarre methods of birth control employed by our forebears. One belief was that breast-feeding minimized the risk of getting pregnant, which might explain why well-to-do women who could afford to hire a wet nurse to suckle their children often had more children than those of the lower orders.

Other advocated 19th-century contraceptive methods included inserting a vaginal sponge moistened with water before sex; 'douching' to dislodge semen following sex; the good-old fashioned withdrawal method; and the rhythm method. One of the men who supported the latter, a medical student named Charles Drysdale, went so far as to give the times of the 'safe period' when couples could have sex without fear of conception. Unfortunately, his research was wrong, and countless couples who followed his guide received a nasty shock. Vaginal pessaries, once used in ancient England, made a comeback towards the end of the 19th century, one such concoction being made up of quinine and cocoa-nut butter. Chapman's article relates the story of one doctor, Dr H. A. Allbutt of Leeds, who published *The Wife's Handbook*, which included a chapter on the contraceptive methods mentioned above. He was struck off the medical register not for the detail included, or the illustrations, but for selling the book so cheaply that it could be afforded by working men and women.

All very strange to us now. But then, had some of these methods actually worked, a fair few of us might not be here now.

Any number of reasons can be attributed as to why the size of families declined towards the end of the Victorian era. The growth of the middle classes is one: the wealthier tended to have smaller

> **But even if children got through the first year of their life, infectious diseases threatened them before they reached maturity.**

families so they could invest money in their children's education and hire domestic staff. Another reason was the increasing number of women going to work, particularly in areas dominated by the textile industry. But even well into the 20th century it was common for working-class families, particularly in rural areas or the mining community, to be vast in size. Dan's grandfather, born in 1904, was one of twelve children, whilst Nick's grandfather, born in 1906, was one of eight.

As mentioned earlier, the high infant mortality was a motivating factor for couples to produce more children. While only 2 per cent of children now die before the age of five, in the first years of the Victorian era it was as high as 28 per cent. Most family historians scanning the death certificate indexes at the Family Records Centre are shocked to see the number 0 so many times in the 'Age at Death' column. Since that peak the rate has decreased, thanks in the main to better sanitation, better nutrition, control of disease and improvement in childbirth techniques – many of the children who died through complications during birth would have survived today.

But even if children got through the first year of their life, infectious diseases threatened them before they reached maturity. Smallpox was a major killer until vaccination was introduced in 1853 (though not made compulsory until 1967). Measles, now controlled, replaced smallpox as one of the main causes of infant mortality, as did scarlet fever, whooping cough, diphtheria and tuberculosis – a disease that claimed hundreds of thousands of adult victims too. All these diseases make regular, almost monotonous appearances on the death certificates of our ancestors.

At the other end of the spectrum, far fewer people lived to old age than do now. It is only in the second half of the 20th century that the proportion of elderly people in the population rose dramatically, to the point where the concern for modern demographers is an elderly population with too few working adults to support and provide for them. This was not a problem faced by our ancestors. In 1871 those more than 60 years of age were only 7.5 per cent of the population, and it actually fell to 7.4 by 1901. And of those most would have been members of the well-fed, well-bred upper classes. Few working-class people were offered the luxury of retiring; they tended to work until the day they died, even if afflicted by ill health. Take our William Towers for example: he died aged 45 (about the average life expectancy of someone of his class and status at that time) in 1906. His death certificate suggests that he had been suffering from the disease that eventually claimed his life for eight years, yet the 1901 census makes no mention of him being retired. William probably laid bricks until his body prevented him from doing so. The old-age pension was not introduced until 1909, and then its terms were extremely narrow. One had to be 70 to collect it for a start, an age which very few workers reached.

Hearth and Home

Family, immediate and extended, were the main focus of our ancestors' lives. It would probably be correct to say that for many it was also the bane. The working classes, as we have seen, tended to have the biggest families, but they also lived in the smallest houses. Imagine the family dynamics of a group of eight people, two adults and six children, living in a one- or two-bedroom house. Rows, falling outs and fraternal fights were commonplace. The streets of the 19th and 20th centuries echoed with the sound of children playing from dawn to dusk; there was simply no room in the house so most of their leisure time was spent playing in the street.

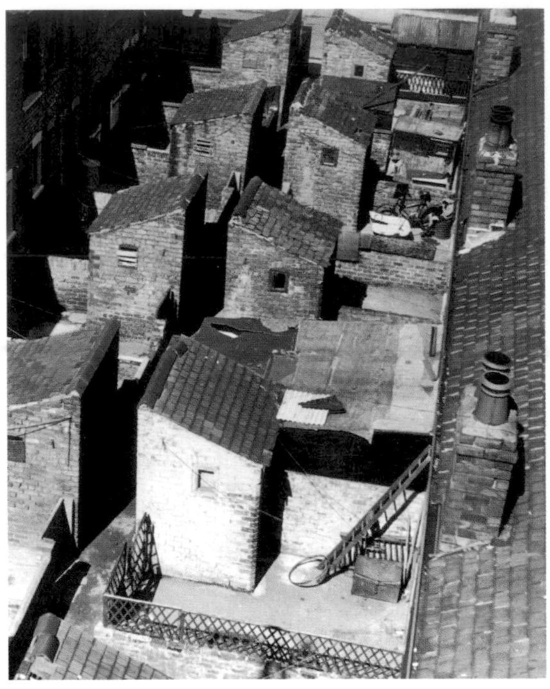

Above: *The Bath Street area of Grimsby – a slum area scheduled for demolition.*

Above: *A typical suburban semi-detached house of the late 19th century.*

The housing conditions of Victorian England did improve, thanks to Public Health Acts and improvements in sanitation. Many of the urban slums that blighted so many towns and cities were cleared, especially during the late 19th century. Where before existing properties were divided up so that they could accommodate more than one family, the 1875 Public Health Act stipulated that each house must be self-contained with its own sanitation and water. Following this act, many long streets of terraced

housing were built, many of which we can still see and some of us live in today.

The middle classes built their houses away from the centres of towns and cities, moving away from the smoke and the pollution and the noise, to what became known as the suburbs. The height of this building came in the late 19th and early 20th centuries: semi-detached mock-Tudor villas with large gardens on leafy streets, spacious rooms, bay windows – all these features marked a house out as a home for the reasonably affluent. By the late 1930s more than 300,000 houses were being built every year. Between the end of the First World War and the beginning of the Second World War four million were constructed. The specifications for a semi-detached house erected in the 1930s, with three bedrooms and a sale price of around £750, included electric fires throughout, tiled bathrooms, a porcelain bath suite, airing cupboards and separate toilets. Many of us will have grown up in one. The people who bought these houses were the progenitors of the boom in gardening and DIY.

Above: *Terraced housing satisfied the growth of housing regulations and bye-laws and complemented the public sanitation systems which had been put in place.*

The middle classes built their houses away from the centres of towns and cities, moving away from the smoke and the pollution and the noise, to what became known as the suburbs.

Above: *Eton College courtyard in 1825: Eton was founded in 1440 by Henry VI but education for the masses was not a popular cause until the late 19th century.*

Education

When we trawl through the birth, marriage and death certificates of our ancestors, many if not all of us will discover that the majority of people born in the 19th century were unable to read or write: where a signature is required, there is often a mark, a scrawled 'X' in its stead. Standards of literacy among the masses were extremely low for much of the 1800s. There was no law compelling children to go to school in early Victorian Britain; children of working families sent their offspring to work in the factories instead because they could not afford to pay for them to be educated (and to boost their own income; though many factories did provide rudimentary schooling – especially schools run by the Unitarians). From 1833 the government gave money to churches and charities to set up schools that more people could afford. Again, for most people, this was too expensive. Instead most children went to schools in which they were trained for industry as well as being taught; these institutions became commonly known as 'Ragged Schools'.

In 1852 Charles Dickens wrote an article for the *Daily News* after visiting a ragged school in Field Lane (now Farringdon Road), a poverty-stricken area. Dickens was appalled by the conditions he witnessed:

I offer no apology for entreating the attention of the readers of the Daily News to an effort which has been making for some three years and a half, and which is making now, to introduce among the most miserable and neglected outcasts in London, some knowledge of the commonest principles of morality and religion; to commence their recognition as immortal human creatures, before the Gaol Chaplain becomes their only schoolmaster; to suggest to Society that its duty to this wretched throng, foredoomed to crime and punishment, rightfully begins at some distance from the police office; and that the careless maintenance from year to year, in this, the capital city of the world, of a vast hopeless nursery of ignorance, misery and vice; a breeding place for the hulks and jails: is horrible to contemplate.

This attempt is being made in certain of the most obscure and squalid parts of the Metropolis, where rooms are opened, at night, for the gratuitous instruction of all comers, children or adults, under the title of RAGGED SCHOOLS. The name implies the purpose. They who are too ragged, wretched, filthy, and forlorn, to enter any other place: who could gain admission into no charity school, and who would be driven from any church door; are invited to come in here, and find some people not depraved, willing to teach them something, and show them some sympathy, and stretch a hand out, which is not the iron hand of Law, for their correction.

Dickens's aim was to alert the authorities to the desperate plight of the children who attended ragged schools, and to encourage them to offer some form of help. Though appalled by what he saw, he did admit that what these schools provided, imperfect as it was, was better than nothing. Thankfully for Dickens, and thanks to his campaigning, it would not be too long before the government acted. (Ironically he died in 1870, the

Above: *Social reformer, the Rev. Thomas Guthrie, at the blackboard of his Ragged School in a church hall in Princes Street, Edinburgh.*

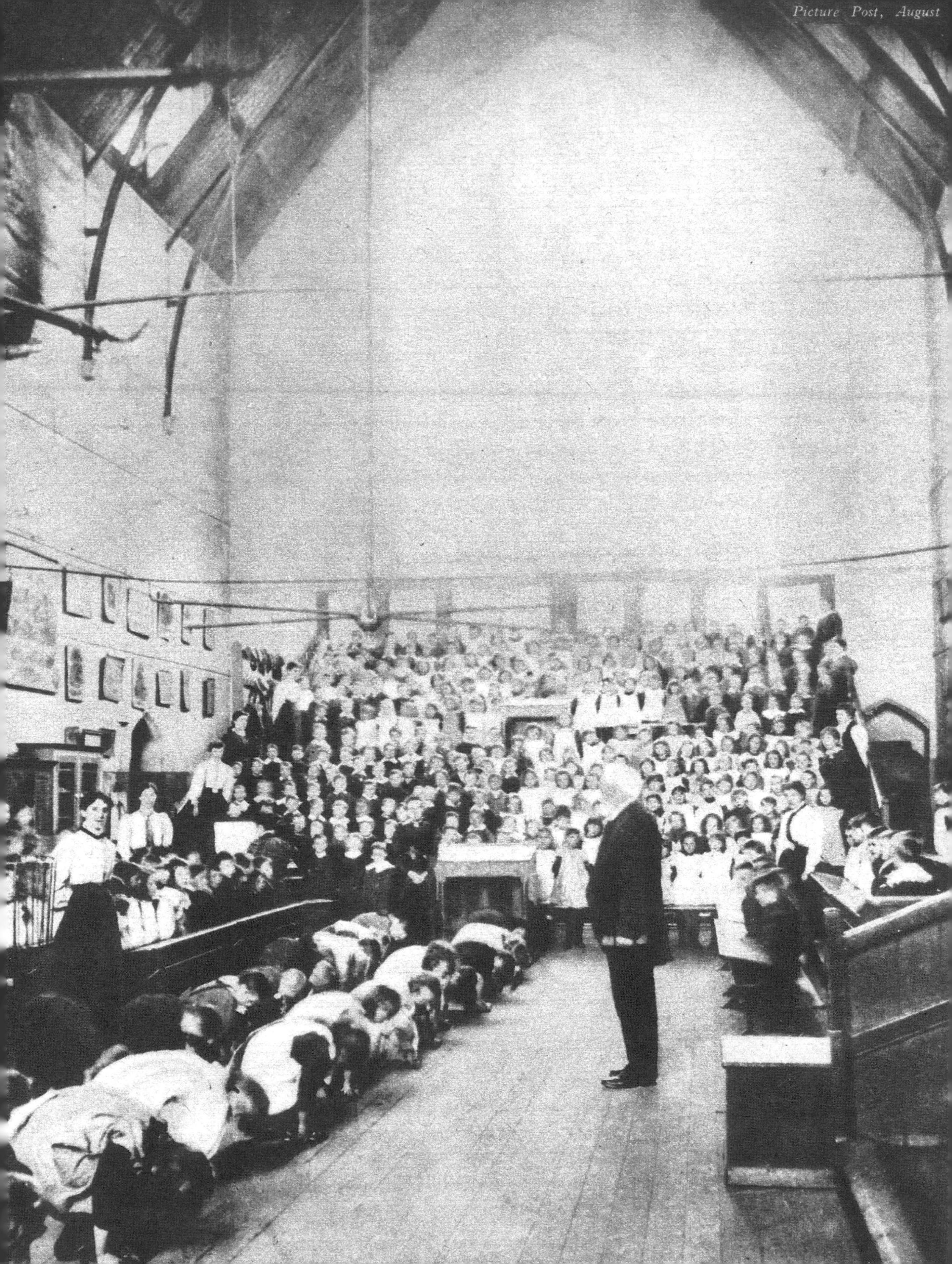

Picture Post, August

same year as the Education Act which was seen as the first great step towards universal education.) Field Lane still stands today, a Christian charity offering accommodation and support for homeless families, the elderly and the disabled.

If the conditions outlined by Dickens were the reality for many of the poor, it was a different matter for the wealthy. When young, the children of the rich were schooled by governesses or a master who lived in their homes. At seven or eight the boys might have been sent away to boarding school where they were given a rounded education to prepare them for the world of work, while the girls remained at home to be schooled and taught by the governess, the lessons focusing on housekeeping, and being a good mother and wife. There were few girls' boarding schools or high schools until late into the Victorian era, and examples of young women progressing to university were extremely rare.

The 1870 Education Act was a watershed in the history of this country. It stipulated that all children aged between five and ten should attend school, though it was not made compulsory. There was one problem with the plan, however: there were not enough schools to house these children. New schools were built – Board Schools as they became known after the local elected boards tasked with providing them – and made available for children for only a few pence. But even that was beyond the reach of some parents until they were made free in 1891. It was not until 1880 that all children were compelled to go to school until the age of 10 – raised to 11 in 1893 and 12 in 1899 – except for those employed in agriculture. The effects took some time to trickle through, but by 1893 almost 95 per cent of married couples were able to sign the marriage register. The days of the 'mark' were receding.

Opposite: *The whole school being taught in one cold room whilst other children take turns to exercise to keep warm (1880s).*

It was a different matter for the wealthy. When young, the children of the rich were schooled by governesses or a master who lived in their homes.

Board schools had a transforming effect on many communities, particularly in poorer areas where previously the only schooling a child might receive was at Sunday school. Rather than children milling in the street all day, or being packed off for work, they were dressed and sent to school. Charles Booth noted the positive results in his notebooks on London life. He was in Notting Dale, Kensington, an area known among many, including Dickens, as a place of appalling poverty and squalor.

Booth noted this, however:

> *Sirdar Road (late St Clements Road) is black as far north, on both sides, as Kenilworth Street, common lodging houses. As we passed the children were coming out of the Board School. Cold morning, some looked blue and peaked but majority well-fed and clothed though many hatless and girls with frayed skirts. Many children of dark, gypsy type.*
>
> *On the west side opposite the end of Bangor Street is the St Agnes soup*

kitchen, busy; a tail of school children along the pavement, girls one side and boys the other, about 30 boys and 40 girls waiting to get in, inside was full, inside they get bread, a thick vegetable soup, some bring it away 'these have to pay a trifle'.

The redeeming feature of the Bangor Street area is the appearance of the roadway and that of the children. For the greater number of those seen going out of the St Clement's School (in the Sirdar Road) were clean, well fed and fairly dressed: and this is the school which draws its children from the poorer street.

Above: *An inspector from the School Board tests two cottage children to check their mother is teaching them correctly.*

Following the 1902 Education Act, standards of education continued to improve: teachers' salaries rose, attracting better recruits; secondary-school provision was introduced, albeit slowly at first (the school day was still organized so that children could also hold down a job, a practice not ended until 1918). Control of the schools was taken out of the hands of the boards and given to local education authorities. By the end of the First World War education was on its way to becoming a right rather than a privilege.

Higher education was a different matter, however. By the First World War only 22,000 went to university, and of these a mere 1,000 came from state rather than public schools. The situation was improved by the growth of the new 'red-brick' universities in cities such as Liverpool, Newcastle, Manchester, Sheffield and Bristol.

Secondary-school provision grew immeasurably between the World Wars, but the act that transformed education in this country was the 1944 Butler Act. The act raised the school-leaving age to 15 and provided universal free schooling in three different types of schools: grammar, secondary modern and technical. Butler hoped that these schools would cater for the different academic levels and other aptitudes of children. Entry to these schools was based on the 11+ examination.

By the First World War only 22,000 went to university, and of these a mere 1,000 came from state rather than public schools.

Religion and Worship

Above: *The whole household, including the maidservants, gather for bible reading and prayer (1850s).*

It's a common myth to believe that our 19th-century ancestors were all pious, God-fearing folk living in dread of eternal damnation. The fact is that not everyone went to church – though attendances were far higher than they are now – and not everyone believed in God. What was true, particularly during Queen Victoria's reign, was that religion shaped the way ordinary people lived, provided a moral framework and defined the attitude of communities. One only has to look at issues such as contraception and illegitimacy to see how religious beliefs pervaded our ancestors' private lives. While not everyone worshipped God, Victorian England was one of the most moral eras this country has experienced.

The good burghers of Victorian Britain were given a nasty shock in 1851 following the first and only ever census of religious worship in England and Wales. It revealed that more than half of the population did not go to any religious service at all. It also revealed that a large number of those who did attend were not Church of England. In addition to Roman Catholics, the nonconformists covered a

Above: A Victorian christening ceremony, with parents and godparents at the baptism font (1860).

wide range of beliefs: Wesleyans, Quakers, Unitarians, Congregationalists, Baptists and Methodists to name a few – each had their chapels where believers attended services.

But while most people did not attend church or chapel services, the vast majority of the population considered themselves to be Christians and paid lip service to their faith by praying. Where the church and chapel played a central role in people's life was leisure time. Almost every child visited a Sunday School, where they were given an introduction to the Bible. Sporting clubs were often founded by the church. The names of two of the best-known cricket clubs in the country, Pudsey St Lawrence and Pudsey Congs, illustrate this. The former was the team that belonged to the local parish church, while Congregationalists founded the latter. Religious festivals provided most of the holidays and were events to be celebrated, such as Whitsuntide, while Sunday, or the Sabbath as it was commonly known, was a day of rest across the country. In some circles even reading books was frowned upon: the only book you were expected to read on Sunday was the Bible. When in 1896 Parliament voted for art galleries and museums to be opened on Sunday, the religious authorities were indignant.

The effect churches and chapels had on community life was a powerful one. They were certainly anti-hedonistic, which showed itself in the temperance movement (see box overleaf). The basic tenets were self-improvement, self-discipline and self-restraint. It was common practice for the upper and middle classes in Victorian England to gather for family prayers

But as the 19th century wore on, the grip that religion had on the nation was loosened. Charles Booth in his notebooks witnessed this: the only religious institution the poor had any dealings with were missions set up to help clothe and feed them, while the working man rarely attended church. Of course that was in London, which has always had more than its fair share of 'heathens', but while attendances did not shrink to anywhere nearly as low as they did throughout the 20th century, churches and chapels had to compete, for the first time, with other leisure pursuits.

Opposite: A Purim party at the Jewish Free School in 1908; the first Jewish Free School was founded for orphans in 1732.

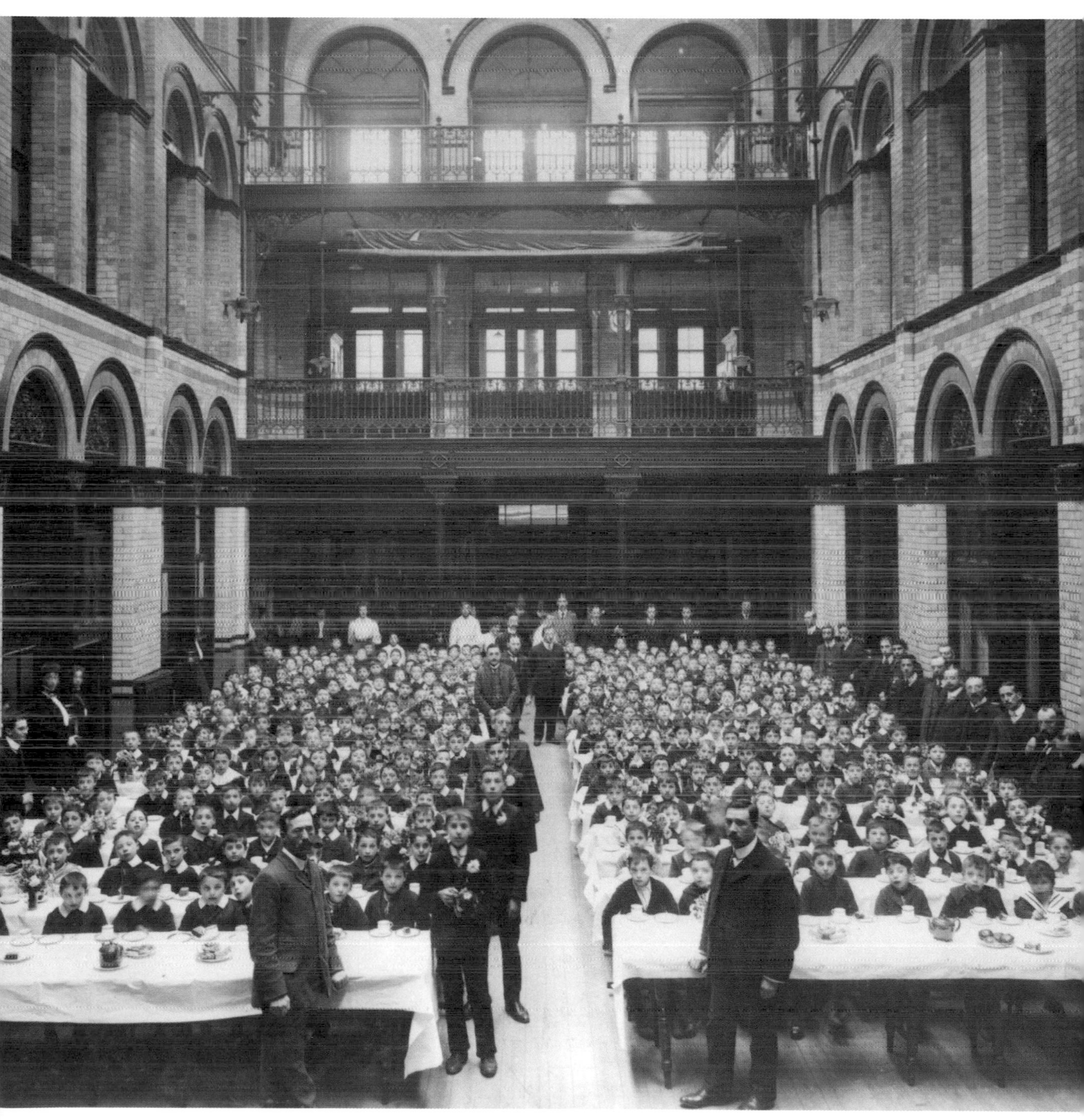

Temperance

In 1832 Joseph Livesey, a cheesemaker, and seven other men from Preston signed a pledge stating that never again would alcohol pass their lips. Other working men followed Livesey's example, and as a result the British Association for the Promotion of Temperance was formed three years later.

At first temperance usually involved a promise not to drink spirits; members continued to consume wine and beer. However, by the 1840s, temperance societies began to advocate teetotalism: a pledge to abstain from all alcohol for life and a promise not to provide it to others. Nonconformists were at the forefront. Drink was blamed as a senseless waste of money that could otherwise be spent on clothing and feeding families, for causing domestic violence and injuries in the workplace. (It was common for men to drink beer in the breaks at work, and agricultural labourers had long enjoyed being paid part of their wages in cider, though this was less an indication of the country's tendency towards inebriation, and more a recognition that the water supply was too poor to drink – beer and

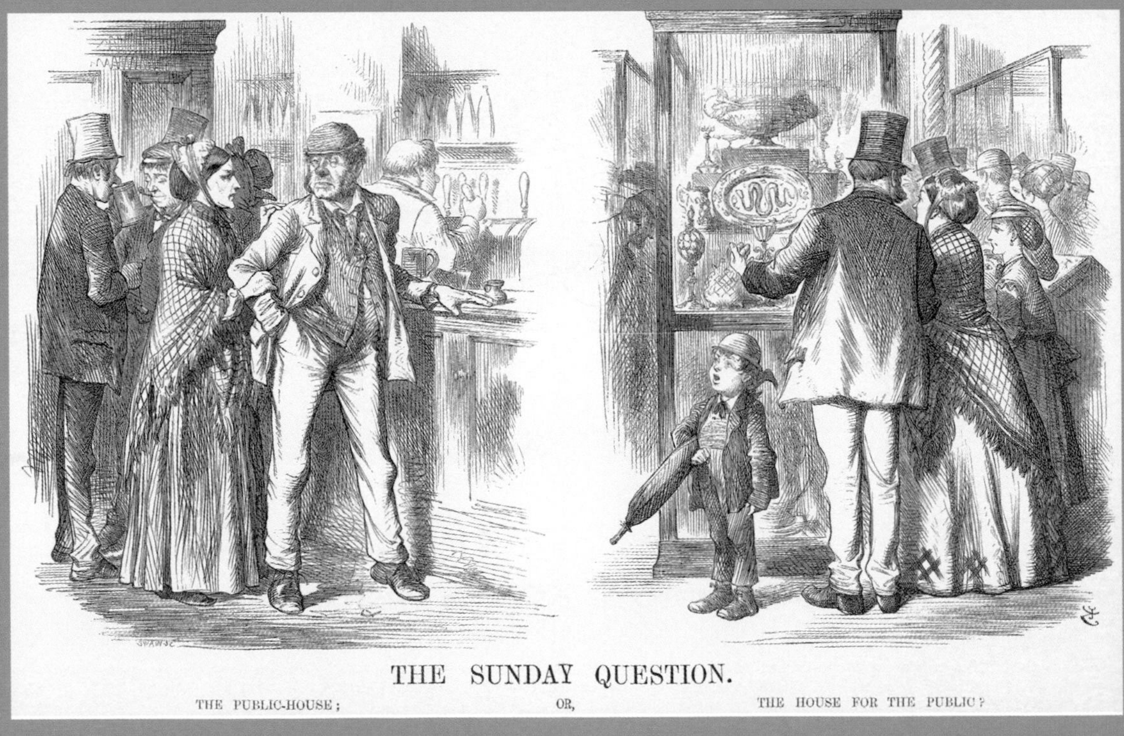

THE SUNDAY QUESTION.

THE PUBLIC-HOUSE; OR, THE HOUSE FOR THE PUBLIC?

ale had been common mealtime drinks dating back to the Middle Ages.)

Since Georgian times, the problem of inner-city drunkenness had exercised the minds of those who dwelt on the greater good. The widespread availability and cheap price of gin meant that the sight of the poor – men, women and children – staggering around drunk in the middle of the day was not uncommon. That great chronicler of 18th-century London life, William Hogarth, particularly in his painting *Gin Lane*, graphically depicted these everyday scenes of public dissolution.

Hogarth's cudgel was taken up by the artist, George Cruikshank, who produced a series of illustrations showing the impact of alcohol on families (his father, Isaac, had died of alcoholism); these included *The Bottle* (1847), an eight-part series which sold 1,000 copies, *The Drunkard's Children* (1848) and *The Worship of Bacchus* (1862). Another important figure was the Catholic priest Theobald Matthew, who persuaded thousands of people in Ireland to sign the pledge. Members of the British Women's Temperance Association set out to make men promise never to drink, while The Band of Hope, a temperance organization that taught working-class children the 'evils of drink', and had been founded in Leeds in 1847, also helped to increase the number of abstainers. Members were enrolled from six years of age.

Pressure was put on politicians and parliament to restrict the sale of alcohol, backed by the Quakers and members of the Salvation Army. As a result, in some parts of Britain public houses were forced to close on Sundays and publicans found it nigh on impossible to get permission to open a new pub. The National Temperance Federation, formed in 1884, forged close ties with the Liberal Party, whereas the Tories resisted it, mainly to support the interests of the drink trade.

Nonconformists were very active in the temperance movement. A survey in 1886 of 1,900 Baptist ministers revealed that 1,000 were total abstainers, while another study during that period showed that 2,500 out of 3,000 Congregational ministers had signed the pledge. It has been estimated that by 1900 about a tenth of the adult population were total abstainers from alcohol.

__Opposite:__ A Punch cartoon from 1869, 'The Sunday Question'. Attempts had been made to close public houses on Sundays, a side effect would be to perhaps allow more time for family outings.

Pressure was put on politicians and Parliament to restrict the sale of alcohol, backed by the Quakers and members of the Salvation Army.

Above: The Woolwich Arsenal football team in 1895: this was the first southern team to gain entry to the football league.

Sport and Pastimes

The weekend as we know it – Saturday and Sunday freed from work to do as we please – was unfamiliar to our ancestors, our 19th-century ones in particular. For a start many of them worked on Saturdays, albeit sometimes just a half-day. The Sabbath was strictly observed, though most people donned their Sunday best even if they weren't going to church and promenaded in the many parks built during the Victorian era.

But coming towards the close of the 19th-century, the rising standard of living and shorter working hours gave people the means to spend money and the time to do it. The question was: what? Sport was one: during Victoria's reign football, both codes of rugby, cricket, tennis and boxing were all either invented or reached prominence, while walking and cycling became popular pastimes.

Finishing work at Saturday lunchtime encouraged the rise of sport, amateur and professional. It is still the case across the country that league cricket games begin in the afternoon, a practice dating back to the early 20th century, to allow players to travel to the match after completing half a day's work.

The most popular of these sports, in terms of attendances at least, was football. The rules of the game had been formulated in 1863, based on a game played by Cambridge undergraduates. Ironic, then, that the sport became so massively popular, initially at least, in the industrial strongholds of the North. England played Scotland in the first international match in 1872; against Wales for the first time in 1879; and versus Ireland in 1882. The Football League was founded in 1888 by 12 clubs from the Midlands and the North. By 1901 football had become so popular that the Cup Final of that year, between Tottenham Hotspur and Sheffield United, attracted a crowd of 110,820.

Cricket, which had been played for several decades by the late 19th century, entered the professional stage, though the gate money it made was peanuts when compared with football. But it was made a popular craze by the feats of Dr W.G. Grace – born in 1848, during 1870–1876 he was at his crowd-pleasing peak. The Australians first arrived to play in this country in 1878, creating further interest, and the Ashes were born when they defeated the MCC on the 1882 tour and *The Times* pronounced the death of English cricket, a ritual repeated in two-yearly cycles ever since. The County Championship was founded in 1889 and proved very popular.

Rugby also became popular in the North, and in 1895 the game became a professional sport with the formation of the Northern Rugby Union. Rugby Union, the national sport of Wales by the end of the 19th century, clung on to its amateur roots, relenting only in the last decade or so. Horse racing attracted large crowds, thanks in main to the railways, which made travelling to race days so much easier. The so-called 'Sport of Kings', it was the one pastime that united the working man and the wealthy, though the latter was in a far better position when it came to squandering money with bookmakers. The favoured pastimes of the rich during the late Victorian and Edwardian era, however, were country sports, such as shooting, fishing and hunting. But by the time of the First World War an interloper arrived that captured the attention of the middle and upper classes: golf. Previously seen as a strange game played by a few Scots, the founding of the Westward Ho! and Hoylake clubs in the 1860s introduced it to England. By the turn of the century it had grown in popularity, boosted further by the introduction of the rubber-covered ball in 1908. Courses sprang up, and a number of middle-class women took up the game; it proved a far less expensive pastime than hunting and shooting. This was true of tennis, too. A certain Major Wingfield took a patent out for it in 1874, fully intending for reasons best known to himself to call it Sphairistike. In 1877 the Wimbledon Croquet Club annexed the sport, made some revisions and it became known as lawn

Rugby also became popular in the North, and in 1895 the game became a professional sport with the formation of the Northern Rugby Union.

Right: *A Victorian tennis party.*

tennis. All you needed to play it was a good-size garden, and it spread like wildfire, played in country houses across the nation.

Of course, many of these sports had been around in one form or another for centuries, but it was only in this period that they became widespread and taken up by the masses; the earliest football-related injury comes from a 13th-century document when a man was killed playing football because he fell on his shears.

The invention of the 'safety' bicycle in 1885 and its introduction a couple of years later meant the 1890s were a paradise for cyclists, and people of all classes and both sexes took to the road with glee. Cycling clubs sprang up across the land, and a trip out on a bike became a pastime indulged in by millions. Unfortunately the arrival of the motor car, which became the ultimate status symbol of Edwardian England, in the early 1900s, and the dust and dirt cars kicked up on roads not built to suit them made the hobby somewhat less enjoyable, and put the brakes on the cycling boom.

Pubs and Booze

The British have always liked their beer. The question has been where they choose to drink it. In 1801, almost half the beer consumed in this country was brewed at home; a hundred years later, hardly any was. People in the new industrial towns simply did not have the space to brew it, so they needed a place in which they could. The answer was the public house.

Inns, taverns and coaching houses had been a fixture of British history for centuries, places for weary travellers on a bruising coach journey lasting days to rest up, have some food and a drink, perhaps even a bed to sleep in. But of course, the advent of the railways changed all that. People could now get between towns in hours not days, and the need to stop off was not so urgent (though look at every railway station of reasonable size and you will find a pub, or old hotel, across the road from it; even a few hours on a train made travellers thirsty).

Between 1830 and 1881 the number of public houses in England and Wales doubled. By the beginning of the 20th century, there were 100,000 alehouses in the country, and 12,000 off-licences, a recent innovation in response to the creation of

Left: *Society ladies cycling in Hyde Park, London (1896).*

cheap bottled beers. Most of these pubs were owned by the breweries, which were able to transport their beers over considerable distances thanks to the railway. By the turn of the century they had also managed to beat off the attentions of the temperance movement, which had sought – and for a period succeeded – to cut the number of pubs.

George Sims, the social reformer and journalist, said, 'Drink gave the poor the Dutch courage they needed to go on living.' And it is true that throughout the 19th century and for most of the 20th century, pubs were places for working men and women to let down their hair. The poorer the area, the more pubs there were likely to be. But they were more than simple places to drink; they were informal working men's clubs. Trade unions, Masonic lodges and friendly societies all met there; it was a place where journeymen and casual workers could hear about upcoming work; bands, choirs, sports teams and all manner of clubs and groups used them as a place to gather. Weddings, wakes, new jobs, new children, promotion or the sack, all these events and more were celebrated or drowned out at the pub. As much as the church, the pub was the focal point of many urban, working-class communities.

Pubs were open most of the day and well into the night. It was not until the First World War that late-morning opening hours and being forced to close in the mid-afternoon for a few hours until evening were introduced. In England it was still possible to get a drink on Sunday, but Scottish and Welsh drinkers were less fortunate. Of course, this meant drunkenness then, as now, was a problem; in 1908–9 more than 62,000 people were convicted and sent to prison for public drunkenness. Drink was a major cause of violence and misery in working-class communities. Binge drinking is by no means a new phenomenon.

***Above:** An East End pub in 1828.*

It was common in many pubs during the mid-19th century to have an evening's entertainment, called the 'free and easy', in which customers would sing or recite songs. These shindigs were seen as the beginnings of the music-hall. Enterprising publicans tacked on a room in which they would put on entertainment. John Balmbra established a music-hall at his pub in Newcastle (which is still there, named after him) where, in 1862, the Geordie anthem 'The Blaydon Races' was performed for the first time. By 1866 London had 20 music-halls, rising to 300 by 1875. All the major industrial towns had them, as well as theatres showing plays. The working and lower-middle classes continued to go to music-hall and variety shows in their thousands until well into the 20th century, when cinema arrived and stole their thunder.

James Garrod:
'The Elusive Lily Burnand: Music Hall Queen'

'Lovely, lively' Lily Burnand was a music-hall artiste who flourished in the 1890s and 1900s and seems to have lived a colourful life befitting her profession. Born Eleanor Elizabeth Day in the East End of London in 1865, her stage career began when she was 15, forming a duo with another girl, known as the Sisters Burnand. Soon, however, Lily went solo, travelling to Europe where it seems she toured for several years. It was there she met William Doris, whose stage name was Will Kendall. Their first child, Lillian, was born in Paris in 1884. But when Will became ill, they returned to England where their second daughter, Marie, was born, in July 1890, in Poplar.

Will died in 1892, and in 1893 on a tour of the USA, Lily married Michel Kirschen. In June 1896 a baby girl was registered, Ellen Elizabeth, and the mother's name given as 'Ellen Elizabeth Kirschen, formerly Day, a burlesque actress'. The child was born on 21 December in Bloomsbury; no mention was made of a father on the certificate. Had Michel left? The 1900 US census mentions a Michael Kirschen in prison in New York ...

I scoured the 1901 census for Lily, without success. I had heard she lived in Brixton, then an affluent area where many of the stars of the music hall lived; I looked in a street directory and found a Burnand living at Barrington Road. In the census for that address I found an entry for an Elizabeth Paris, 32, music-hall artiste, a Lillian Paris, 17, born in France, and a Marie Paris, born in Poplar.

Where had that surname come from? Perhaps the enumerator had become confused between the name Doris – the real name of Lily's first husband, which she might have been using if her second had been jailed – and Paris, which was Lillian's birthplace. But where was the third child, born in Bloomsbury in late 1895? Even more curiously, there were

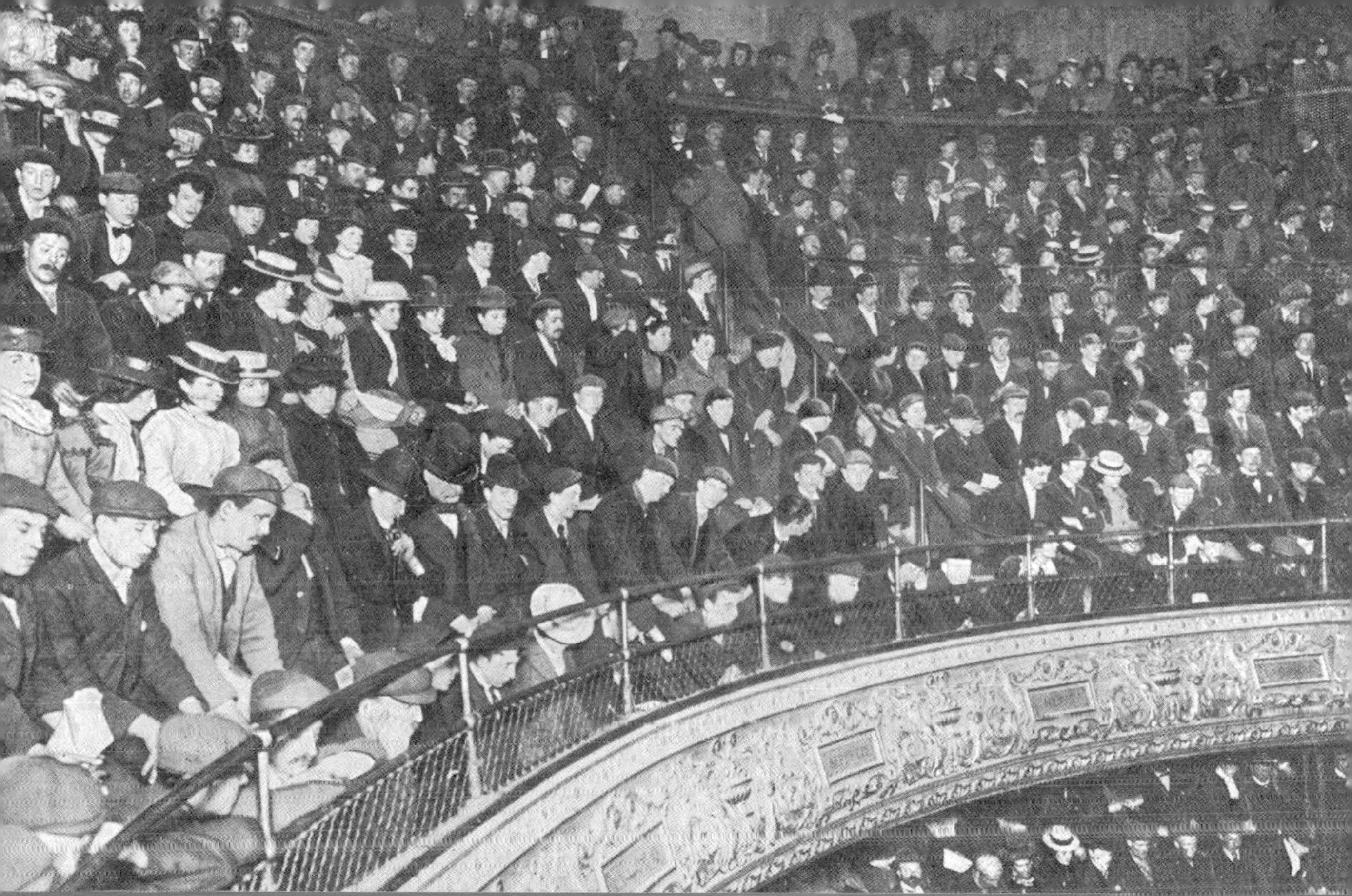

two boarders mentioned at the address: Asher Simmons, a 58-year old commercial traveller, and five-year-old Queenie Simmons.

I looked up Asher Simmons in the 1881 census; there was a man with that name and around that age living as an art dealer in Soho with a wife and seven children. If that was the same guy, how had he ended up in Brixton with a young child and nothing more?

Queenie Simmons's birth certificate revealed that she was born on 31 December 1895. The father's name was given as Asher Simmons, a commercial traveller, and the mother as Elizabeth Simmons, former Day. It was Lily. But what had happened? The conclusion we came up with was that Ellen Elizabeth Kirschen and Queenie Simmons were the same child, and had been registered twice.

In 1908 Lily married again, this time to Will Pogany, a well-known book illustrator. They moved to America in 1914, where it seems she and her family finally settled. But given her complicated past, who knows?

Above: *The end of Victoria Pier, South Shore, Blackpool (1905)*

Travel

The rich pioneered the concept of foreign travel. The Grand Tour, a trip into Europe, was the privilege of a rare few. For the rest of the population, in early 19th-century England and Wales, a holiday was not even a concept. Working hours were long and hard and pay was poor. Plus, where could you go?

As with so many things in the 19th century, the railways changed all that. Allied to shorter working days and rising prosperity, people could travel cheaply to the seaside for a day. Resorts catering to working people began to pop up: Skegness, Southend and, perhaps most famously of all, Blackpool.

The likes of Blackpool, which boomed in the second half of the 19th century thanks to the expansion in the number of working-class people taking holidays, offered 'pleasure palaces', as the popular journalist G. R. Sims called them. They combined music-hall entertainment, variety and dancing with zoos, opera houses, theatres, aquaria, pleasure gardens and exhibitions. Blackpool's Tower and Winter Gardens embody this, though their faded glamour stands as a testament to how holidaymaking tastes in this country altered once the era of air travel came into being.

Such large-scale commercial entertainments seldom paid satisfactory dividends even in their heyday, outside Blackpool, and they, along with the great Victorian seaside hotels, were particularly vulnerable to changes in popular taste and in the economics of the entertainment industry from the 1950s onwards. But they were ribald, rowdy places, where those who worked hard came to play even harder.

Thomas Cook – Travel Pioneer

Thomas Cook is one of this country's biggest and most successful travel agents. It is also the oldest. Have you ever wondered who Thomas Cook was? Born in Melbourne, Derbyshire, in 1808, Cook was brought up a strict Baptist. At 17, Thomas joined the local Temperance Society and over the next few years spent his spare time campaigning against the consumption of alcohol.

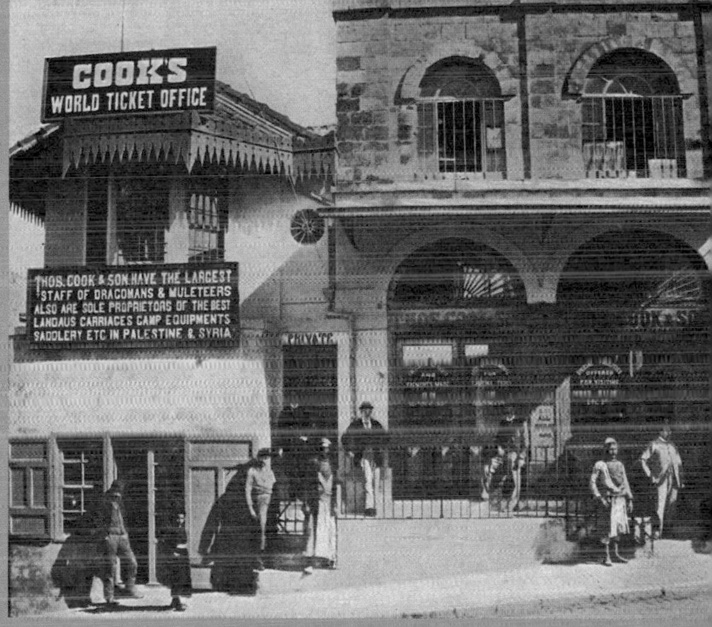

It was his view that working men and women be given other ways to spend their money and leisure time other than consuming alcohol (allied, too, to a cool business brain, which saw a gap in the market). In 1841 Cook came up with the idea of arranging an 11-mile rail excursion from Leicester to a Temperance Society meeting in Loughborough on the newly extended Midland Railway. Cook charged his customers one shilling, including the cost of the rail ticket and the food on the journey. The venture was a great success; Cook decided to start his own business running rail excursions.

In 1846 he took 500 people from Leicester on a tour of Scotland. His greatest achievement came in 1851 when he arranged the transportation of more than 165,000 people to see the Great Exhibition in Hyde Park. In 1865 Cook moved his business to London where he arranged his first overseas tours, to Egypt. He drafted in his son John, who managed the London office of the company that was now known as Thomas Cook & Son. By 1872 Thomas Cook & Son was able to offer a 212-day round-the-world tour for 200 guineas. The journey included a steamship across the Atlantic, a stagecoach from the east to the west coast of America, a paddle steamer to Japan, and an overland journey across China and India. He retired in 1879, and died in 1892, leaving behind him a legacy of travel that survives today. The moral man in him, teetotal and brimming with religious conviction, would probably not have approved of package trips such as Club 18–30, but the businessman would have.

Sheila Hancock

Ever since the death of her mother, actor Sheila Hancock has been in possession of an old, sepia-tinted photograph of a portrait of an unknown woman. Like many aspects of her past, Sheila knew few details about the painting's handsome, rather exotic-looking subject, though a distant relation was at least able to furnish her with a suitably evocative name: Madam Zurhorst. Beyond that, the woman remained a mystery. Sheila had the picture framed – if nothing else, it proved a wonderful talking point – but she had never taken any steps towards discovering who the enigmatic Madam Zurhorst actually was. Here was her chance.

Sheila guessed that the woman in the picture must be a relative of her maternal grandmother, known to her as Grandma Woodward. Through Grandma Woodward's marriage certificate, Sheila was able to discover the identity of her own great-grandfather, James Joseph Allum. At this point, the mystery apparently began to unravel. By hunting out Great-Grandfather James's marriage certificate, the maiden name of his wife came as a welcome surprise: Louisa Octavius Zurhorst. Case closed? Possibly. But a niggling fact remained: Louisa would, of course, have become an Allum when she married James, while the middle-aged woman from the painting was known to be a Zurhorst. Sheila would need to go back a further generation, and James and Louisa's marriage certificate gave her the starting point she needed: Louisa's father, the wonderfully named Hamnett Pinkey Octavius Zurhorst. Surely *his* wife would be the elusive Madam Zurhorst?

Sheila's next port of call was the 1861 census, where she found Hamnett Zurhorst listed, along with his wife Louisa. Subsequent censuses offered snapshots of how the couple's lives had been played out over the following decades. In 1871, Hamnett was an iron trimmer in an iron works. Ten years later, he appeared as a book keeper, while the record for 1891 shows him to be a retired foundry turner and book keeper living in 'Penn's Almshouses' – accommodation provided by the firm for any employees who had

***Right:** The elusive Madame Zurhorst.*

fallen on hard times. Given Hamnett's recorded expertise working with iron, it seemed likely that he had worked in a variety of positions for John Penn, a major manufacturing firm which had pioneered a system of steam propulsion used in the first modern warship, HMS *Warrior*. From the available facts, it seemed fair to assume that Hamnett, having worked at John Penn for most of his life, had retired with no savings or source of income, and so was housed by the factory's almshouses. But what of his wife? Had Sheila finally found the handsome Madam Zurhorst from the painting?

Hamnett's apparently modest financial situation would suggest otherwise, since only a genuinely wealthy Victorian man would have had the means to commission an expensive portrait of his wife. The search for the real Madam Zurhorst continued, though Sheila knew she was on the right track.

Her next step was to try to fix a date for when the portrait might have been painted. From the distinctive clothes worn by Madam Zurhorst in the picture, an expert at Sotheby's estimated that the subject had been painted some time between 1830 and 1835. Could the woman be Hamnett Zurhorst's mother? Sheila's problem was that Hamnett was born before 1837 – the era of civil registration – meaning that a birth certificate carrying the required information would not exist. So, she logged onto the International Genealogical Index, a website run by the Church of the Latter Day Saints (more commonly known as Mormons), a huge resource which contains records of millions of christenings and marriages entered from parish records. There she and her daughter Jo discovered that a certain Fredrick William Zurhorst was Hamnett's father (and therefore Sheila's great, great, great-grandfather) and that he had married one Ann-Judith Williams.

At the London Metropolitan Archive, Sheila tried to flesh out the lives of the Zurhorsts. Fredrick appeared in a trade directory as a shipping agent, and later as a broker; a member of one of the City's liveried companies, and a freeman of the City of London. Among the documents confirming his status, a mention was made of Frederick's father Herman Zurhorst, 'a native of Rotterdam who came to Ireland' and eventually landed in London. Other documents

Left: *Sheila begins the search for Madame Zurhorst in Greenwich*

Right: Emma Hancock, Sheila's 'rather grand' grandma is pictured here. Her past had always been somewhat of a mystery.

indicated that Ann-Judith had at least 13 children, and remarkably ran her own business, independent of her husband, a linen warehouse on the banks of the Thames, a fact which resonated with Sheila, who lives beside the great river and feels a strong affinity with it. Perhaps this need to be by the water resides in her Zurhorst genes?

From here, the search switched to the Continent. Sheila was lucky enough to establish, through a member of the Dutch branch of the Zurhorsts, that the clan Zurhorst was known to have bought land from monks in Germany during the reign of Charlemagne, way back in 803. Very few of us will be able to trace any lines of our family back beyond the beginning of the eighteenth century at best, so to go back more than 1,200 years was extraordinary. Contacting a distant Dutch relative, August – gamely keeping up the Zurhorst tradition of exotic Christian names – Sheila discovered that Fredrick and Ann-Judith had moved to Guernsey in their dotage, which suggested that there might be more information to be found closer to home. From records in Guernsey, she learned that Ann Judith was a woman of independent means – probably the reason they had moved to the Channel Islands in the first place, given that it was then, as now, a tax haven. Here, as a wealthy woman of leisure, is where the portrait of Ann-Judith Zurhorst was almost certainly created. She died in 1850, aged 68, and rather fittingly Sheila was able to locate her grave, and pay her respects to the woman whose distinctive portrait had led to such an amazing journey.

Madam Zurhorst was not the only remarkable person that Sheila encountered on her genealogical quest. She recounts growing up in the suburbs of London with her parents and two of her grandparents: Grandma Hancock and Grandma Woodward, both of whom shared a room despite being worlds apart, and (perhaps not surprisingly) bickered constantly.

Sheila describes Grandma Hancock as 'rather grand and a bit mad', who had once been found dancing with a lamp post outside their house. Grandma Woodward, on the other hand, was altogether more down to earth; a hard worker with few airs and graces. Sheila was interested to find out more about the stories of these two remarkable, but very different, women.

Above: *Sheila's great-grandparents. Benjamin Croft, pictured here on the right, was the superintendent of one of London's largest sewage works.*

Grandma Hancock's background was a complete mystery to Sheila; she admits to not even knowing the Christian name of her grandfather, though she was aware that he had worked for Thomas Cook, the travel agent. After a little digging, it turned out that George Thomas Hancock, to give him his full name, was the son of a station master, George Hancock, and indeed had at one point been an agent for Thomas Cook, based in the bustling northern Italian city of Milan. As for George's wife Emma – that is to say, Grandma Hancock – she was the daughter of a sewage station superintendent. This last piece of information caused Sheila some amusement, given her grandmother's grand manner, until she discovered that Emma's father, Benjamin, would have had around twenty men in his charge. The pumping station he worked at in Pimlico would have played a major part in the sanitisation of Victorian London, transformed since the era of 'The Great Stink' of 1858 by the sewage system masterminded by Joseph Bazalgette.

Keen to get a flavour of what George and Emma Hancock's lifestyle might have been like in turn-of-the-century Italy, Sheila travelled to Milan. Given George's job as a travel agent, they would have mixed in suitably well-heeled circles, escorting and guiding rich tourists through the delights of the city, such as La Scala and the Poldi Pezolli museum. Cook agents were almost honorary consuls, to all intents and purposes de facto members of the diplomatic service and would have had to converse in several languages. There would have been grand dinners, trips to the opera, and perhaps even brushes with royalty and other dignitaries. No wonder Grandma Hancock had airs and graces. And yet despite the reflected opulence of their time in Italy, George retired without a pension, which might explain how Emma came to be sharing a room with Sheila's other grandmother in her latter years.

Right: *George Hancock, pictured here in the middle, was a travel agent working in Milan for Thomas Cook.*

Above: *The Pumping House. Grandma Hancock grew up here, just ten yards from the sewage station run by her father.*

Grandma Woodward, with whom Sheila enjoyed a very good relationship, had ostensibly led a less eventful, and certainly less salubrious life. Born Louisa Elizabeth Allum, she was married in 1887 to Alfred Woodward, a cutler. But from the various certificates and census documents that Sheila used to trace Grandma Woodward's life, she encountered some shocking information. In the space of just seventeen tragic months, Louisa and Alfred had lost a pair of twins. Daisy Octavius had died just one month after her premature birth, her twin sister Violet Hetty succumbing to whooping cough just over a year later. The couple had had three children in total, but only one had survived: Sheila's mother. Understandably, Sheila found this news extremely moving, though it also gave her a more rounded understanding of the manner and character of her grandmother. 'Well, what it does is make these people live for you,' she said after learning about this tragedy buried in her family's past. 'I just thought of an old grandma who told me off a lot and was busy, busy, busy. But she was hiding huge grief. Because you don't get over something like that, do you? Losing two children?'

Left: *Sheila's father, Enrico, pictured here on the right, with his hand on the shoulder of Louisa Woodward. Enrico's mother, Emma Hancock, is seated on the left of the picture below her husband George.*

Section 3

Directory

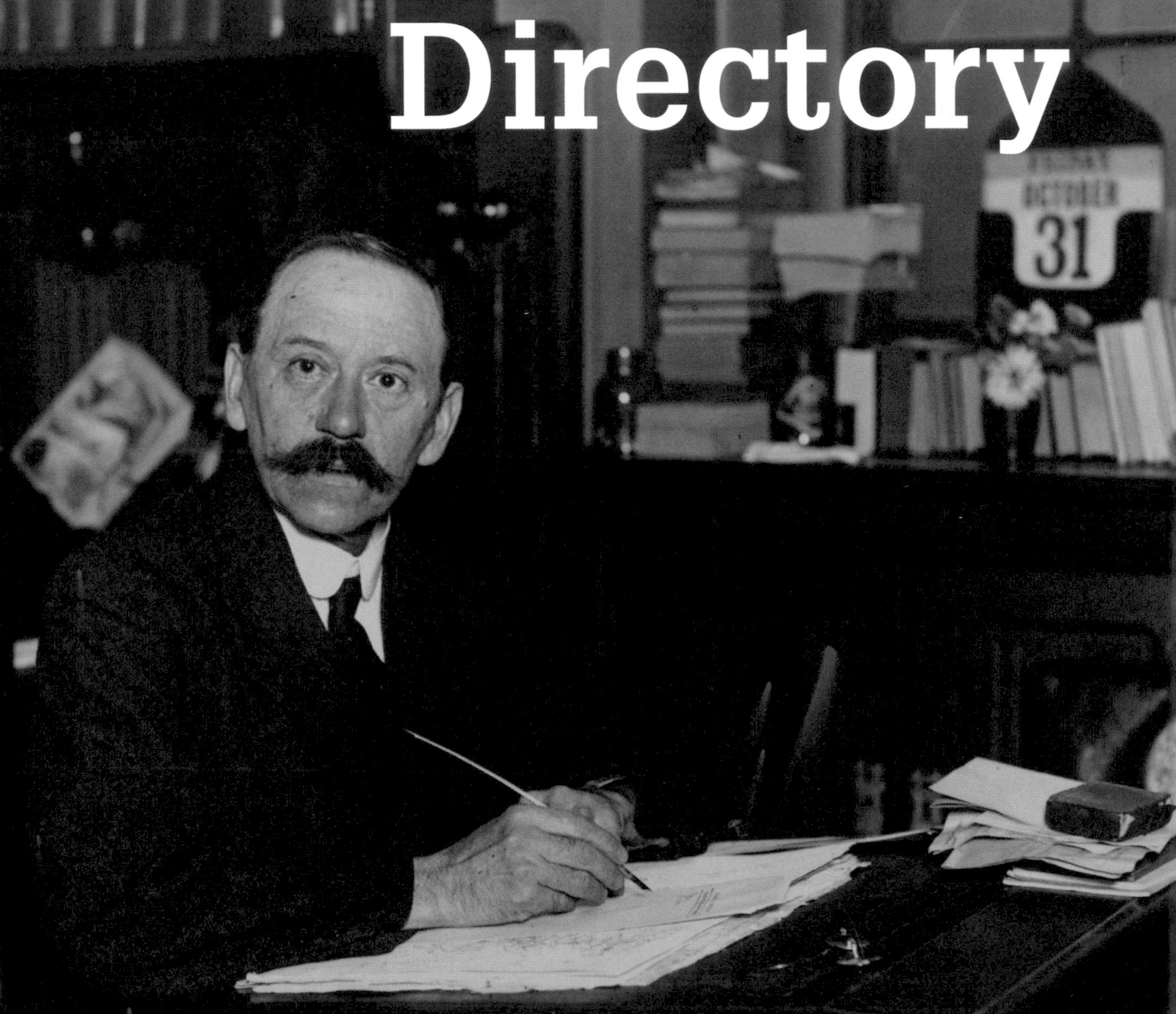

Getting Started

Your first step on your voyage of discovery is often the hardest part, and to help you navigate through the somewhat daunting range of institutions and websites, here are the top ten contact details of a few key places you'll need to visit or access at some stage.

First steps: basic sources include civil registration indexes, census returns and PCC wills pre-1858
Family Records Centre
1 Myddelton Street, London EC1R 1UW
www.nationalarchives.gov.uk
www.gro.gov.uk

A slightly more advanced place of research, with records concerning how and where your ancestors lived, plus a wide range of 'life' sources
The National Archives
Ruskin Avenue, Kew, Richmond,
Surrey TW9 4DU
www.nationalarchives.gov.uk

Modern wills post 1858
Principal Registry of the Family Division,
Probate Searchroom
First Avenue House, 42–49 High Holborn,
London WC1V 6NP
www.courtservice.gov.uk

Has someone done any research before you?
The Society of Genealogists has an extensive library and range of pedigrees, family trees and notes. The Guild of One Name Studies are also located here.
Society of Genealogists
14 Charterhouse Buildings, Goswell Road,
London EC1M 7BA
www.sog.org.uk
www.one-name.org

Joining a family history society is one of the most important ways of finding and sharing information.
Federation of Family History Societies
c/o Administrator, PO Box 2425,
Coventry CV5 6YX
www.ffhs.org.uk

Access to Archives
searchable catalogues from UK archives
www.a2a.org.uk

1837 Online
civil registration indexes
www.1837online.com

Ancestry
census records 1861–1901, plus other datasets
www.ancestry.co.uk

Familysearch
the online International Genealogical Index
www.familysearch.org

Moving Here
online information about tracing immigrant ancestors
www.movinghere.org.uk

'Skeletons' Records

If you are tracking down your ancestors and stumble across a family secret, it can come as a great surprise. Once you have discovered that there is a mystery to be solved, the skill lies in peeling back the layers that have cloaked your ancestor in secrecy: shearing the 'black sheep' of the family, as it were. These documents should help you know where to look to sketch in the details.

Official registration documents
Tracing BMDs gives you an indication of how many children a family may have had, including birth and death certificates for those that were born but failed to survive infancy. These can be viewed at the Family Records Centre (England and Wales), General Register Office (Scotland) or General Register Office of Northern Ireland (N. Ireland). Indexes can be viewed online for England and Wales, whilst some Scottish certificates can be viewed over the Internet.
http://www.familyrecords.gov.uk/topics/bmd_3.htm
http://www.1837online.com
http://www.scotlandspeople.gov.uk

Census returns
Important information about the day-to-day life of our ancestors is recorded in the census: the house in which they lived, an exact address to help you trace whether the house is still standing, and the people who lived in surrounding houses. Returns between 1851-1901 can be viewed at the Family Records Centre (England and Wales), General Register Office (Scotland) or Public Record Office of Northern Ireland (N. Ireland). Some census records are available online.
http://www.familyrecords.gov.uk/topics/census.htm
http://www.scotlandspeople.gov.uk
http://www.ancestry.gov.uk

Registered wills
Bequests to 'natural' children are often made in wills, with provision for their education or welfare. These can be viewed at the National Archives (Prerogative Court of Canterbury pre-1858), the Borthwick Institute (Prerogative Court of York pre-1858), the Probate Searchroom of the Principal Registry of the Family Division (England and Wales after 1858), the National Archives of Scotland (Scotland) or Public Record Office of Northern Ireland (N. Ireland). Early local wills are housed at the relevant diocesan record office or county archive.
http://www.familyrecords.gov.uk/topics/wills.htm
http://www.documentsonline.nationalarchives.gov.uk/wills.asp
http://www.york.ac.uk/inst/bihr

Parish registers
Baptisms of illegitimate children are often noted in the local parish register – they are often referred to as 'bastards' or 'base born' – where you can find other genealogical information on marriages and burials. Records are usually deposited in the relevant local archive.
http://www.familyrecords.gov.uk/topics/religious.htm
http://www.familysearch.org

Quarter session returns
Information on illegitimacy, such as bastardy bonds, can be found in quarter session returns. These are stored at the relevant county record office.
http://www.nra.nationalarchives.gov.uk/nra
http://www.a2a.org.uk

Divorce records

Records of historic divorce proceedings are available at the National Archives, whilst modern information is available from the Principal Registry of the Family Division of the Supreme Court.
http://www.catalogue.nationalarchives.gov.uk/RdLeaflet.asp?sLeafletID=53

You can obtain certified copies of decree nisi after 1858 from the Principal Registry of the Family Division, Decree Absolute Section, First Avenue House, 42–49 High Holborn, London WC1V 6NP. For a fee they will search a union name index.

Bigamy prosecutions

Bigamous marriages were often tried in assize courts, and you can research them at the National Archives or National Library of Wales (before 1830).
For further information:
http://www.catalogue.nationalarchives.gov.uk/RdLeaflet.asp?sLeafletID=156
http://www.catalogue.nationalarchives.gov.uk/RdLeaflet.asp?sLeafletID=158
http://www.catalogue.nationalarchives.gov.uk/RdLeaflet.asp?sLeafletID=154

Adoption records

From 1927 in England, 1930 in Scotland and 1931 in Northern Ireland, a national register of adoptions was introduced. Before registration, adoption was often arranged privately and facilitated by charities such as Dr Barnado's.
For further information:
http://www.familyrecords.gov.uk/topics/adoption.htm

Hospital and asylum records

Most historic medical records are closed for 100 years, and are likely to be deposited at the relevant county record office. More modern papers may be with the hospital trust that took over the administration of historic hospitals.
http://www.catalogue.nationalarchives.gov.uk/RdLeaflet.asp?sLeafletID=166
http://www.nationalarchives.gov.uk/hospitalrecords
http://www.wellcome.ac.uk

Lunatic records in Chancery

The State took an interest in people deemed to be 'lunatics' or 'idiots', and many records concerning individuals can be found at the National Archives in the court of Chancery.
http://www.catalogue.nationalarchives.gov.uk/RdLeaflet.asp?sLeafletID=166
http://www.catalogue.nationalarchives.gov.uk/RdLeaflet.asp?sLeafletID=164

Criminal trial proceedings

Criminal ancestors can be researched via court records, principally those of the itinerant assize judges. The records are at The National Archives (England) or the National Library of Wales (Wales). Separate records of the sheriffs' courts exist for Scotland in the National Archives of Scotland.
http://www.catalogue.nationalarchives.gov.uk/researchguidesindex.asp

Central criminal court records

Records of the Central Criminal Court at the Old Bailey are to be found at the National Archives. This is where serious crimes were brought to trial for the Greater London area.
http://www.catalogue.nationalarchives.gov.uk/RdLeaflet.asp?sLeafletID=172
http://www.catalogue.nationalarchives.gov.uk/RdLeaflet.asp?sLeafletID=365
http://www.catalogue.nationalarchives.gov.uk/RdLeaflet.asp?sLeafletID=120

Assize and trial records
Local assize documents can be located for England at the National Archives. Records for Wales before 1830 are stored at the National Library of Wales, whilst criminal records for Scotland are at the National Archives of Scotland. For further information:
http://www.catalogue.nationalarchives.gov.uk/RdLeaflet.asp?sLeafletID=156
http://www.catalogue.nationalarchives.gov.uk/RdLeaflet.asp?sLeafletID=158
http://www.catalogue.nationalarchives.gov.uk/RdLeaflet.asp?sLeafletID=154
http://www.nas.gov.uk/family_history.htm

For further information on sources for convicts in England and Wales:
http://www.catalogue.nationalarchives.gov.uk/RdLeaflet.asp?sLeafletID=253

Coroners' reports
In cases of unusual or suspicious deaths, a coroner was required to hold an inquest into the circumstances. Whilst many records no longer survive, local newspapers often carried transcripts of the inquest.
http://www.bl.uk/collections/newspapers.html
http://www.nra.nationalarchives.gov.uk/nra
http://www.a2a.org.uk

For coroners' inquests linked to murder trials:
http://www.catalogue.nationalarchives.gov.uk/RdLeaflet.asp?sLeafletID=175

USEFUL ADDRESSES

The National Archives
Ruskin Avenue, Kew, Richmond, Surrey TW9 4DU
http://www.nationalarchives.gov.uk

Family Records Centre
1 Myddelton Street, London EC1R 1UW
http://www.familyrecords.gov.uk/frc.htm

General Register Office for Scotland
New Register House, Edinburgh EH1 3YT
http://www.gro-scotland.gov.uk

General Register Office of Ireland
8–11 Lombard Street, Dublin 2
http://www.groireland.ie

General Register Office of Northern Ireland
Oxford House, 49–55 Chichester Street, Belfast BT1 4HL
http://www.groni.gov.uk

National Archives of Scotland
HM General Register House, Edinburgh EH1 3YY
http://www.nas.gov.uk

National Archives of Ireland
Bishop Street, Dublin 8
http://www.nationalarchives.ie

Public Record Office of Northern Ireland
66 Balmoral Avenue, Belfast BT9 6NY
http://proni.nics.gov.uk

Principal Registry of the Family Division, Decree Absolute Section
First Avenue House, 42–49 High Holborn, London WC1V 6NP

Principal Registry of the Family Division, Probate Searchroom
First Avenue House, 42–49 High Holborn, London WC1V 6NP

National Library of Wales
Aberystwyth, Dyfed SY23 3BU
http://www.llgc.org.uk

British Newspaper Library
Colindale Avenue, London NW9 5HE
http://www.bl.uk/collections/newspapers.html

Borthwick Institute of Historical Research
University of York, Heslington, York, YO10 5AR
http://www.york.ac.uk/inst/bihr

Military Records

Few other records are as detailed and useful to family historians as those kept by the military. Your main resource for these records, at the outset of your search at least, should be the National Archives in Kew. The perfect place to start is with the easy-to-follow leaflets they have produced, guiding you through the records they hold and the information they contain. We have linked to the online version of these guides here where relevant. When you visit TNA, do not hesitate in asking a member of staff for guidance should you get stuck. They will be able to point you in the right direction.

SPECIFIC DOCUMENT RESOURCES

Army

Service records
The collected records relating to a soldier's career from enlistment to discharge often contain biographical information. Before 1923, records are with the National Archives; records after this date are with the Ministry of Defence.
Further information:
http://www.catalogue.nationalarchives.gov.uk/researchguidesindex.asp

Pension records
Medical notes and service summaries are often provided when a soldier was discharged to pension after completing his period of service. Before 1923, records are with the National Archives; records after this date are with the Ministry of Defence.
Further information:
http://www.catalogue.nationalarchives.gov.uk/researchguidesindex.asp

Musters and pay lists
Each regiment compiled quarterly or monthly pay lists and musters. These can be used to find out where your ancestor served. Records from the 18th to the late 19th century are at the National Archives.
Further information:
http://www.catalogue.nationalarchives.gov.uk/researchguidesindex.asp

Operational records
Information on particular military campaigns in which your ancestors took part can be found in regimental or unit war diaries. While it is rare to find other ranks mentioned by name, deeds of gallantry may be referred to.
Further information:
http://www.catalogue.nationalarchives.gov.uk/researchguidesindex.asp
http://www.armymuseums.org.uk

Royal Navy and Marines

Naval service records
Records of continuous service were introduced in 1853, although earlier service documents survive. They include important biographical information, as well as details of vessels on which your ancestor served. Before 1923, records are with the National Archives; records after this date are with the Ministry of Defence.
Further information:
http://www.catalogue.nationalarchives.gov.uk/researchguidesindex.asp

Naval pension records
Many ex-sailors applied for naval pensions, whilst widows of officers were also eligible for payments. However, few records have survived. Those before 1923 are with the National Archives; records after this date are with the Ministry of Defence.
Further information:
http://www.catalogue.nationalarchives.gov.uk/researchguidesindex.asp

Royal Marines

A variety of historical records survive that allow you to trace service in the Royal Marines. Attestation, discharge and pension documents for the various divisions can be found at the National Archives, but records for anyone who enlisted after 1925 are still with the Ministry of Defence.
Further information:
http://www.catalogue.nationalarchives.gov.uk/researchguidesindex.asp

Ships' musters and pay lists

Ships' musters contain biographical information on their crew and are stored at the National Archives. You can also use them to track the vessels on which your ancestor served.
Further information:
http://www.catalogue.nationalarchives.gov.uk/researchguidesindex.asp

Operational records

Information on naval battles and voyages in which your ancestors took part can be found in ships' logs or captains' letters. Surgeons' logs can reveal conditions on board ship, and may include the names of sailors who were treated.
Further information:
http://www.catalogue.nationalarchives.gov.uk/researchguidesindex.asp
http://www.royalnavalmuseum.org

Royal Air Force

Service records

The RAF was created in April 1918 from the Royal Flying Corps (RFC) and Royal Naval Air Service (RNAS). RAF service records between 1918 and 1923 are with the National Archives; records after 1923 are with the Ministry of Defence. Earlier service records for the RFC or RNAS are with the relevant army or navy records.
Further information:
http://www.catalogue.nationalarchives.gov.uk/researchguidesindex.asp

Operational records

You can use material such as Operation Record Books (ORBs) to investigate the history of the squadron or base where your ancestor served. These records, as well as other sources such as casualty reports, can be found at the National Archives, and the RAF Museum at Hendon also holds a wide range of operational material.
Further information:
http://www.catalogue.nationalarchives.gov.uk/researchguidesindex.asp
http://www.rafmuseum.org.uk

East India Company

Army pension and service records

Before 1858, the British East India Company (EIC) governed India and, to ensure its authority, the EIC had separate armies for each of the three main Presidencies that it ruled, namely Bengal, Madras and Bombay. However, there are few 'service records' as such, mainly summaries of service and payment ledgers of the various military funds that served as pensions for ex-officers and soldiers. Surviving material can be found at the Oriental and India Office Library at the British Library.
For further information:
http://www.bl.uk/collections/orientaloffice.html

Musters and pay lists

As well as service histories, you can look for surviving regimental musters and pay lists for the EIC's army. However you need to know which army your ancestor served in; whether they were with the native infantry or cavalry; and then which regiment. Printed sources such as the *Indian Army List* can help. These records can be found at the Oriental and India Office Library at the British Library.
For further information:
http://www.bl.uk/collections/orientaloffice.html

Operational records and official histories

Many important military men in EIC service wrote memoirs or kept diaries which tell you about the life and times of an army in the field, whilst you can also access printed official histories written about many campaigns fought in India. The best place to start looking for such material is at the Oriental and India Office Library at the British Library.
For further information:
http://www.bl.uk/collections/orientaloffice.html

GENERAL RESOURCES

Medals

Military personnel were often awarded medals for taking part in a specific campaign, whilst other medals were granted for specific acts of gallantry. Nominal medal rolls and the *London Gazette* (where gallantry awards were published) can be examined at the National Archives.
Further information:
http://www.catalogue.nationalarchives.gov.uk/researchguidesindex.asp

War dead

The Commonwealth War Graves Commission provides burial information for all armed forces. their website boasts a searchable database of the 1.7 million men and women who died during the wars. Where possible, it will even tell you where your ancestor is buried. You can also find nominal rolls of war dead, as well as regimental births, marriages and deaths, at the National Archives and Family Records Centre.
Further information:
http://www.catalogue.nationalarchives.gov.uk/researchguidesindex.asp
http://www.cwgc.org.uk

Military memorabilia

Context is an important part of your research, and military memorabilia can be found at local (eg regimental) and national museums. In particular, photographs, uniforms, weaponry and equipment provide an indication of their life and times in the armed forces.
Further information:
http://www.royalnavalmuseum.org
http://www.national-army-museum.ac.uk
http://www.iwm.org.uk

Newspaper and media reports

Coverage of wars and military operations can be found in contemporary newspapers. From the 20th century onwards, you should also look for television and radio coverage at places such as the National Sound Archive at the British Library.
Further information:
www.bl.uk

USEFUL ADDRESSES

The National Archives
Ruskin Avenue, Kew, Richmond, Surrey TW9 4DU
http://www.nationalarchives.gov.uk

The Oriental and India Office Library
The British Library, 96 Euston Road,
London NW1 2DB
http://www.bl.uk/collections/orientaloffice.html

British Newspaper Library
Colindale Avenue, London NW9 5HE
http://www.bl.uk/collections/newspapers.html

Imperial War Museum
Lambeth Road, London SE1 6HZ
http://www.iwm.org.uk

The Imperial War Museum
Duxford, Cambridgeshire CB2 4QR
http://www.iwm.org.uk/duxford

RAF Museum
Hendon Aerodrome, London NW9 5LL
http://www.rafmuseum.org.uk

National Army Museum
Royal Hospital Road, London SW3 4HT
http://www.national-army-museum.ac.uk

National Maritime Museum
Romney Road, London SE10 9NF
http://www.nmm.ac.uk

Royal Naval Museum
HM Naval Base (PP66), Portsmouth, Hampshire, PO1 3NH
http://www.royalnavalmuseum.org

Fleet Air Arm Museum
Box D6, RNAS Yeovilton, Ilchester, Somerset BA22 8HT
http://www.fleetairarm.com

Immigration and Emigration Records

Throughout the past 500 years or so, all immigrants that moved to this country, and everyone that has left these shores, have at some stage been touched by the hand of authority; some lightly, some oppressively. Although our ancestors might not have welcomed this contact, it does make it easier for us to trace their inward and outward journeys.

SPECIFIC DOCUMENT RESOURCES

Immigration

Census returns
From 1851, census returns often indicate the country of origin if someone was born outside Britain, or whether they had become naturalized British citizens. Census returns for England and Wales are held at the Family Records Centre, whilst those for Scotland are at the General Register Office and those for Ireland at the National Archives, Dublin.
Further information:
http://www.familyrecords.gov.uk/frc.htm
http://www.scotlandspeople.gov.uk
http://www.nationalarchives.ie
http://www.ancestry.gov.uk

Change of name
Many settlers in Britain decided to anglicize their name. A selection of surviving records can be found at the National Archives.
Further information:
http://www.catalogue.nationalarchives.gov.uk/researchguidesindex.asp

Inward passenger lists
Between 1878 and 1890, it is possible to look at the lists of people who arrived in Britain by ship from destinations outside Europe and the Mediterranean.
Further information:
http://www.catalogue.nationalarchives.gov.uk/researchguidesindex.asp

Naturalization and denization papers
Records of naturalization and denization applications, and duplicate certificates, can be found at the National Archives. Many documents contain information on places of origin.
Further information:
http://www.catalogue.nationalarchives.gov.uk/researchguidesindex.asp

Emigration

Outward passenger lists

The National Archives holds the passenger lists of ships travelling outside Europe and the Mediterranean from 1890–1960. It helps if you know the port of departure.
Further information:
http://www.catalogue.nationalarchives.gov.uk/researchguidesindex.asp
http://ellisisland.org – arrivals in the US
http://www.blaxland.com/ozships – arrivals and departures to Australia

Passports

There are some historical records at the National Archives, whilst the UK Passport Office undertakes limited searches of its historical records.
Further information:
http://www.catalogue.nationalarchives.gov.uk/researchguidesindex.asp
http://www.ukpa.gov.uk

Records of colonial administration

The records generated by the British administration in each colony can be used to trace the history of British ex-patriots abroad. You may also need to contact the relevant national archive for the country where your ancestor settled.
Further information:
http://www.catalogue.nationalarchives.gov.uk/researchguidesindex.asp
http://www.bl.uk/collections/orientaloffice.html
http://www.sas.ac.uk/commonwealthstudies

Transportation

Records relating to the transportation of convicts to penal colonies abroad can be found at the National Archives.
Further information:
http://www.catalogue.nationalarchives.gov.uk/researchguidesindex.asp

Assize and trial records

Sentences of transportation can be located in the English trial papers held at the National Archives. Records for Wales before 1830 are stored at the National Library of Wales.
For further information:
http://www.catalogue.nationalarchives.gov.uk/RdLeaflet.asp?sLeafletID=156
http://www.catalogue.nationalarchives.gov.uk/RdLeaflet.asp?sLeafletID=158
http://www.catalogue.nationalarchives.gov.uk/RdLeaflet.asp?sLeafletID=154

For further information on sources for convicts:
http://www.catalogue.nationalarchives.gov.uk/RdLeaflet.asp?sLeafletID=253

Transportation records

Records relating to the transportation of prisoners can be found at the National Archives. These include the name of the prisoner, the vessel they sailed on, the destination and date of departure.
For further information:
http://www.catalogue.nationalarchives.gov.uk/RdLeaflet.asp?sLeafletID=347

Many prisoners died during the voyage. Conditions on board ship can be researched via surgeons' logs.
For further information:
http://www.catalogue.nationalarchives.gov.uk/ link to surgeons' logs leaflet

Penal colony records

Records relating to the administration of penal colonies often include census returns and information on the families of the convicts who voluntarily elected to accompany them.
For further information:
http://www.catalogue.nationalarchives.gov.uk/RdLeaflet.asp?sLeafletID=74
http://www.catalogue.nationalarchives.gov.uk/RdLeaflet.asp?sLeafletID=377

Newspaper and media reports

The arrival of citizens from abroad to these shores was reported extensively at the time, particularly the wave of Commonwealth immigrants following the Second World War, and a good place to start your research is the British Newspaper Library, Colindale.
For further information:
http://www.bl.uk/collections/newspapers.html

Irish history

Historical Irish records are divided between the Public Record Office of Northern Ireland, Belfast and the National Archives of Ireland, Dublin.
http://proni.nics.gov.uk
http://www.nationalarchives.ie
It might be best to contact the Irish Genealogical Research Society:
http://www.igrsoc.org

Poor law relief

Many Irish immigrants who arrived in England sought poor law relief. Papers are usually held at the local record office.
For further information:
http://www.catalogue.nationalarchives.gov.uk/RdLeaflet.asp?sLeafletID=116
http://www.catalogue.nationalarchives.gov.uk/RdLeaflet.asp?sLeafletID=167

Black and Asian history

The following websites offer advice about researching black and Asian roots.
http://www.movinghere.org.uk
http://www.rootsweb.com
http://www.sas.ac.uk/commonwealthstudies
http://www.nationalarchives.gov.uk/pathways/blackhistory
http://www.bl.uk/collections/orientaloffice.html

Jewish history records

Jewish refugees were often welcomed into established Jewish communities, in particular in London and the east coast of Britain. Apart from religious records kept by the relevant synagogue, there are a range of sources that can be used to trace the development of Jewish communities from the late 19th century onwards.
For further information:
http://www.catalogue.nationalarchives.gov.uk/RdLeaflet.asp?sLeafletID=249
http://www.catalogue.nationalarchives.gov.uk/RdLeaflet.asp?sLeafletID=312
http://www.movinghere.org.uk/galleries/roots/jewish/jewish.htm
The following websites offer advice about researching Jewish ancestors.
http://www.movinghere.org.uk
http://www.rootsweb.com
http://www.jewishgen.org
http://www.jgsgb.ort.org
http://www.cityoflondon.gov.uk

Child Emigration

Child Migrant Central Information Index

If you or an ancestor was sent abroad under one of the 20th century child emigration schemes, you can use the Child Migrant Central Information Index to trace the agency that holds personal records.
For further information:
http://www.voluntarychild.org

Children's Overseas Reception Board

Surviving records of the Children's Overseas Reception Board are stored at the National Archives in series DO131.
For further information:
http://www.catalogue.nationalarchives.gov.uk/RdLeaflet.asp?sLeafletID=292

USEFUL ADDRESSES

The National Archives
Ruskin Avenue, Kew, Richmond, Surrey TW9 4DU
www.nationalarchives.gov.uk

Jewish Genealogical Society of Great Britain
PO Box 13288, London N3 3WB
http://www.jgsgb.ort.org

The Oriental and India Office Library
The British Library, 96 Euston Road,
London NW1 2DB
http://www.bl.uk/collections/orientaloffice.html

National Archives of Ireland
Bishop Street, Dublin 8, Ireland
http://www.nationalarchives.ie

National Archives of Scotland
HM General Register House, Edinburgh, EH1 3YY
http://www.nas.gov.uk

General Register Office for Scotland
New Register House, Edinburgh EH1 3YT
http://www.gro-scotland.gov.uk

National Library of Wales
Aberystwyth, Dyfed SY23 3BU
http://ww.llgc.org.uk

The Society of Genealogists
14 Charterhouse Buildings, Goswell Road,
London EC1M 7BA
http://www.sog.org.uk

Black Cultural Archives
378 Coldharbour Lane, London SW9 8LF

Family Records Centre
1 Myddelton Street, London EC1R 1UW
http://www.familyrecords.gov.uk/frc.htm

Huguenot Library
University College, Gower Street,
London WC1E 6BT
http://www.ucl.ac.uk/library/huguenot.htm

Immigration and Nationality Department
Nationality Office, B4 Division, India Buildings,
Water Street, Liverpool L2 0QN
http://www.ind.homeoffice.gov.uk

Institute of Commonwealth Studies
University of London, 28 Russell Square,
London WC1B 5DS
http://www.sas.ac.uk/commonwealthstudies

UK Passport Office
Discharge of Information Section, Aragon Court,
Peterborough PE1 1QG
http://www.ukpa.gov.uk

Index